ESSENTIAL GUIDE TO BIBLE VERSIONS

ESSENTIAL GUIDE TO

# BIBLE VERSIONS

PHILIP W. COMFORT, Ph.D.

TYNDALE HOUSE PUBLISHERS, INC. WHEATON, ILLINOIS

Visit Tyndale's exciting Web site at www.tyndale.com

Copyright © 2000 by Philip W. Comfort. All rights reserved.

Scripture quotations marked KJV are taken from the *Holy Bible*, King James Version.

Scripture quotations marked ASV are taken from the *Holy Bible*, American Standard Version.

Scripture quotations marked RSV are taken from the *Holy Bible*, Revised Standard Version, copyright © 1946, 1952, 1971 by the Division of Christian Education of the National Council of the Churches of Christ in the United States of America, and are used by permission. All rights reserved.

Scripture quotations marked NASB are taken from the *New American Standard Bible*, © 1960, 1962, 1963, 1968, 1971, 1972, 1973, 1975, 1977 by The Lockman Foundation. Used by permission.

Scripture quotations marked "NKJV" are taken from the New King James Version. Copyright © 1979, 1980, 1982 by Thomas Nelson, Inc. Used by permission. All rights reserved.

Scripture quotations marked NRSV are taken from the New Revised Standard Version of the Bible, copyrighted, 1989 by the Division of Christian Education of the National Council of the Churches of Christ in the United States of America, and are used by permission. All rights reserved.

Scripture quotations marked NIV are taken from the *Holy Bible*, New International Version®. NIV®. Copyright © 1973, 1978, 1984 by International Bible Society. Used by permission of Zondervan Publishing House. All rights reserved.

Scripture quotations marked NJB are taken from *The New Jerusalem Bible*. Copyright © 1985 by Darton, Longman & Todd Ltd. and Doubleday & Co., Inc.

Scripture verses marked NEB are taken from *The New English Bible*, copyright © 1970, Oxford University Press, Cambridge University Press.

Scripture quotations marked REB are taken from *The Revised English Bible*. Copyright © 1989 by Oxford University Press and Cambridge University Press.

Scripture quotations marked TEV are taken from *Good News Bible*, Today's English Version. Copyright © 1976 by American Bible Society. Used by permission.

Scripture quotations marked CEV are taken from *Holy Bible*, Contemporary English Version. Copyright © 1995 by American Bible Society. Used by permission of Thomas Nelson, Inc.

Scripture quotations marked NLT are taken from the *Holy Bible*, New Living Translation, copyright © 1996. Used by permission of Tyndale House Publishers, Inc., Wheaton, Illinois 60189. All rights reserved.

Edited by S. A. Harrison

Cover photograph copyright © 2000 by William Koechling. All rights reserved.

Cover designed by Jenny Destree

---

**Library of Congress Cataloging-in-Publication Data**

Comfort, Philip Wesley.
The essential guide to Bible versions / Philip Wesley Comfort.—Expanded trade & classroom ed.
p. cm.
Rev. ed. of: The complete guide to Bible versions. c1996.
Includes bibliographical references and index.
ISBN 0-8423-3484-X (sc)
1. Bible. English—Versions. I. Comfort, Philip Wesley. Complete guide to Bible versions. II. Title.
BS125.C65 2000
220.5'2—dc21 00-037787

---

Printed in the United States of America

05 04 03 02 01 00
8 7 6 5 4 3 2

# CONTENTS

# INTRODUCTION

MODERN readers of the Bible, exposed to a multitude of English translations, find it difficult to determine which translation they should read. Since the Bible is such an important book—in fact, *the* most important book—readers want to be sure that they are using an accurate and understandable translation of the original text. It would be wonderful if everyone could read the Bible in the original languages: Hebrew, Aramaic, and Greek. Since so very few have learned these ancient languages, nearly everyone depends on translations.

This book serves as a guide to the English Bible and English Bible translations. This guide should help you understand how we got the Bible, what are the important ancient **manuscripts**,* and what are the significant English translations that have been made throughout history. This book should also guide you in your selection of Bible **versions** and give you direction in using each one.

A modern English translation of the Bible has more to it than meets the eye. Let's say you just picked up a copy of the New International Version or the New Living Translation and

*This bold type is used throughout the text to indicate that the word or phrase is defined in the Glossary (page 271).

started reading the Gospel of Luke. As you read along, enjoying the account of John the Baptist's miraculous birth, then Jesus' even more miraculous birth, and so on, you probably don't realize how many people have been at work to bring this wonderful Gospel to you in contemporary, understandable English.

Many people have been at work, over a long period of time, to make this Gospel text available to you: (1) Luke, the writer who produced the **autograph**; (2) **scribes** who produced copies upon copies of this work; (3) archaeologists and/or **paleographers** who have discovered these copies and published transcriptions of them; (4) **textual critics** who have compared the copies and compiled **critical editions** of the Greek text; and (5) translators who produced an English translation of the Greek text.

The purpose of this book is to explain (1) how the Bible text was originally written—both for the Hebrew Bible and the Greek New Testament; (2) how the text was transmitted copy after copy; (3) what significant manuscripts have been discovered and published; (4) how textual critics have understood **textual transmission** and employed textual criticism to produce editions of the Hebrew Bible and Greek New Testament; and, finally, (5) how translators throughout the ages have employed different translation techniques to produce versions in a multitude of languages.

The issues pertaining to the Hebrew Old Testament text, **canon**, and manuscripts are covered in chapter 1. The issues pertaining to the Greek New Testament text, canon, and manuscripts are covered in chapter 2. Chapter 3 provides a well-rounded discussion on the theories and practices of Bible translation. Thereafter, the book focuses on actual translations of the Bible.

Beginning in chapter 4, I have provided a survey of several of the most significant early versions of the Old Testament and New Testament in languages other than English. This includes discussions about the Samaritan Pentateuch; the Septuagint; the Greek versions of Aquila, Symmachus, and Theodotian; Origen's *Hexapla*; the Aramaic Targums; Syriac versions; Coptic versions; the Armenian version; the Gothic translation of Ulfilas; and Latin versions. This is followed by a history of the earliest versions of the English Bible, up until the King James Version.

The rest of the book focuses on English translations from the King James Version to the present. Chapter 5 is dedicated to an analysis of the King James Version and all the revisions of this translation, including the English Revised Version, the American Standard Version, the Revised Standard Version, the New American Standard Version, the New King James Version, and the New Revised Standard Version.

Chapter 6 presents an analytical survey of more than twenty translations of the twentieth century, including such noteworthy versions as *The New English Bible,* the New International Version, and the New Living Translation. In chapter 7, I provide a close comparative study of several modern translations of the prologue to John's Gospel. This study is designed to help readers see the kinds of differences Bible readers encounter and why. In this chapter, I focus on the portions of the New Testament that were included in the King James Version but are usually excluded from modern translations. Finally, in chapter 8, I discuss so-called "extra verses" in traditional translations—that is, verses that were included in earlier English versions but have been excluded from more recent translations for textual reasons.

# TIMELINE

| | |
|---|---|
| ca. 2000 B.C. | The birth of Abraham |
| ca. 1447 B.C. | The Exodus (early date) |
| ca. 1400 B.C. | The Israelites enter the Promised Land (early date) |
| ca. 1270 B.C. | The Exodus (late date) |
| ca. 1230 B.C. | The Israelites enter the Promised Land (late date) |
| ca. 1010 B.C. | David is crowned king of all the Israelite tribes |
| 931 B.C. | The kingdom is divided into Israel and Judah |
| 722 B.C. | Exile of the northern kingdom of Israel |
| 597–586 B.C. | Exile of the southern kingdom of Judah |
| 538 B.C. | Many Jews return from exile |
| 516 B.C. | Completion of the Second Temple |
| 457 B.C. | Ezra arrives in Jerusalem |
| 444 B.C. | Nehemiah arrives in Jerusalem |
| ca. 160 B.C. | Judas Maccabeus dies |
| ca. 6/5 B.C. | Jesus Christ is born |
| ca. A.D. 30 | Jesus' crucifixion and resurrection |
| ca. A.D. 49 | Council of Jerusalem |
| ca. A.D. 60 | Paul is imprisoned in Rome |
| A.D. 70 | The destruction of the Temple in Jerusalem |
| ca. A.D. 90 | John the apostle is exiled to Patmos |
| A.D. 324 | Constantine secures his rule over the Roman Empire |
| A.D. 395 | The Roman Empire is divided into East and West |
| ca. A.D. 400 | Jerome completes the Latin Vulgate |
| A.D. 410 | Barbarians attack Rome |
| A.D. 800 | Charlemagne is crowned emperor of the Holy Roman Empire |
| ca. A.D. 1008 | The Masoretes produce the Leningrad Codex |
| A.D. 1054 | The church officially splits, separating Roman Catholicism from Eastern Orthodoxy |
| A.D. 1066 | William of Normandy conquers England |
| ca. A.D. 1450 | Johannes Gutenberg invents his printing press |
| A.D. 1517 | Martin Luther nails his Ninety-five Theses to the chapel door in Wittenburg |
| A.D. 1534 | Henry VIII establishes the Church of England |

| | |
|---|---|
| A.D. 1536 | William Tyndale is strangled and burned at the stake for translating the New Testament into English without Church permission |
| A.D. 1563 | The Council of Trent is adjourned |
| A.D. 1611 | The King James Version is completed |
| A.D. 1616 | William Shakespeare dies |
| A.D. 1620 | The Pilgrims arrive in America |
| A.D. 1776 | The American Revolution |
| A.D. 1881 | Westcott and Hort publish the first critical edition of the *Greek New Testament* |
| A.D. 1918 | World War I ends |
| A.D. 1945 | World War II ends |
| A.D. 1947 | Discovery of the Dead Sea Scrolls |

CHAPTER ONE

# The Old Testament Text

## THE INSPIRATION OF THE OLD TESTAMENT

Thousands of years ago, God chose certain men—such as Moses, David, Isaiah, Jeremiah, Ezekiel, and Daniel—to receive his words and write them down. What they wrote became books, or sections, of the Old Testament.

God gave his words to these men in many different ways. Certain writers of the Old Testament received messages directly from God. Moses was given the Ten Commandments inscribed on a stone when he was in God's presence on Mount Sinai. When David was composing his psalms to God, he received divine **inspiration** to foretell certain events that would occur a thousand years later in the life of Jesus Christ. God told his prophets—Isaiah, Jeremiah, and others—exactly what to say; therefore, when they gave a message, it was God's word, not their own. This is why many prophets often said, "Thus says the Lord." (This statement appears over two thousand times in the Old Testament.) God communicated his message to other prophets, such as Ezekiel and Daniel, through visions and dreams. They recorded exactly what they saw, whether they understood it or not. And other writers, such as Samuel and Ezra, were directed by God to record events in the history of Israel.

Four hundred years after the last book of the Old Testament (Malachi) was written, God's Son, Jesus Christ, came to earth. In his talks, he affirmed the divine authorship of the Old Testament writings—even down to the very letter (see Matt. 5:17-18; Luke 16:17; John 10:35-36). Furthermore, Jesus often pointed to passages in the Old Testament as having predicted events in his life (see Luke 24:27, 44).

The New Testament writers also affirmed the divine inspiration of the Old Testament text. The apostle Paul was directed by God to write, "All Scripture is inspired by God" (2 Tim. 3:16, NLT). Quite specifically, he was speaking of the Old Testament. A translation of Paul's statement closer to the original language (Greek) would be, "All Scripture is God-breathed" (NIV). This tells us that every word of the Bible was breathed out from God. The words of the Bible came from God and were written by men. The apostle Peter affirmed this when he said, "No prophecy of Scripture came about by the prophet's own interpretation. For prophecy never had its origin in the will of man, but men spoke from God as they were carried along by the Holy Spirit" (2 Pet. 1:20-21, NIV).

## THE LANGUAGES OF THE OLD TESTAMENT

### HEBREW

Most of the Old Testament was written in Hebrew. It was one of several Canaanite dialects, which included Phoenician, Ugaritic, and Moabite. Such dialects were already present in the land of Canaan before its conquest by the Israelites.

Hebrew belongs to the **Semitic** family of languages; these languages were used from the Mediterranean Sea to the

### The Hebrew Alphabet
*(Square Script)*

| Letter | Name | Gloss |
|---|---|---|
| א | aleph | ’ (glottal stop) |
| ב | beth | b |
| ג | gimel | g |
| ד | daleth | d |
| ה | heh | h |
| ו | vav | v/w |
| ז | zayin | dz |
| ח | heth | kh |
| ט | teht | t |
| י | yodh | y |
| כ | kaph | k |
| ל | lamedh | l |
| מ | mem | m |
| נ | nun | n |
| ס | samekh | s |
| ע | ayin | ‘ (smooth stop) |
| פ | pe | p |
| צ | tsadhe | ts |
| ק | qoph | q (guttural k) |
| ר | resh | r |
| שׁ | shin | sh |

mountains east of the Euphrates River valley, and from Armenia (Turkey) in the north to the southern extremity of the Arabian Peninsula. Semitic languages are classified as Southern (Arabic and Ethiopic), Eastern (Akkadian), and Northwestern (Aramaic, Syriac, and Canaanite).

The Hebrew alphabet consists of twenty-two consonants; signs for vowels were devised and added late in the language's history.

The origin of the alphabet is unknown. The oldest examples of a Canaanite alphabet were preserved in the Ugaritic

Cuneiform alphabet of the fourteenth century B.C. The old style of writing the letters is called the Phoenician or **paleo-Hebrew script**. The script used in modern Hebrew Bibles (Aramaic or **square script**) came into vogue after Israel's exile into Babylon (sixth century B.C.). The older style was still used sporadically in the early Christian era on coins and for writing God's name, Yahweh, as the **tetragrammaton** YHWH (יהוה). Hebrew has always been written right to left.

## ARAMAIC

A few sections of the Old Testament were written in Aramaic: Daniel 2:4b–7:28; and Ezra 4:8–6:18; 7:12-26. Aramaic phrases and expressions also appear in Genesis (31:47), Jeremiah (10:11), and the New Testament. Aramaic has perhaps the longest continuous living history of any language known. It was used during the Bible's patriarchal period and is still spoken by a few people today. Aramaic and its cognate, Syriac, evolved into many dialects in different places and periods. Characterized by simplicity, clarity, and precision, it adapted easily to the various needs of everyday life. It could serve equally well as a language for scholars, pupils, lawyers, or merchants. Some have described it as the Semitic equivalent of English.

The origin of Aramaic is unknown, but it seems to have been closely related to Amorite and possibly to other ancient Northwest Semitic dialects barely known to scholars. By the eighth century B.C., King Hezekiah's representatives requested the spokesmen of the Assyrian king Sennacherib to "speak to your servants in Aramaic, since we understand it" (2 Kings 18:26, NIV). By the Persian period, Aramaic had become the language of international trade in the Mediterranean world.

The Jews probably adopted Aramaic during their captivity for the sake of convenience. They certainly used Aramaic in commerce, while Hebrew became confined to scholarly and religious use. After the Babylonian exile, Aramaic was widely used in the land of Palestine. Nehemiah complained that children from mixed marriages were unable to speak Hebrew (Neh. 13:24). The Jews seem to have continued using Aramaic widely during the Persian, Greek, and Roman periods. Jesus spoke in Aramaic: several of the Gospels, though written in Greek, retain some of Jesus' actual wording in Aramaic.

Eventually, the Hebrew Scriptures were translated into Aramaic paraphrases, called **Targums**, some of which have been found among the **Dead Sea Scrolls**.

## OLD TESTAMENT CANON

The **canon** designates those books in the Jewish and Christian Bible that are considered to be Scripture and therefore authoritative in matters of faith and doctrine. The term canon comes from a Greek word (*kainon*) that means "a rule," or "measuring rod." A canon is a list to which other books are compared and by which they are measured. Only those writings that met the standard were accepted as "Scripture," the word of God, worthy of reading by God's people.

The criteria for selecting the books in the Old Testament canon are not known, but they clearly had to do with their worth in the religion of the Jewish nation. Jews call their thirty-nine books of Scripture the **Tanakh**—an acronym formed from the first letters of *Torah* (Law), *Naviim* (Prophets), and *Kethubim* (Writings). These are called the "Law of Moses, the Prophets and the Psalms" in Luke

24:44 (NIV) (the first book of the Writings in the Hebrew Bible is the Psalms).

Jewish religion existed for a millennium, from Moses to Malachi, without a **closed canon**, an exclusive list of authoritative books. Never in their history did the people of the Old Testament have the entire thirty-nine books of the Old Testament. The exact date for the closing of their canon is not known. Some scholars think it occurred at the Council of Jamnia in A.D. 90, but others point out that we did not have our first list of thirty-nine books until A.D. 170, in a list produced by Melito of Sardis. That list included no books written after the time of Malachi (ca. 430 B.C.).

The thirty-nine books of the modern Old Testament were originally divided into only twenty-four according to the uniform testimony of early Hebrew tradition. The **Talmud**, **rabbinic literature**, and probably the book of 4 Esdras testify to this arrangement, which included five books of the Law, eight of the Prophets, and eleven of the Writings. Modern Hebrew Bibles reflect this tripartite arrangement that was used in the first three printed editions (Soncino, 1488; Naples, 1491–1493; Brescia, 1492–1494).

Of the three sections of the Hebrew Bible, the most important to the Israelites has always been the Law. Another name for the Law is the **Pentateuch** (literally, "five in a case"—referring to five scrolls in a case). The Pentateuch contains the first five books of the Bible: Genesis, Exodus, Leviticus, Numbers, and Deuteronomy. The Pentateuch, said to be written by Moses, provided the Israelites with basic teachings and principles for personal, social, and spiritual life.

The second section, "the Prophets," comprises a very large segment of the Hebrew Bible. This includes four historical books (Joshua, Judges, Samuel, and Kings), the books of the three major prophets (Isaiah, Jeremiah, and Ezekiel), and the books of the twelve minor prophets (Hosea, Joel, Amos, Obadiah, Jonah, Micah, Nahum, Habbakuk, Zephaniah, Haggai, Zechariah, and Malachi). The prophetic books are a record of God's oracles to his people concerning past, present, and future events.

In the Hebrew Bible, the last section is "the Writings," which are of two kinds. The first kind is "Wisdom Writings"; this set includes Psalms, Proverbs, Job, the Song of Songs, Lamentations, and Ecclesiastes. Most of these books are poetic in form and thought, and many of them, especially Job, Proverbs, and Ecclesiastes, purport "wisdom" as a central theme. The second kind of "Writings" includes historical books, specifically Esther, Daniel, Ezra, Nehemiah, and Chronicles.

## OLD TESTAMENT AUTHORSHIP

Traditionally, authorship of the Pentateuch has been ascribed to Moses. Several Old Testament writers considered him to be the author (2 Kings 14:6; Ezra 3:2; Dan. 9:11), as did Jesus (Luke 24:44) and Paul (1 Cor. 9:9). Traditionally, Joshua is thought to be the author of the book that bears his name, although the book itself does not say this. Judges is thought to have been written by Samuel on the basis that he was the last of the judges. He did not write 1 and 2 Samuel (originally one book) inasmuch as his death is recorded in 1 Samuel, making it impossible for him to record the events of 2 Samuel. The "Samuel" who wrote the books 1 and 2 Samuel is most likely Samuel the Prophet, whose writing is mentioned in 1 Chronicles 29:29—*The Record of Samuel the Seer.* We do not know who wrote Ruth, Esther, or 1 and

2 Kings. The rest of the historical writings (1 and 2 Chronicles, Ezra, and Nehemiah) were probably written by Ezra, a knowledgeable and well-trained scribe.

As for the poetic books, it is thought that Job was written by Job, but we do not know this with certainty. The Psalms were composed by a number of individuals, including Korah, Asaph, and David, whose names are mentioned in the titles to their psalms. Most of the proverbs probably came from Solomon, and a few were authored by Agur and Lemuel. The Song of Songs is said to be Solomon's (1:1). Solomon is usually credited with Ecclesiastes, but scholars are uncertain about this.

The authorship of the prophets is more certain because the prophet's name is specifically identified in each of the books—usually in the first verse.

The grouping and ordering of the books in the Hebrew Bible is different from what Christians have in their Bibles because the Christian Bible adopted the order in the **Septuagint**, a Greek translation of the Hebrew Bible. The Septuagint, the first translation of the Hebrew Bible, was made in the third century B.C. by Jewish scribes versed in Hebrew and Greek. This translation became very popular among Jews in the first two centuries before Christ because many Jews in those days did not understand Hebrew. Their ancestors had left Israel centuries before, and succeeding generations gradually lost the ability to read the Scriptures in Hebrew. Many of the Jews in Jesus' day used the Septuagint as their Bible. Quite naturally, the early Christians also used the Septuagint in their meetings and for personal reading; and many of the apostles quoted it when they wrote the Gospels and Epistles in Greek.[1]

---

[1] For further discussion on the Old Testament canon, see R. T. Beckwith, "The Canon of the Old Testament" in Comfort, ed., *Origin of the Bible*, 51-64.

The Christian Old Testament can be divided into five sections, as follows:

**The Old Testament Books and Their Authors**

| Book | Author |
|---|---|
| **The Pentateuch (the Law)** | |
| Genesis | Moses |
| Exodus | Moses |
| Leviticus | Moses |
| Numbers | Moses |
| Deuteronomy | Moses |
| **Historical Writings** | |
| Joshua | Joshua |
| Judges | Samuel (?) |
| Ruth | Anonymous |
| 1 and 2 Samuel | Anonymous |
| 1 and 2 Kings | Anonymous |
| 1 and 2 Chronicles | Ezra |
| Ezra | Ezra |
| Nehemiah | Ezra |
| Esther | Anonymous |
| **Wisdom Literature / Poetry** | |
| Job | Job (?) |
| Psalms | Korah, Asaph, David, and others |
| Proverbs | Solomon, Agur, and Lemuel |
| Ecclesiastes | Solomon (?) |
| Song of Songs | Solomon (?) |
| **Major Prophets** | |
| Isaiah | Isaiah |
| Jeremiah | Jeremiah |
| Lamentations | Jeremiah |
| Ezekiel | Ezekiel |
| Daniel | Daniel |
| **Minor Prophets** | |
| Hosea | Hosea |

| | |
|---|---|
| Joel | Joel |
| Amos | Amos |
| Obadiah | Obadiah |
| Jonah | Jonah (?) |
| Micah | Micah |
| Nahum | Nahum |
| Habbakuk | Habbakuk |
| Zephaniah | Zephaniah |
| Haggai | Haggai |
| Zechariah | Zechariah |
| Malachi | Malachi |

## THE TEXT OF THE OLD TESTAMENT

### THE SCRIBES

In Old Testament times, professional scribes were employed as secretaries in Palestine, Egypt, Mesopotamia, and the Greco-Roman Empire. Court scribes would sometimes rise to positions of social prestige and considerable political influence, much as a secretary of state today. There were schools for the training of such scribes. To master the difficult art of writing on clay probably required as much time then as it takes students now to develop the ability to read and write. Would-be scribes could either enter a regular school or work as an apprentice under a private teacher, though most of them apparently followed the latter procedure. Scribes who were willing to teach could be found everywhere—even in the smaller towns. In fact, most scribes had at least one apprentice, who was treated like a son while learning the profession. Such students learned not only from private tutoring but also from the example of their teacher. This kind of education was sufficient to equip young scribes for the normal commercial branches of the craft. They were fully prepared to handle various kinds of legal and business documents, and they could easily take dictation for private correspondence.

For additional study and training, however, it was necessary to attend the regular schools. For example, only the schools adjacent to the temples had the proper facilities to teach the sciences (including mathematics) and literature, which the more advanced scribes had to master. There, a budding scribe could even study to become a priest. In the ruins of ancient cities, archaeologists have discovered "textbooks" used by pupils. Excavators have also uncovered schoolrooms with benches on which the students sat. Some of the ancient Near Eastern texts that have been unearthed are schoolboy exercises or student copies of originals. These copies are usually not as beautiful or as legible as the originals, which were written by master scribes.

When the teacher wanted to give the students an assignment, he had available in the temple school virtually every type of text imaginable. For elementary work he could have the students practice writing a list of **cuneiform** signs, much like our learning the letters of the alphabet—except that there were some six hundred signs! Another simple assignment would have been to copy dictionaries containing lists of stones, cities, animals, and gods. After such preparatory work, the students could then move to literary texts and, for example, accurately reproduce a portion of one of the great epics, a hymn, or a prayer. Through arduous study and a lengthy program of instruction and practice, a gifted student could become qualified for scribal service in almost any field.

The Jewish scribe undertook a wide range of writing tasks. Often the scribe sat at the gate of the city or in an open area undertaking numerous kinds of writing tasks for illiterate citizens, including correspondence and the writing of receipts and contracts. More officially, the scribe kept records and wrote annals. Religious scribes copied the Scriptures. Several of these men are mentioned in the Old Testament: Shebna (2 Kings 18:18, 37), Shaphan (2 Kings 22:8-12), Ezra (Ezra 7:6, 11; Neh. 8:1, 9-13; 12:26, 36), Baruch (Jer. 36:26, 32), and Jonathan (Jer. 37:15, 20).

From the Old Testament itself, we learn of two exemplary scribes, Baruch and Ezra. Baruch was the scribe for the prophet Jeremiah. During the reign of King Jehoiakim of Judah (605/604 B.C.), Baruch wrote down Jeremiah's prophecy of the judgment that God was going to bring upon Judah unless the nation repented (Jer. 36:1-4). Baruch read the words of Jeremiah's prophecy to the people and to the officials (Jer. 36:9-19). The message finally reached Jehoiakim, who destroyed the scroll and demanded Baruch's and Jeremiah's arrest (Jer. 36:21-26). As a fugitive, Baruch again wrote down Jeremiah's prediction of Judah's destruction (Jer. 36:27-32).

Ezra was called a priest and a scribe (Ezra 7:11-12; Neh. 8:9; 12:26). In the commission of the Persian king Artaxerxes to Ezra, the king described him as "scribe" (Ezra 7:6-11). But Ezra was not a mere copyist; he was a diligent and profound student of God's law (Ezra 7:11-12). It was Ezra who began the tradition of the scribe being a religious teacher, a "scholar." Scribes such as Ezra were qualified to teach and preach the Scriptures, as well as interpret them.

## THE WRITING MATERIALS

Writers used a **stylus** for writing cuneiform ("wedge-shaped" characters) on clay tablets. For writing on **ostraca** (potsherds, or pottery fragments), **papyrus**, and **parchment**, writers split or cut a reed to function as a brush. In Egypt, rushes were used to form a brush. Ink was usually a black carbon (charcoal) mixed with gum or oil for use on parchment or with a metallic substance for use on papyrus. It was kept in an inkhorn as a dried substance, in which the scribe would dip or rub his moistened pen.

The ancient Hebrews probably used leather and papyrus for writing materials. The Dead Sea Scrolls, for example, were sheets of leather sewed together with linen thread. Metal scrolls also existed (e.g., copper). Parchment, a refined leather made from sheep and goat skins, began to replace leather as early as the third century B.C. To prepare parchment, the hair was removed from the skins and the latter rubbed smooth.

The most common form of book for Old Testament documents was evidently a roll or scroll of papyrus, leather, or parchment. The average length of a scroll was about 30 feet, though the famous Harris Papyrus is 133 feet long. Scrolls were often stored in pottery jars (Jer. 32:14) and were frequently sealed.

## THE MANUSCRIPTS

Not one of the original writings (called the **autographs**) of any book in the Old Testament exists or is **extant** today. Fortunately, Jewish scribes throughout the ages have made copies of God's word. If a scroll wore out or if there was a need for copies in various synagogues, Jewish scribes would make additional copies. These scribes were usually the "readers" (or what is technically known as **lectors**) of Scripture in the meetings of the Jews. Thus, their task was to keep good copies of the Scriptures and to read them to the congregation on each Sabbath day.

### Significant Masoretic Manuscripts

Beginning in the sixth century and continuing into the tenth century A.D., European Jewish scribes called the **Masoretes** worked carefully to preserve the Old Testament text as they transmitted it from copy to copy. The Hebrew word *masora* means “that which is transmitted,” “that which is handed down”; hence, the name, Masoretes.

The Masoretes came from Tiberias on the Sea of Galilee. Their scholarly school flourished between A.D. 500 and 1000. They standardized the traditional **consonantal text** by adding **vowel pointing** and marginal notes. And they produced countless copies of the Old Testament Scriptures. Several of the manuscripts they produced still exist.

The Masoretic Text (denoted as MT) as it exists today owes much to the ben Asher family. For five or six generations, from the second half of the eighth century to the middle of the tenth century A.D., this family played a leading role in the Masoretic work at Tiberias. A faithful record of their work can be found in the oldest existing Masoretic manuscripts. The oldest dated Masoretic manuscript is Codex Cairensis (A.D. 895), which is attributed to Moses ben Asher. The other major surviving manuscript attributed to the ben Asher family is the Aleppo Codex (see below).

There are quite a number of less important manuscript **codices** that reflect the Masoretic tradition: the Petersburg Codex of the prophets and the Erfurt Codices. There are also a number of manuscripts that no longer exist but were used by scholars in the Masoretic period. One of the most prominent is Codex Hillel, traditionally attributed to Rabbi Hillel ben Moses ben Hillel about A.D. 600. This **codex** was said to be very accurate and was used for the revision of other manuscripts. Readings of this codex are cited repeatedly by the early medieval Masoretes.

Codex Muga, Codex Jericho, and Codex Jerushalmi, also no longer extant, were cited by the Masoretes. These manuscripts were likely prominent examples of unpointed texts that had become part of a standardizing consensus in the first centuries

A.D. These laid the groundwork for the work of the Masoretes of Tiberias.[1]

*The Cairo Codex of the Prophets (Codex Cairensis) (ca. A.D. 895)* This manuscript contained both the Former Prophets (Joshua, Judges, Samuel, and Kings) and the Latter Prophets (Isaiah, Jeremiah, Ezekiel, and the twelve Minor Prophets). The rest of the Old Testament is missing from this manuscript. It was probably written by Moses ben Asher for the Akraite Jew, Yabes ben Shelomo, in 895. Thereafter, it was well preserved by the Karaite Synagogue of Cairo.

*The Aleppo Codex (tenth century A.D.)* According to the manuscript's concluding note, Aaron ben Moses ben Asher was responsible for writing the Masoretic notes and pointing the text. This manuscript contains the entire Old Testament and dates from the first half of the tenth century A.D. It was reportedly destroyed in anti-Jewish riots in 1947, but this proved to be only partly true. A majority of the manuscript survived and has been used as the basis for a new critical edition of the Hebrew Bible to be published by the Hebrew University in Jerusalem.

*The Leningrad Codex (Codex Leningradensis) (A.D. 1008–1009)* This manuscript originally contained the entire Old Testament, but a quarter of it is now missing. Presently stored in the Leningrad Public Library, this manuscript is of special importance as a witness to the ben Asher text. According to a note on the manuscript, it was copied in A.D. 1008 from texts written by Aaron ben Moses ben Asher. Since the oldest complete Hebrew text of the Old Testament (the Aleppo Codex) was not available to scholars earlier in this century, Codex Leningradensis (as the

[1] For more on the Masoretes and their work, see Würthwein, *Text of the Old Testament*, 12-37.

Leningrad Codex is called in Latin) was used as the textual base for the popular Hebrew texts of today: *Biblia Hebraica* (1929–1937), edited by R. Kittel, and its revision, *Biblia Hebraica Stuttgartensia* (1967–1977), edited by A. Alt, O. Eissfieldt, and P. Kahle.

*The Leningrad Codex of the Prophets* This codex, made in A.D. 916, contains the Major Prophets.[1]

*The British Museum Codex Oriental 4445* This ninth- or tenth-century codex, housed in the British Museum, contains a large portion of the Pentateuch in 186 **folios**. It appears that 129 of these folios reflect an early form of the text made by ben Asher around A.D. 895. The other 55 folios were added later, around 1540.

*The Firkowitsch Codex* This is the oldest complete codex of the Old Testament, dated A.D. 1010.

### Other Significant Old Testament Manuscripts

*The Nash Papyrus* This papyrus was unearthed from Egypt at the beginning of the twentieth century. When it was compared with Aramaic papyri and **ostraca** (texts written in ink on pottery) from Egypt and with Herodian inscriptions, it was determined that the Nash Papyrus was written in the Maccabean period, about 100 B.C. This papyrus shows a striking similarity of script with the scrolls of the Qumran manuscripts of the Old Testament. It contains the Ten Commandments and the Jewish *Shema* (Deut. 6:4-5): "Hear, O Israel: The LORD our God *is* one LORD: And thou shalt love the LORD thy God with all thine heart, and with all thy soul, and with all thy might" (KJV). This manuscript was not a part of a parchment scroll but a separate leaf used in teaching. W. L. Nash acquired it in

[1] Further descriptions of extant Masoretic manuscripts can be found in Würthwein, 34-37.

Egypt in 1902 and later donated it to the Cambridge University Library.

*Cairo Genizah Fragments* Near the end of the nineteenth century, many fragments from the sixth to the eighth centuries were found in an old synagogue in Cairo, Egypt, which had been Saint Michael's Church until A.D. 882. They were found there in a **genizah**, a storage room where worn or faulty manuscripts were hidden until they could be disposed of properly. This genizah had apparently been walled off and forgotten until its recent discovery. In this small room, as many as two hundred thousand fragments were preserved, including biblical texts in Hebrew and Aramaic. The fact that the biblical fragments date from the fifth century A.D. makes them invaluable for shedding light on the development of the Masoretic work prior to the standardization instituted by the great Masoretes of Tiberias.

### The Dead Sea Scrolls

In 1947 and in 1948, the year Israel regained its national independence, there was a phenomenal discovery. A Bedouin shepherd boy found scrolls in a cave west of the Dead Sea. These scrolls, known as the **Dead Sea Scrolls**, are dated between 100 B.C. and A.D. 100. They are nearly a thousand years earlier than any of the Masoretic manuscripts. The Dead Sea Scrolls contain significant portions of the Old Testament. Every book except Esther is represented. The largest portions come from the Pentateuch (especially Deuteronomy: twenty-five manuscripts), the major Prophets (especially Isaiah: eighteen manuscripts), and Psalms (twenty-seven manuscripts). The Dead Sea Scrolls also have portions of the Septuagint, the **Targums** (an Aramaic paraphrase of the Old Testament), some **apocryphal** fragments, and a commentary on Habakkuk.

The scribes who made these scrolls were members of a community of ascetic Jews who lived in Qumran from the third century B.C. to the first century A.D.

*Significance of the Dead Sea Scrolls* Even though the Dead Sea Scrolls are nearly a thousand years older than the Masoretic manuscripts, there are not as many significant differences between the two groups of manuscripts as one might expect. Normally, a thousand years of copying would have generated thousands of differences in wording. But this is not the case when one compares most of the Dead Sea Scrolls with the Masoretic manuscripts. This shows that Jewish scribes for over a millennium copied one form of the text with extreme fidelity.

The greatest importance of the Dead Sea Scrolls lies in the discovery of biblical manuscripts dating back to only about three hundred years after the close of the Old Testament canon. That makes them one thousand years earlier than the oldest manuscripts previously known to biblical scholars. The texts found at *Wadi Qumran* (as the area is called) were all completed before the Roman conquest of Palestine in A.D. 70, and many predate this event by quite some time. Among the Dead Sea Scrolls, the Isaiah Scroll has received the most publicity, although the collection contains fragments of all the books in the Hebrew Bible with the exception of Esther.

*History of the Dead Sea Scrolls' Discovery* Because the discovery of the Dead Sea Scrolls is so important for Old Testament textual criticism, a short history and description of these recent discoveries is appropriate. Before the Qumran find, few manuscripts had been discovered in the Holy Land. The early **church father** Origen (third century A.D.) mentioned using Hebrew and Greek manuscripts that had been stored in jars in caves near Jericho. In the ninth century A.D., a patriarch of the

Eastern church, Timothy I, wrote a letter to Sergius, Metropolitan (Archbishop) of Elam, in which he, too, referred to a large number of Hebrew manuscripts found in a cave near Jericho. For more than one thousand years since then, however, no other significant manuscript discoveries were forthcoming from caves in that region near the Dead Sea.

The history of the Dead Sea manuscripts, both of their hiding and of their finding, reads like a mystery adventure story. It began with a telephone call on Wednesday afternoon, February 18, 1948, in the troubled city of Jerusalem. Butrus Sowmy, librarian and monk of Saint Mark's Monastery in the Armenian quarter of the Old City of Jerusalem, was calling John C. Trever, acting director of the American Schools of Oriental Research (ASOR). Sowmy had been preparing a catalog of the monastery's collection of rare books. Among them he found some scrolls in ancient Hebrew which, he said, had been in the monastery for about forty years. Could ASOR supply him with some information for the catalog?

The following day, Sowmy and his brother brought a suitcase containing five scrolls or parts of scrolls wrapped in an Arabic newspaper. Pulling back the end of one of the scrolls, Trever discovered that it was written in a clear, square Hebrew script. He copied several lines from that scroll, carefully examined three others, but was unable to unroll the fifth because it was too brittle. After the Syrians left, Trever told the story of the scrolls to William H. Brownlee, an ASOR fellow. Trever further noted in the lines he had copied from the first scroll the double occurrence of an unusual negative construction in Hebrew. In addition, the Hebrew script of the scrolls was more archaic than anything he had ever seen.

Trever then visited Saint Mark's Monastery. There he was introduced to the Syrian Archbishop, Athanasius Samuel, who gave him permission to photograph the scrolls. Trever and Brownlee compared the style of handwriting on the scrolls with a photograph of the Nash Papyrus. The two ASOR scholars concluded that the script on the newly-found manuscripts belonged to the same period. When ASOR director, Millar Burrows, returned to Jerusalem from Baghdad a few days later, he was shown the scrolls, and the three men continued their investigation. Only then did the Syrians reveal that the scrolls had been purchased the year before, in 1947, and had not been in the monastery for forty years as was first reported.

The true history is that sometime during the winter of 1946/1947, three Bedouins were tending their sheep and goats near a spring in the vicinity of Wadi Qumran. One of the herdsmen, throwing a rock through a small opening in the cliff, heard the sound of the rock evidently shattering an earthenware jar inside. Another Bedouin later lowered himself into the cave and found ten tall jars lining the walls. Three manuscripts (one of them in four pieces) stored in two of the jars were removed from the cave and were thereafter offered to an antiquities dealer in Bethlehem.

Several months later, the Bedouins secured four more scrolls (one of them in two pieces) from the cave and sold them to another dealer in Bethlehem. During Holy Week in 1947, Saint Mark's Syrian Orthodox Monastery in Jerusalem was informed of the four scrolls, and Metropolitan Athanasius Samuel offered to buy them. The sale was not completed, however, until July 1947 when the four scrolls were bought by the Monastery. They included a complete Isaiah scroll, a commentary on Habakkuk, a scroll containing a Manual of Discipline of the religious community at Qumran, and the *Genesis Apocryphon* (an Aramaic paraphrase of Genesis).

In November and December of 1947, an Armenian antiquities dealer in Jerusalem informed E. L. Sukenik, then Professor of Archaeology at the Hebrew University in Jerusalem, of the first three scrolls found in the cave by the Bedouins. Sukenik then secured the three scrolls and two jars from the antiquities dealer in Bethlehem. They included an incomplete scroll of Isaiah, the Hymns of Thanksgiving (containing twelve columns of original psalms), and the War Scroll. (That scroll, also known as "The War of the Children of Darkness," describes a war, actual or spiritual, of the tribes of Levi, Judah, and Benjamin against the Moabites and Edomites.)

On April 1, 1948, the first news release appeared in newspapers around the world, followed by another news release on April 26 by Sukenik about the manuscripts he had already acquired at the Hebrew University. In 1949, Athanasius Samuel brought the four scrolls from Saint Mark's Monastery to the United States. They were exhibited in various places and finally were purchased on July 1, 1954, in New York for $250,000 by Sukenik's son on behalf of the nation of Israel and sent to the Hebrew University in Jerusalem. Today they are on display in the "Shrine of the Book" Museum in Jerusalem.

Because of the importance of the initial discovery of the Dead Sea Scrolls, both archaeologists and Bedouins continued their search for more manuscripts. Early in 1949, G. Lankester Harding, director of antiquities for the Kingdom of Jordan, and Roland G. de Vaux, of the Dominic Ecole Biblique in Jerusalem, excavated the cave (designated Cave 1 or 1Q—"Q" is for Qumran) where the initial discovery was made. Several hundred caves were explored the same year.

*Contents of the Dead Sea Scrolls* So far, eleven caves in the Wadi Qumran have yielded treasures. Almost 600 manuscripts have been recovered, about 200 of which are biblical material. The fragments number between 50,000 and 60,000 pieces. About 85 percent of the fragments are leather; the other 15 percent are papyrus. The fact that most of the manuscripts are leather contributed to their preservation.

The second most important cave (next to Cave 1) is Cave 4 (designated 4Q), which has yielded about 40,000 fragments of 400 different manuscripts, 100 of which are biblical.

In addition to biblical materials, many sectarian scrolls peculiar to the religious community that lived at Qumran were also found. They furnish historical background on the nature of pre-Christian Judaism and help fill in the gaps of intertestamental history. One of the scrolls, the Damascus Document, had originally turned up in Cairo, but manuscripts of it have now been found at Qumran. The Manual of Discipline was one of the seven scrolls from Cave 1. Fragmentary manuscripts of it have been found in other caves. The document gives the group's entrance requirements, plus regulations governing life in the Qumran community. The Thanksgiving Hymns include some thirty hymns, probably composed by one individual.

There were also many commentaries on different books of the Old Testament. The Habakkuk commentary was a copy of the first two chapters of Habakkuk in Hebrew accompanied by a verse-by-verse commentary. The commentary gives many details about an apocalyptic figure called the "Teacher of Righteousness" who is persecuted by a wicked priest.

A unique discovery was made in Cave 3 (3Q) in 1952. It was a scroll of copper, measuring about eight feet long and a foot wide. Because it was brittle, it was not opened until 1966, and then only by cutting it into strips. It contained an inventory of some sixty locations where treasures of gold, silver, and incense were hidden. Archaeologists have not been able to find any of it. That list of treasures, perhaps from the Jerusalem temple, may have been stored in the cave by Zealots (a revolutionary Jewish political party) during their struggle with the Romans in A.D. 66–70.

During the Six-Day War in June 1967, Sukenik's son, Yigael Yadin of the Hebrew University, acquired a Qumran document called the Temple Scroll. That scroll measures twenty-eight feet and is the longest scroll found so far in the Qumran area. A major portion of it is devoted to statutes of the kings and matters of defense. It also describes sacrificial feasts and rules of cleanliness. Almost half of the scroll gives detailed instructions for building a future temple, supposedly revealed by God to the scroll's author.

*Dating the Dead Sea Scrolls* Early conclusions about the antiquity of the first Dead Sea Scrolls were not accepted by everyone. Some scholars were convinced that the scrolls were of medieval origin. A series of questions relate to the dating problem. When were the texts at Qumran composed? When were they deposited in the caves? Many scholars believe the manuscripts were placed in the caves by members of the Qumran community when Roman legions were besieging Jewish strongholds. That was shortly before the destruction of Jerusalem in A.D. 70. Many other scholars think the scrolls were taken to the Dead Sea caves by Jewish scribes fleeing Roman persecution in the period prior to the destruction of Jerusalem or around the time of the Bar-Kochba revolt (A.D. 132).

Careful study of the contents of a document sometimes reveals its authorship and the date when it was written. An example of using such **internal evidence** for dating a nonbiblical work is found in the Habakkuk commentary. It gives hints about the people and events in the days of the commentary's author, not in the days of the prophet Habakkuk. The commentator described the enemies of God's people as the Kittim. Originally that word denoted Cyprus, but later came to refer more generally to the Greek islands and the coasts of the eastern Mediterranean. In Daniel 11:30 the term is used prophetically, and most scholars seem to identify the Kittim with the Romans. Thus, the Habakkuk commentary was probably written about the time of the Roman capture of Palestine under Pompey in 63 B.C.

Another significant way to date a manuscript is by **paleography**, the study of ancient handwriting. That was the method initially employed by Trever when he compared the script of the Isaiah Scroll with the Nash Papyrus, thus dating it to the pre-Christian era. His conclusions were confirmed by William F. Albright, then the foremost American archaeologist. The evidence of paleography clearly dates the majority of the Qumran scrolls in the period between 200 B.C. and A.D. 200.

Archaeology provides another kind of **external evidence**. The pottery discovered at Qumran dates from the late Hellenistic and early Roman periods (200 B.C.–A.D. 100). Earthenware articles and ornaments point to the same period. Several hundred coins were found in jars dating from the Greco-Roman period. A crack in one of the buildings at Qumran is attributed to an earthquake that, according to Josephus (a Jewish historian who wrote during the first century A.D.), occurred in 31 B.C. The excavations at Khirbet Qumran (the caves of Qumran) indicate that the general period of their occupation was from about 135 B.C. to A.D. 68, the year the Zealot revolt was crushed by Rome.

Finally, radiocarbon analysis has contributed to dating the finds. Radiocarbon analysis is a method of dating material from the amount of radioactive carbon remaining in it. The process is also known as carbon 14 dating. Applied to the linen cloth in which the scrolls were wrapped, the analysis gave a date of A.D. 33 plus or minus two hundred years. A later test bracketed the date between 250 B.C. and A.D. 50. Although there may be questions concerning the relation of the linen wrappings to the date of the scrolls themselves, the carbon 14 test agrees with the conclusions of both paleography and archaeology. On the basis of all of these dating methods, the general period in which the Dead Sea Scrolls can be safely dated is between about 150 B.C. and A.D. 100.

Before the Qumran discoveries, the oldest existing Hebrew manuscripts of the Old Testament were the Masoretic manuscripts noted above, along with the Nash Papyrus and Cairo Genizah fragments. The oldest complete manuscript was the Firkowitsch Codex from A.D. 1010. The greatest importance of the Dead Sea Scrolls, therefore, lies in the discovery of biblical manuscripts dating back to only about three hundred years after the close of the Old Testament canon. That makes them a thousand years earlier than the oldest manuscripts previously known to biblical scholars. The most frequently represented Old Testament books are Genesis, Exodus, Deuteronomy, Psalms, and Isaiah. The oldest text is a fragment of Exodus dating from about 250 B.C. The Isaiah Scroll from Cave 1 dates from about 100 B.C.

Whatever differences may have existed between the community at Qumran and the mainstream of Jews from which it separated, it is certain that both used common biblical texts. Thus, the manuscripts could have originated from either Jerusalem, the Qumran community, or both.[1]

---

[1] The section on the Dead Sea Scrolls and their dating was excerpted and adapted from M. Norton, "The Text of the Old Testament," in Comfort, *Origin of the Bible*, 156-161, 171-173. Used by permission.

### Significant Dead Sea Scroll Manuscripts

Among the hundreds of biblical manuscripts discovered in the eleven caves around the Dead Sea, there are some very significant ones—especially for textual studies.

Over eight hundred manuscripts have been discovered in the caves at Qumran. The vast majority of the manuscripts are poorly preserved. Often, only a few columns of text survive. Many times only a few barely legible scraps can be identified; but the quantity of material offers a treasure of information from a period and region that previously yielded little manuscript evidence. There are about two hundred fifty Qumran biblical manuscripts, mostly in Hebrew, but some in Aramaic and Greek.

Some of the more significant manuscripts are briefly described below. When a manuscript is described as being **proto-Masoretic**, this means that its text largely agrees with that found later in Masoretic manuscripts. Other manuscripts will be described as having affinities with the Samaritan Pentateuch or the Septuagint (designated LXX).

In the names of the Qumran manuscripts, the first number signifies the cave, Q indicates Qumran, the abbreviation for the biblical book follows, often followed by a superscript letter for successive manuscripts containing the same book.

*1QIsa$^{a}$* This is the first Dead Sea Scroll to receive widespread attention. It is dated to ca. 100 B.C. The text, which includes most of Isaiah, is proto-Masoretic with some significant variants. The RSV committee, which was nearing completion of their work at the time, adopted thirteen readings from 1QIsa$^{a}$. Many translations published since the RSV have also adopted readings from this manuscript.

*1QpaleoLev(+Num) (= 1Q3)* This manuscript contains portions of Leviticus and Numbers (Lev. 11; 19–23; Num. 1). Some scholars categorize it as three different manuscripts, which are designated as $1QpaleoLev^a$, $1QpaleoLev^b$, and 1QpaleoNum. The **paleo-Hebrew script** (archaic Hebrew handwriting) is difficult to date, since the scribe was probably imitating an older style of writing. Richard S. Hanson dates it somewhere between 125 and 75 B.C.[1]

*$1QIsa^b$* The text, which includes most of Isaiah, is proto-Masoretic. It is dated from 25 B.C. to A.D. 50.

*2QJer* This manuscript is dated from 25 B.C. to A.D. 50 and has portions of Jeremiah chapters 42–49. It has some readings that follow the Septuagint (LXX), while it follows the order of chapters found in proto-Masoretic texts. For the book of Jeremiah, the Septuagint and Masoretic Text are quite different: the Septuagint is one-eighth shorter and has a different arrangement of chapters.

*$4QpaleoExod^m$* This manuscript, containing most of Exodus, is dated quite early, 200–175 B.C., primarily because it displays paleo-Hebrew script. As such, it has provided scholars with some interesting insights into the early history of the **textual transmission** of Exodus and the Pentateuch. The manuscript shows many similarities with the Samaritan Pentateuch (described below).

*$4QNum^b$* This manuscript, dated 30 B.C.–A.D. 20, contains most of Numbers. The book of Numbers existed in three distinguishable textual traditions: the Masoretic Text, the Samaritan Pentateuch, and the Septuagint. This manuscript, $4QNum^b$, shows similarities with the Samaritan Pentateuch and the Septuagint, while having its own unique readings.

---

[1] Hanson, *Paleo-Hebrew Scripts*, 41.

*4QDeut^a* Though it contains only a few verses of Deuteronomy (23:26(?); 24:1-8), this manuscript is one of the earliest copies of Deuteronomy found at Qumran. Harold Scanlin said, "The text appears to be quite close to the presumed original form of the text of Deuteronomy."[1]

*4QSam^a* This manuscript, containing about a tenth of 1 and 2 Samuel, is dated ca. 50–25 B.C. This manuscript, showing some similarities with the Septuagint, is believed to have several readings that are superior to the Masoretic Text. Scanlin said, "The MT of Samuel is generally considered to be quite problematic, with numerous omissions. This Qumran manuscript demonstrates the existence of a Hebrew text that is considered to be superior to the MT in many passages."[2]

*4QJer^a* This manuscript, containing portions of Jeremiah 7–22, dates ca. 200 B.C. It generally concurs with the Masoretic Text.

*4QJer^b* This manuscript, dated ca. 150–125 B.C., follows the arrangement of the Septuagint, as well as its brevity. The significance of this is that two different texts of Jeremiah were used in the pre-Christian era—one that was proto-Masoretic (as with 4QJer^a) and one that was like the Septuagint.

*4QDan^a* This manuscript, containing portions of many chapters in Daniel, dates to the late Hasmonean or early Herodian period. In Daniel 1:20 there appears to be a gap in the extant fragments that would be about the size necessary to include the longer text found in the Greek manuscript 967 (Chester Beatty Papyrus IX).

*5QPs* This manuscript from the first century A.D. contains Psalm 119:99-101, 104, 113-120, 138-142. The first letters in

---

[1] Scanlin, *Dead Sea Scrolls*, 60.

[2] Ibid., 64.

the right margin of two columns show that the manuscript of this Psalm preserved the original acrostic arrangement, which means that each new stanza began with successive letters of the Hebrew alphabet.

*11QPs[a]* This manuscript, dated ca. A.D. 25–50, preserves many psalms. However, these are not in the traditional sequence found in the Hebrew Bible. Furthermore, the manuscript has an additional psalm, known as Psalm 151. Prior to the Qumran discovery, this psalm was known only through ancient translations (LXX, Latin, and Syriac). The Hebrew text indicates two separate poems, which the translations combined. The first poem (designated by Sanders as 151a) is a commentary on 1 Samuel 16:1-13. It relates how David was set over his father's flocks but was made king over God's people after God had looked upon his heart. The second poem (151b) is a commentary on 1 Samuel 17 and deals with David and Goliath. It is thought by some to show the bravery of David in contrast to his humility as is shown in 151a.[1]

### Scroll Discoveries at Wadi Murabba'at

In 1951, Bedouins discovered more manuscripts in caves in the *Wadi Murabba'at,* which extends southeast from Bethlehem toward the Dead Sea, about eleven miles south of Qumran. Four caves were excavated there in 1952 under G. Lankester Harding and Roland G. de Vaux. They yielded biblical documents and important materials, such as letters and coins, from the time of the Second Jewish Revolt under Bar Kochba in A.D. 132–135. Among the biblical manuscripts was a scroll containing a Hebrew text of the Minor Prophets, dating from the second century A.D. This manuscript corresponds almost perfectly with the

---

[1] Further descriptions of the Dead Sea Scrolls can be found in Scanlin's *Dead Sea Scrolls,* 43-83.

Masoretic Text, hinting that by the second century, a standard consonantal text was already taking shape. Also found in Wadi Murabba'at were fragments of the Pentateuch and of Isaiah.

## TEXTUAL CRITICISM OF THE OLD TESTAMENT

The task of the textual critic can be divided into a number of general stages: (1) the collection and collation of existing manuscripts, translations, and quotations; (2) the development of theory and methodology that will enable the critic to use the gathered information to reconstruct the most accurate text of the biblical materials; (3) the reconstruction of the history of the transmission of the text in order to identify the various influences affecting the text; and (4) the evaluation of specific **variant readings** in light of textual evidence, theology, and history.

### MANUSCRIPT TRADITIONS

All the primary sources of the Hebrew Scriptures are handwritten manuscripts, usually written on animal skins, **papyrus**, or sometimes metal. The fact that the manuscripts are handwritten creates the need for textual criticism. Human error and editorial tampering are the source of the many variant readings in Old and New Testament manuscripts. The fact that the ancient manuscripts are written on skins or papyrus is another source of difficulty. Due to natural decay, most of the surviving ancient manuscripts are fragmentary and difficult to read.

There are many secondary witnesses to the ancient Old Testament text, including translations into other languages, quotations used by both friends and enemies of biblical religion, and evidence from early printed texts. Most of the secondary witnesses have suffered in ways similar to the primary ones. They, too, contain numerous variants due to both intentional and accidental scribal errors and are fragmentary as a result of natural decay. Since variant readings do exist in the surviving ancient manuscripts, these must be collected and compared. The task of comparing and listing the variant readings is known as **collation**.

Both Old and New Testament textual critics undertake a similar task and face similar obstacles. They both seek to recover a hypothetical "original" text with limited resources that are at varying degrees of deterioration. But the Old Testament textual critic faces a more complex textual history than does his New Testament counterpart. The New Testament was written primarily in the first century A.D., and complete New Testament manuscripts exist that were written only a hundred years later. The Old Testament, however, is made up of literature written over a thousand-year period, the oldest parts dating to the twelfth century B.C., or possibly even earlier. To make matters even more difficult, until recently, the earliest known Hebrew manuscripts of the Old Testament were medieval. This left scholars with little witness to the Old Testament's textual development from ancient times to the Middle Ages, a period of over two thousand years.

The Masoretic manuscripts, as old as they are, were written between one and two thousand years after the original **autographs**. Until the discovery of the Dead Sea Scrolls in the 1940s and 1950s, secondary Aramaic, Greek, and Latin translations served as the earliest significant witnesses to the early Hebrew Scriptures. Since these are translations, and subject to sectarian alterations, editorial tampering, and **interpolations**, their value to the textual critic, though significant, is limited.

The discoveries of the Dead Sea Scrolls and other early

manuscripts have provided primary witnesses to the Hebrew Old Testament in earlier times. The textual evidence of Dead Sea Scrolls has helped scholars understand that there were, at least, three lines of textual transmission prior to the first century B.C. They know this because some of the manuscripts discovered in Qumran, especially two manuscripts of 1 Samuel, show greater affinity with the Septuagint than with the Masoretic Text; and other manuscripts from Qumran, especially one manuscript of Exodus, resemble the **Samaritan Pentateuch**. Thus, there must have been some different forms of the text other than the one appearing in most of the Dead Sea Scrolls and then later in the Masoretic manuscripts.

One line of transmission of the Old Testament text has been manifest in the Greek translation of the Hebrew Old Testament known as the **Septuagint**. (The majority of Old Testament quotations in the New Testament are from the Septuagint). That translation was made about 250 B.C. and ranks second in importance to the Masoretic Text for reconstructing an authentic Old Testament text. In the past, some scholars attributed differences between the Septuagint and the Masoretic Text to imprecision, subjectivity, or laxity on the part of the Septuagint's translators. Now it seems that many of those differences resulted from the fact that the translators were following a slightly different Hebrew text. Some Hebrew texts from Qumran correspond to the Septuagint and have proved helpful in solving textual problems. Septuagint manuscripts have also been found among the Dead Sea Scrolls.

Another line of Old Testament transmission has been manifest in the Samaritan preservation of the Hebrew text of the Pentateuch dating from the second century B.C. The copies of the Samaritan Pentateuch were written in the same script used in some of the Dead Sea Scrolls found at Qumran. Some of the Hebrew biblical texts among the Qumran documents have closer affinities with the text of the Samaritan version than with the text handed down by the Masoretic scholars. All of the manuscripts have shed new light on grammatical forms, spelling, and punctuation.

Another line of textual transmission led up to the kind of text that is found in most of the Dead Sea Scrolls and then in the Masoretic Text. The Masoretes standardized the traditional consonantal text by adding vowels and marginal notes (the ancient Hebrew alphabet had no vowels). Some scholars dated the origin of the consonantal Masoretic Text to the editorial activities of Rabbi Akiba and his colleagues in the second century A.D. The discoveries at Qumran, however, proved them wrong, by showing that the Masoretic Text went back several more centuries into antiquity and had been accurately copied and transmitted. Although there are some differences in spelling and grammar between the Dead Sea Scrolls and Masoretic Text, the differences have not warranted any major changes in the substance of the Old Testament. Yet they have helped biblical scholars gain a clearer understanding of textual differences.

Various scholars attempted to account for such diversity by **local text theories**. Frank M. Cross, the first editor assigned to most of the biblical manuscripts in Qumran's Cave 4, developed a **three-recension theory** with **text types** being created in three different geographic regions: (1) Egypt (the Septuagint), (2) Palestine (the Samaritan Pentateuch), and (3) Babylon (the proto-Masoretic text). Cross's theory was quite influential in shaping the discussion about textual witnesses.[1]

Shemaryahu Talmon adjusted Cross's text type theory by arguing that the groupings should be sociological rather than

[1] Cross, "New Directions."

geographical. His contention was that three text groups survived because the groups that preserved them survived: (1) Jews (the proto-Masoretic text), (2) Samaritans (the Samaritan Pentateuch), and (3) Christians (who adopted the Septuagint as their edition of the Old Testament).[1]

In recent years, scholars have been less prone to affirm three clear-cut types of texts. Instead, they point out that several of the Dead Sea Scrolls show a mixture of text types. For example, the Old Testament textual critic Emanuel Tov, expressing a typical view among contemporary Old Testament textual critics, has observed the mixed nature of some important Qumran biblical manuscripts:

> We suggest that the Samuel scrolls from Cave 4, 11QpaleoLev, as well as many other texts from Qumran, reflect such early texts [not three recensions] of the OT, insofar as they do not agree exclusively with one tradition, but agree now with this and then with that text (MT, LXX, and Samaritan Pentateuch), and in addition contain a significant number of exclusive readings. In our view, the traditional characterization of the LXX as a text type is imprecise and misleading. In the case of the Samuel scrolls, the recognition of a relatively large number of "LXX readings" made it easy for scholars to label some of these scrolls as "Septuagintal," and this characterization was readily accepted in scholarship which had become used to viewing the textual witnesses of the OT as belonging to three main streams. However, . . . this view should now be considered outdated.[2]

---

[1] Talmon, "Old Testament Text."

[2] Tov, *Texts of Samuel*, 64–65.

Many contemporary Old Testament textual critics think that the varying degrees of textual fidelity probably show that the autographs were subject to editorial adjustments soon after they were originally composed. Indeed, the earliest scribes seemed to have functioned as editors or **redactors**, who thought it their function to improve the original work by adding minor details and other interpolations. According to Tov, this was a kind of intermediary stage between the original composition and the copying of the book. One could call it a "compositional-transmissional" or "editorial-scribal" stage.

Thus, the period of textual unity reflected in the assumed pristine texts of the biblical books was brief at best. Tov believed that most of the textual changes in the Hebrew Bible were created by editors during the **compositional-transmissional stage**, and not by later scribes in the **textual-transmission stage**. In this regard, Tov wrote:

> The amount of deliberate changes inserted by scribes was probably smaller than believed . . . [because] many of the pervasive changes in the biblical text, pertaining to whole sentences, sections and books should not, according to our description, be ascribed to copyists, but to earlier generations of editors who allowed themselves such massive changes in the formative stage of the biblical literature.[1]

Another prominent view among contemporary scholars is that some of the extreme textual differences in certain books of the Old Testament can be traced—not to the **recensional** work of scribes—but to early editions of the same work.

[1] Tov, *Textual Criticism*, 265-266.

Scanlin, for example, thinks there is clear evidence of at least two ancient editions for 1 and 2 Samuel.[1] Sharing the same view, Eugene Ulrich makes the following comments:

> For 1 Samuel 1–2, we find in the earlier edition (which, I would suggest, is the MT) a straightforward account with one portrait of Hannah. In the secondary edition (the LXX), we find the intentional and consistent reshaping of that account, arguably for theological motives and possibly for misogynous motives, to give a changed portrait of Hannah. When we turn to 1 Samuel 17–18, in the earlier edition (the LXX this time), we find a single version of the story; whereas in the secondary edition (here the MT), we find a composite version.[2]

The current view about the transmission of the Old Testament text is that, after several centuries of textual plurality in the books of the Hebrew Bible, a period of uniformity and stability can be discerned, beginning as early as the third century B.C. and becoming firmly fixed by the end of the first century A.D. This text has been called the proto-Masoretic text because it anticipates the Masoretic Text of Medieval times. During this period (200 B.C.–A.D. 100), the Hebrew text did not change much because it was copied with painstaking accuracy. It is known that scribes would count the number of letters on the new copy and compare it with the **exemplar** in an attempt to find even one letter difference between the two. If the copy was in error, it would be corrected or destroyed. This practice continued generation after generation and century after century. Beginning in the sixth century and into the tenth century

[1] Scanlin, *op. cit.*, 211-213.

[2] Ulrich, "Double Literary Editions," 103-105.

A.D., the Masoretes worked carefully to preserve the Old Testament text as they transmitted it from copy to copy. Thus, it is evident that the period of textual stability greatly curbed scribal creativity—meaning scribes had to keep themselves from interacting with the text.

Standardization as practiced by the Masoretes meant identifying one text as normative and copying carefully from that text. It also meant correcting existing texts by the normative text. The next stage in the transmission of the Old Testament text was standardization of punctuation and vowel patterns. That process, which began fairly early in the Christian era, extended over a period of one thousand years. A long series of Masoretes provided annotations known as *masora,* which, in Hebrew, means "tradition." Two different motivations are evident in their work. One was their concern for accurate reproduction of the consonantal text. For that purpose a collection of annotations on irregular forms, abnormal patterns, the number of times a form or word was used, and other matters was gathered and inserted in the margins or at the end of the text.

A second concern of the Masoretes was to record and standardize the **vocalization** (pronunciation) of the consonantal text for reading purposes. Up until that time, scribes had been prohibited against inserting vowels to make the vocalization of the text clear. Because of this, a proper reading of the text depended on the oral tradition passed down from generation to generation. The Masoretes designed a system of **vowel pointing** in which the vowels were represented above and below the consonantal text by small marks, rather than by letters inserted into the consonantal text.

The origins of vocalization reflect differences between Babylon and Palestine. The Tiberian Masoretes (scholars working in Tiberias in Palestine) provided the most complete and exact system of vocalization. The earliest-dated manuscript from that tradition is a codex of the Prophets from the Karaite synagogue of Cairo dated A.D. 896.

Standardization of both the consonantal text and vocalization succeeded so well that the manuscripts that have survived display a remarkable agreement. Most of the variants, being minor and attributable to scribal error, do not affect interpretation.

## METHODOLOGY OF OLD TESTAMENT TEXTUAL CRITICISM

The search for an adequate methodology to handle the many variant readings found in manuscripts is inseparably intertwined with our understanding of the history of transmission. The basic issue in textual criticism is the method used to decide the relative value of those variant readings. Many factors must be evaluated in order to arrive at a valid decision.

Modern science has provided a number of aids for deciphering a manuscript. Scientific dating procedures help to determine the age of the writing materials. Chemical techniques help clarify writing that has deteriorated. Ultraviolet light enables a scholar to see traces of ink (carbon) in a manuscript even after the surface writing has been effaced.

Each manuscript must be studied as a whole, for each has a "personality." It is important to identify the characteristic errors, characteristic carelessness or carefulness, and other peculiarities of the scribe(s) who copied the manuscript. Then the manuscript must be compared with other manuscripts to identify the "family" tradition with which it agrees. Preservation of common errors or insertions in the text is a clue to relationships. All possible details of date, place of origin, and authorship must be ascertained.

### Types of Scribal Errors

Scribal errors fall into several distinct categories. The first large category is that of *unintentional errors.* Unintentional errors fall into the following types:

1. Confusion of similar consonants and the **transposition** of two consonants are frequent errors.
2. Corruptions also resulted from an incorrect division of words (many early manuscripts omitted spaces between words in order to save space).
3. Confusion of sounds occurred particularly when one scribe read to a group of scribes making multiple copies.
4. In the Old Testament, the method of vocalization (addition of vowels to the consonantal text) created some errors.
5. Omissions (**haplography**) of a letter, word, or phrase created new readings. Omission could be caused by the eye of a scribe slipping from one word to a similar word or ending. Omissions by **homoioteleuton** (Greek meaning "similar endings") were quite common. This occurred when two words that were identical, similar, or had identical endings were found close to each other, and the eye of the copyist moved from the first to the second, omitting the words between them.
6. Repetition (**dittography**) of a letter, word, or even a whole phrase was also common, caused by the eye skipping backward, perhaps to a word with a similar ending (homoioteleuton).
7. In the Old Testament, errors were at times caused by the use of consonants as vowel letters in some ancient

texts. Copyists unaware of this usage of vowel letters would copy them in as aberrant consonants.

Normally, unintentional errors are fairly easy to identify because they create nonsense readings. **Intentional alterations** are much more difficult to identify and evaluate. **Harmonizations** from similar materials occurred with regularity. A thinking scribe might attempt to "improve" a difficult reading. Objectionable expressions were sometimes eliminated or smoothed out. Occasionally synonyms were employed. **Conflation** (resolving a discrepancy between two variant readings by including both of them) often appears.

Becoming aware of these common problems is the first step in detecting and eliminating the more obvious errors and identifying and eliminating the peculiarities of a particular scribe. Then more subtle criteria for identifying the reading most likely to be the original must be employed. Procedures for applying such criteria are similar in both Old Testament and New Testament work.

### General Characteristics of Various Text Types

The basic text for primary consideration is the Masoretic Text because of the careful standardization it represents.[1] That text is compared with the testimony of the ancient versions. The Septuagint, by reason of age and basic faithfulness to the Hebrew text, carries significant weight in all decisions. The **Targums** (Aramaic paraphrases) also reflect the Hebrew base but exhibit a tendency to expansion and paraphrase. The Syriac (**Peshitta**), Latin (**Vulgate**), Old Latin, and **Coptic** (Egyptian) versions add **indirect evidence**, although translations are not always clear witnesses in technical details. Use of

[1] Würthwein makes a strong case for this in his *Text of the Old Testament*, 114–116.

such versions enables scholars to do **comparative philology** in textual decisions and thus expose early errors for which the original reading probably has not survived. (Each of these versions is discussed in chapter 5.)

## General Methodological Principles

Through the work of textual critics in the last several centuries, certain basic principles have evolved. The primary principles for the Old Testament can be summarized briefly.

1. *The reading that best explains the origin of other variants is preferable.* Information from reconstruction of the history of transmission often provides additional insight. Knowledge of typical scribal errors enables the critic to make an educated decision on the sequence of variants.
2. *The shorter reading is preferable.* The scribes frequently added material in order to solve problems with style or syntax and seldom abridged or condensed material.
3. *The more difficult reading is more likely to be the original one.* This principle is closely related to the second. Scribes did not intentionally create more complex readings. Unintentional errors are usually easy to identify. Thus, the easier reading is normally suspect as a scribal alteration.
4. *Readings that are not* **harmonized** *or* **assimilated** *to similar passages are preferable.* Copyists had a tendency to correct material on the basis of similar material elsewhere (sometimes even unconsciously).
5. *When all else fails, the textual critic must resort to* **conjectural emendation**. To make an "educated guess" requires intimate acquaintance with the Hebrew

> language, familiarity with the author's style, and an understanding of culture, customs, and theology that might color the passage. Use of conjecture must be limited to those passages in which the original reading has definitely not been transmitted to us.

It should be noted that textual criticism operates only when two or more readings are possible for a specific word or phrase. For most of the biblical text, a single reading has been transmitted. Elimination of scribal errors and intentional changes leaves only a small percentage of the text about which any questions occur.

The field of textual criticism is complex, requiring the gathering and skillful use of a wide variety of information. Because it deals with the authoritative source of revelation for all Christians, textual argumentation has often been accompanied by emotion. Yet in spite of controversy, great progress has been made, particularly in the last century. Refinements in methodology have greatly aided our understanding of the accumulated materials. Additional aid has come from accumulations of information in related fields of study such as archaeology, church history, biblical theology, and the history of Christian thought.

The collection and organization of all variant readings has enabled modern textual critics to give strong assurance that the word of God has been transmitted in an accurate and dependable form. Although variant readings have become obvious through the publication of so many manuscripts, the inadequate, inferior, and secondary readings have been largely eliminated. In relatively few places is conjectural emendation necessary. In matters pertaining to the Christian's salvation, clear and unmistakable transmission provides authoritative answers. Christians are thus in debt to the textual critics who have worked, and are working, to provide a dependable biblical text.

To this day, almost all Bible scholars and translators still use the Masoretic Text of the Hebrew Bible as the authoritative, standard text. At the same time, they make use of the findings of the Dead Sea Scrolls, as well as two other important sources: the Septuagint and the Samaritan Pentateuch. During this century, translators have used *Biblia Hebraica* (1929–1937), and its revision, *Biblia Hebraica Stuttgartensia* (1967–1977). At the same time, translators have profited from the work of the Hebrew Old Testament Text Project (sponsored by the United Bible Societies) and the Hebrew University Bible Project, both of which provide textual information on variant readings from all the extant sources. Using these sources has helped translators make decisions about adopting readings that are superior to those in the Masoretic Text.

CHAPTER TWO

# The New Testament Text

## INSPIRATION OF THE NEW TESTAMENT

After the church began, the early believers relied on the words of the apostles to teach them about Jesus' life and ministry. This oral teaching about Jesus, together with the Septuagint, provided the verbal sustenance for the early church. Then certain individuals—the apostles themselves (such as Matthew and John) and those who knew the apostles (Mark and Luke)—were **inspired** by God to write Gospel accounts to substantiate the oral tradition. Luke, for example, explained in the preface to his Gospel (Luke 1:1-4) that he wrote his account to confirm what had been taught **catechetically** about Jesus' life and ministry. Mark, tradition tells us, compiled a Gospel based on Peter's messages about Jesus' ministry. Many scholars believe that John first preached many of the chapters that he later weaved into a Gospel narrative.

We must remember that Jesus himself never wrote anything. We must rely on the writings of the eyewitnesses for the true accounting of his life and words. By way of analogy, we could consider the writings of Plato about Socrates. As far as we know, Socrates wrote nothing. All that we know about Socrates comes from one of his disciples, Plato. All that we know about Jesus comes from a few of his disciples. What kept these disciples—whether of Plato or of Jesus—from composing fabrications? The presence of the other disciples, who could challenge them on anything they said. One among the Twelve could have testified against any falsification. And there was also a group of seventy-two other disciples (Luke 10:1). By the time the church began, the group had grown to one hundred twenty (Acts 1:15). According to 1 Corinthians 15:6, by the time he had finished his ministry, Jesus had at least five hundred followers (those who witnessed a resurrection appearance) and most of these were still alive (Paul said) in the A.D. 60s—the approximate time when the synoptic Gospels were composed.

Before Jesus left this earth and returned to his Father, he told the disciples that he would send the Holy Spirit to them. He told them that one of the functions of the Holy Spirit would be to remind them of all the things that Jesus had said and then to guide them into more truth (see John 14:26; 15:26; 16:13-15). Those who wrote the Gospels were helped by the Holy Spirit to remember Jesus' exact words, and those who wrote other parts of the New Testament were guided by the Spirit as they wrote.

The **inspiration** for writing the Gospels didn't begin when the authors set pen to papyrus; the inspiration began when the disciples Matthew, Peter (for whom Mark wrote), and John were enlightened by their encounters with Jesus Christ, the Son of God. The apostles' experiences with him altered their lives forever, imprinting on their souls unforgettable images of the revealed God-man, Jesus Christ.

This is what John was speaking of in the prologue to his Gospel when he declared, "The Word became flesh and lived among us, and we have seen his glory" (John 1:14, NRSV). The "we" refers to those eyewitnesses of Jesus' glory—the apostles who lived with Jesus for over three years. John expands upon this reminiscence in the prologue to his first epistle, where he says "we have heard him, touched him, seen him, and looked upon him" (1 John 1:1-2, paraphrased). In both the Gospel and the Epistle, the verbs are in the perfect tense, denoting a past action with a present, abiding effect. John never forgot those past encounters with Jesus; they lived with him and stayed with him as an inspiring spirit until the day—many years later—he wrote of them in his Gospel.

Matthew, as one of the apostles who accompanied Jesus for three years, was also an eyewitness. His profession suited him as a writer. As a custom's collector, he would have regularly used shorthand to keep track of people's taxes. He could easily have employed this practice in taking notes on Jesus' sermons, and then transferred the shorthand form to a fuller, written form. This would not have been unusual in those days. Thus, Matthew's Gospel (in limited form) may have existed in written form (perhaps originally in Aramaic—the language Jesus spoke) as early as the A.D. 30s. Later, Matthew composed an entire Gospel narrative, built around Jesus' sayings. The importance of this is that Matthew's Gospel is an on-the-spot, eyewitness account. In essence, it may have been composed concurrently with the history being observed—much like a traveling journalist would do.

The inspiration for the writing of the Epistles can also be traced to the writers' encounters with the living Christ. The most prominent epistle-writer, Paul, repeatedly claims that his inspiration and subsequent commission came from his encounter with the risen Christ (see, for example, 1 Cor. 15:8-10). Peter also claims that his writings were based upon his experiences with the living Christ (see 1 Pet. 5:1; 2 Pet. 1:16-18). And so does John, who claims to have experienced the God-man visibly, audibly, and palpably (see 1 John 1:1-4). James and Jude make no such claim directly; but since they were the brothers of Jesus who became converts when they saw the risen Christ (this is certain for James—see 1 Cor. 15:7; and presumed for Jude—see Acts 1:14), they too drew their inspiration from their encounters with the living Christ. Thus, all the epistle writers (with the potential exception of the unknown writer of Hebrews) knew the living Christ. This is the relationship that qualified them to write those books which became part of the New Testament **canon**. This made these books distinct from all others.

The writers of the New Testament Epistles were inspired by the Spirit when they wrote. Speaking for all the apostles, Paul indicated that they were taught by the Holy Spirit what to say. The writers of the New Testament did not speak with words "taught by human wisdom," but with words "taught by the Spirit" (see 1 Cor. 2:13, NIV). What they wrote was Spirit-taught. For example, when the apostle John saw that Jesus Christ had come to give eternal life to men, the Spirit helped him express this truth in many different ways. Thus, when the apostle Paul contemplated the fullness of Christ's deity, he was inspired by the Spirit to use such phrasing as "in him dwells all the fullness of the Godhead bodily," "in [him] are hidden all the treasures of wisdom and knowledge," and "the unsearchable riches of Christ" (see Col. 2:9; 2:3; Eph. 3:8, NKJV).

As the Spirit taught the writers, they used their own vocabulary and writing style to express the thoughts of the Spirit. So the Scriptures came as the result of divine and human cooperation. The Scriptures were not **mechanically inspired**—as if God used the men as machines through whom he dictated the divine utterance. Rather, the Scriptures were inspired by God, then written by men. The Bible, therefore, is both fully divine and fully human.

## The Writers of the New Testament

To the best of our knowledge, the authors of the New Testament books are as follows:

| Book | Author |
|---|---|
| **Gospels and Acts** | |
| Matthew | Matthew (the apostle) |
| Mark | Mark (cowriter with Peter) |
| Luke | Luke (Paul's coworker) |
| John | John (the apostle) |
| Acts | Luke (Paul's coworker) |
| **Epistles** | |
| Romans | Paul (the apostle) |
| 1 Corinthians | Paul |
| 2 Corinthians | Paul |
| Galatians | Paul |
| Ephesians | Paul |
| Philippians | Paul |
| Colossians | Paul |
| 1 Thessalonians | Paul |
| 2 Thessalonians | Paul |
| 1 Timothy | Paul |
| 2 Timothy | Paul |
| Titus | Paul |
| Philemon | Paul |
| **General Epistles and Revelation** | |
| Hebrews | Anonymous (Apollos?) |
| James | James (Jesus' brother) |
| 1 Peter | Peter (with Silas) |
| 2 Peter | Peter |
| 1 John | John (the apostle) |
| 2 John | John |
| 3 John | John |
| Jude | Jude (Jesus' brother) |
| Revelation | John |

In none of the Gospels does the author identify himself by name. However, early and widespread tradition indicates who the authors were. The author of the first Gospel was Matthew, one of Jesus' twelve apostles. The second Gospel, probably the first to be written, was composed by John Mark on the basis of Peter's preaching and recollections. We know that the author of the third Gospel is Luke by way of his authorship of the book of Acts, which is the sequel to this Gospel. Luke tells his readers that he based his written Gospel on the accounts given to him by Jesus' eyewitnesses (see Luke 1:1-4). The fourth Gospel was written by Jesus' "beloved disciple," John.

Thirteen New Testament epistles (letters) can be attributed to Paul because they bear his name. The Epistle to the Hebrews is anonymous; many scholars think it was written by Apollos, an early Christian teacher from Alexandria, who was gifted with words. James was written by Jesus' brother James, who had become the primary leader of the church in Jerusalem. 1 Peter was written by Peter with the help of Silas, while 2 Peter was authored by Peter and probably written by some close associate (in much the same way as a book today can be authored by one person, who is the source of the content, while another does the actual writing). Jude was written by another one of Jesus' brothers. 1—3 John, coinciding completely with the style of John's Gospel, were written by John, as was the book of Revelation (1:4).

## THE LANGUAGE OF THE NEW TESTAMENT: KOINÉ GREEK

During its classic period, Greek was the language of one of the world's greatest cultures. During that cultural period, language, literature, and art flourished. The Greek language reflected artistry in its philosophical dialogues, its poetry, and its stately orations. During this period, Greek was also characterized by strength and vigor; classical Greek elaborately developed many forms from a few word roots. Its complex syntax allowed intricate word arrangements to express fine nuances of meaning.

The conquests of Alexander the Great encouraged the spread of Greek language and culture. Regional dialects were largely replaced by Hellenistic or **koiné Greek**. Koiné Greek is a dialect preserved and known through thousands of papyrus writings reflecting all aspects of daily life. The koiné dialect added many **vernacular** expressions to classical Greek, thus making it more cosmopolitan. Simplifying the grammar also better adapted it to a worldwide culture. The new language, reflecting simple, popular speech, became the common language of commerce and diplomacy. The Greek language lost much of its elegance and finely shaded nuance as a result of its evolution from classic to koiné. Nevertheless, it retained its distinguishing characteristics of strength, beauty, clarity, and logical-rhetorical power.

During the centuries immediately before Christ, the Hebrew Scriptures were translated into Greek. This Greek translation, known as the **Septuagint**, later had a strong influence on Christian thought. A consequence of Hebrew writers using the Greek language was that Greek forms of thought influenced Jewish culture. The Jews appropriated from the rich and refined Greek vocabulary some expressions for ideas that were beyond the scope of Hebrew terminology. Also, old Greek expressions acquired new and extended meanings in this translation of the Old Testament by Greek-speaking Jews. Thus, the Greek Old Testament was very significant in the development of Christian thought. Often the usage of a Greek word in the Septuagint provides a key to its meaning in the New Testament.

Although most New Testament authors were Jewish, they wrote in Greek, the universal language of their time. In addition, the apostle John seems to have been acquainted with some Greek philosophy, which influenced his style. John used "Word" (Greek *logos*) in reference to Christ (John 1:1), and several other abstract expressions. John may have been influenced by the Egyptian center of Alexandria, where Greek philosophy and Hebrew learning had merged in a unique way. The apostle Paul also was acquainted with Greek authors (Acts 17:28; 1 Cor. 15:33; Titus 1:12). Greek orators and philosophers influenced Paul's language, as did Hebrew prophets and scholars.

Greek words took on richer, more spiritual meaning in the context of Scripture. Influenced by the simplicity and rich vividness of Semitic style, the New Testament was not written in a peculiar "Holy Ghost" language (as some medieval scholars believed) but in koiné Greek by Semitic-thinking authors. Tens of thousands of papyri unearthed in Egypt in the early twentieth century furnish lexical and grammatical parallels to biblical language, revealing that it was part of the linguistic fabric of that era.

## THE NEW TESTAMENT CANON

The way was paved for a New Testament canon early in the church age by the fact that various books were being collected by congregations—especially Paul's epistles and the four Gospels. Because the Gospels were individual publications from their inception, it took a while for a collection of these four books to be made. The collecting process was completed sooner for Paul's epistles.

### EARLY COLLECTIONS OF NEW TESTAMENT WRITINGS

As Paul's epistles circulated to various churches, neighboring churches began to collect copies of these epistles from their neighbors. This is implicit in Colossians 4:16, where Paul asked the church in Colossae to exchange epistles with the neighboring Laodicean church. Most likely, the epistle "from Laodicea" mentioned in Colossians 4:16 is the epistle we call Ephesians, which was an **encyclical** intended for all the churches in that area, including Laodicea, Colossae, and Ephesus. Paul's language indicates that this epistle would be coming *from* Laodicea to Colossae—and then probably on to Ephesus, its final destination. This exchange implies that each church would make copies of an epistle and send the copies on to the other churches.

Paul's epistles were originally sent to the specific churches to which he was ministering: churches in Corinth, Thessalonica, Philippi, Galatia, Asia Minor (including Ephesus and Colossae), and Rome. But the intent of many of these epistles is that they would be read by more than one local church. This is especially true for Ephesians, which was an encyclical. This epistle would have made the rounds from church to church in Asia Minor, each of which would have made a copy to keep.

Collections of Paul's epistles were being made between A.D. 60 and 100. The earliest date for the collecting process comes from a reference in 2 Peter 3:15-16, which indicates a well-known collection of Paul's writings that are categorized as "Scripture." If Peter authored 2 Peter, this had to have been written prior to Peter's death in A.D. 66/67. If 2 Peter was published posthumously, then we have a later date. Either way, the reference in 2 Peter 3:15-16 tells us that Paul's epistles were being collected and read as Scripture in many churches during the second half of the first century. The well-known New Testament scholar, Gunther Züntz, was confident that there was a Pauline **corpus** (collection) by A.D. 100. Züntz quite convincingly argued that the Pauline corpus was produced by the methods of Alexandrian scholarship and/or in Alexandria itself at the beginning of the second century (ca. 100).[1]

The collection of the four Gospels into one **codex** came about later than the collection of the Pauline Epistles. During the first and early second centuries, each Gospel primarily existed independently. But by the middle of the second century, it appears that churches or individuals began to make codex collections of the Gospels. Various church fathers, such as Justin Martyr and Irenaeus, were speaking of a fourfold Gospel collection in the second century.

The collection of various books by the Christian churches for use in worship was an inadvertent way of canonizing them. There is evidence that within thirty years of the apostle Paul's death, all the Pauline letters (excluding the Pastoral Epistles) were collected and used in the major churches. It is true that some of the smaller letters of Paul (as well as those of Peter and John) were being questioned as to their authority in some quarters for perhaps another fifty years, but this was due only to uncertainty about their authorship in those particular locales. This demonstrates that acceptance was not being imposed by the actions of councils but was happening spontaneously through a normal response on the part of those who had learned the facts about authorship. In those places where the churches were uncertain about the authorship or apostolic approval of certain books, acceptance was slower.

## EARLY AFFIRMATIONS OF CANONICAL STATUS

According to early church writers, the criteria of the selection of New Testament books for use in Christian worship revolved around their **apostolicity**. Like the books of the Old Testament,

[1] Züntz, *Text of the Epistles*, 271-272.

the New Testament books were collected and preserved by local churches in the continuing process of their worship and need for authoritative guidance for Christian living. The formation of the canon was a process rather than an event, a process that took several hundred years to reach finality in all parts of the Roman Empire. Local canons were the basis for comparison, and out of them eventually emerged the general canon that exists in Christendom today.

The principle determining recognition of the authority of the canonical New Testament writings was first established within the content of those writings themselves. For example, at the conclusion of 1 Thessalonians, Paul says, "I command you in the name of the Lord to read this letter to all the brothers and sisters" (1 Thess. 5:27, NLT). Earlier in the same letter, Paul commended them for accepting his spoken word as "the very word of God" (2:13, NLT); and in 1 Corinthians 14:37 he speaks similarly of his writings, insisting that they be recognized as commandments from the Lord himself (see also John's statements in Rev. 1:3).

Other statements in the New Testament itself affirm its canonical status. For example, Paul writes in his first epistle to Timothy:

> Let the elders who rule well be considered worthy of double honor, especially those who labor in preaching and teaching; for the scripture says, "You shall not muzzle an ox while it is treading out the grain," and, "The laborer deserves to be paid" (1 Tim. 5:17-18, NRSV).

In giving this instruction, Paul cites two texts. The first citation of Scripture clearly comes from Deuteronomy 25:4, but the second cannot be found anywhere in the Old Testament. It can, however, be found in the Gospel of Luke (10:7). Jesus made this statement in the same context Paul made his—spiritual workers should receive material benefits from those they serve. Thus, Paul ascribed scriptural status to Jesus' statement recorded in the Gospel of Luke. This means that Luke's Gospel, written ca. A.D. 60, was perceived by Paul to be canonical soon after it was published—for Paul wrote 1 Timothy only a few years later (63-64).

In Peter's second epistle, the author states,

> Regard the patience of our Lord as salvation. So also our beloved brother Paul wrote to you according to the wisdom given him, speaking of this as he does in all his letters. There are some things in them hard to understand, which the ignorant and unstable twist to their own destruction, as they do the other scriptures. (2 Pet. 3:15-16, NRSV).

In this statement, we discover that the author unequivocally indicates that Paul's letters are on the same par as "the other scriptures." The statement is even stronger in Greek, for he says, literally, "the rest of the Scriptures"—thereby indicating that Paul's epistles comprise a certain portion of the whole canon. What is also apparent in the Greek is that the author could have been a contemporary of Paul, because he intimates that Paul was presently speaking to the churches through his epistles. The present participle carries this force: "in all his epistles speaking [Greek *lalon*] in them concerning these things." Of course, the author of 2 Peter could have been referring to the abiding effect of Paul's apostolic voice after his decease. Nonetheless, the author of 2 Peter addressed the same audience Paul addressed and bears witness to the fact that there was a Pauline corpus of epistles, which were considered as Scripture.

What we have in these two New Testament portions is quite noteworthy. We have Paul affirming Luke's Gospel as Scripture, and we see Peter affirming Paul's epistles as Scripture. If such affirmations were pronounced by the apostles about various portions of the New Testament, we would assume that some of the early Christians ascribed the same canonical status to these books. What we know from church history is that the Gospels and certain of Paul's epistles were canonized in the minds of many Christians as early as A.D. 90–100—that is, the four Gospels and Paul's epistles were deemed Scripture worthy to be read in church.

## THE DEVELOPMENT OF THE NEW TESTAMENT CANON AFTER A.D. 100

The first notable **church fathers**—Clement, Ignatius, Papias, Justin Martyr, and Polycarp (all writing before A.D. 150)—used the material of the New Testament as authentic, apostolic Scriptures. In A.D. 95, Clement of Rome wrote to the Christians in Corinth using a free rendering of material from Matthew and Luke. He seems to have been strongly influenced by Hebrews and was obviously familiar with Romans and Corinthians. Since Clement's letter was addressed by the entire church of Rome to the church of Corinth, it can be assumed that both of these audiences knew these writings. Therefore, these books that later became part of the New Testament canon were circulating among the churches prior to A.D. 90.

Ignatius, when quoting from the Gospels or Paul's epistles, made a distinction between his own writings and the inspired, authoritative apostolic writings. Papias, Bishop of Hierapolis (ca. 130–140), in a work preserved for us by

Eusebius, specifically mentions the Gospels of Matthew and Mark. His use of them for exposition indicates his acceptance of them as canonical. Near the middle of the second century, Justin Martyr, in describing the worship services of the early church, put the apostolic writings on a par with those of the Old Testament prophets. He stated that the divine voice that spoke through the prophets was the same voice that spoke through the apostles of Christ. Justin was also free in his use of "it is written" with his quotations from New Testament Scriptures.

Polycarp of Smyrna personally knew some of Jesus' eyewitnesses, particularly the apostle John. Near the end of his life, just prior to his martyrdom (155), he wrote his *Epistle to the Philippians.* In this epistle he used a combined Old Testament and New Testament quotation, introduced by the statement, "As it is said in *these Scriptures*" (Polycarp 12:4, emphasis mine). There are no citations from the Old Testament in this epistle, but there are quotations from and allusions to Matthew, Acts, Romans, 1 Corinthians, Galatians, Ephesians, 2 Thessalonians, 1 Timothy, and 1 Peter.

Other writings of the first half of the second century (A.D. 100-150) affirm that the New Testament writings were regarded as Scriptures. The *Didache* (or *Teaching of the Twelve*), perhaps even earlier, makes references to a written Gospel. The *Epistle of Barnabas* (ca. 130) has the formula, "it is written" (Barnabas 4:14), with reference to Matthew 22:14.

During the second half of the second century, more apostolic fathers were affirming that the New Testament writings were Scripture. The writings of Irenaeus serve as a primary example. Near the end of the second century, Irenaeus was affirming a fourfold Gospel text. Irenaeus had been privileged to begin his Christian training under Polycarp, a disciple of the apostles. Then, as a *presbyter* (leader in the church) in Lyons, he had association with Bishop Pothinus, whose own background also included contact with first-generation Christians. Irenaeus quoted from almost all the New Testament on the basis of its authority and asserted that the apostles were endowed with power from on high. They were, he said, "fully informed concerning all things, and had a perfect knowledge . . . having indeed all in equal measure and each one singly the Gospel of God" (*Against Heresies,* 3.3). He was the first to state four Gospels as canon. In *Against Heresies* (3.3) Irenaeus said that Christ "gave us the Gospel in a fourfold shape . . . held together by one Spirit." To these four he also added a list of apostolic writings, quoting all as "Scripture," along with the Old Testament.

In addition to the Gospels, Irenaeus made reference to Acts, 1 Peter, 1 John, all the letters of Paul except Philemon, and the book of Revelation. In his primary work, *Against Heresies,* Irenaeus gave his theology as statements of the Christian faith to refute the heresies of Valentinus (the gnostic) and Marcion. For Irenaeus, the authority of "the faith" was established through the direct line of elders in the church back to the apostles.

Another important document of this time period is the *Muratorian Canon* (dated ca. 170). An eighth-century copy of this document was discovered and published in 1740 by the librarian L. A. Muratori. The manuscript is mutilated at both ends, but the remaining text makes Scripture of the twenty-seven books of the New Testament, while recording doubts about such books as 2 Peter, Jude, 2–3 John, and Revelation.

In the beginning of the fourth century, Eusebius was the chief proponent of establishing the four Gospels as well as other recognized books as comprising the New Testament canon. But it was in the middle of the fourth century that the canon was established once and for all. In his *Festal Letter* for Easter (367), Athanasius of Alexandria included information designed to eliminate once and for all the use of certain apocryphal books. This letter, with its admonition, "Let no one add to these; let nothing be taken away," provides the earliest extant document that specifies the twenty-seven books without qualification.

At the close of the fourth century, the Council of Carthage (397) decreed that "aside from the canonical Scriptures nothing is to be read in church under the Name of Divine Scriptures." This also lists the twenty-seven books of the New Testament, as we have them today.[1]

## NEW TESTAMENT MANUSCRIPTS

Since the original compositions of the various New Testament books are not **extant**, we must rely on copies for recovering the original text. New Testament scholars have a great advantage over classical scholars in the number of manuscripts available to them.

According to current tabulations of New Testament manuscripts, there are 115 papyrus manuscripts, 257 **uncial manuscripts**, 2,795 **minuscule manuscripts**, and 2,200 Greek **lectionaries**. In total, there are over 5,350 manuscript copies of the Greek New Testament or portions thereof. By way of comparison, Homer's *Iliad*, the greatest of all Greek classical works, is extant in about 650 manuscripts; and Euripides' tragedies exist in about 330 manuscripts. The numbers on all the other works of Greek literature are far smaller. Furthermore,

[1] See M. Fisher, "The Canon of the New Testament" in Comfort, *Origin of the Bible*, 69-74, from which portions of this section were adapted.

the gap in time between the original composition and the first surviving manuscript is far less for the New Testament than for any other work in Greek literature. The lapse for most classical Greek works is about eight hundred to a thousand years, whereas the lapse for many books in the New Testament is around one hundred years.

Individual manuscripts do not exist in isolation from all others—no manuscript is an island. Instead, manuscripts tend to group according to families. A family of manuscripts displays similar characteristics, suggesting that there is a historical connection between those manuscripts. When discussing individual manuscripts, it is often necessary to provide information about the textual character of each manuscript in terms of its family—such as "**proto-Alexandrian**," "Alexandrian," "**Western**" or "**D-text**," and "Byzantine" (A table of manuscripts and the symbols used to refer to them is in Appendix B, "New Testament Manuscripts," page 279.

## PAPYRUS MANUSCRIPTS

The papyrus manuscripts are very important witnesses for reconstructing the original text of the New Testament. It is not the material they are written on (**papyrus**) that makes them so valuable, but the date at which they were written. Several of the most significant papyri are dated from the early second century to the early third. These manuscripts, therefore, provide the earliest direct witness to the **autographs**. Among the extant New Testament papyrus manuscripts, four groups are noted below: the Oxyrhynchus Papyri, the Chester Beatty Papyri, the Bodmer Papyri, and other papyri.[1]

[1] Complete descriptions of all the papyri manuscripts dated before A.D. 300 are found in Comfort and Barrett, eds., *Earliest New Testament Manuscripts.* The descriptions in that work include an extensive bibliography. See also Comfort, "New Reconstructions."

### The Oxyrhynchus Papyri

A new era in New Testament study began on January 11, 1897, when B. P. Grenfell and A. S. Hunt began to excavate at Oxyrhynchus, Egypt, one hundred twenty miles south of Cairo. They did not find papyri in ancient cemeteries, churches, or monasteries; rather, they found them in ancient rubbish heaps. Manuscripts found in rubbish heaps are not "rubbish" per se or defective copies. When a manuscript became old and worn, it was customary to replace it with a fresh copy and then discard the old one. The Egyptians are known to have disposed of such copies, not by burning them, but by putting them into rubbish heaps. Excavators looking for ancient Egyptian papyri would search for ancient rubbish heaps in deserted sites on ground higher than the Nile River. Excavators would also look in tombs, cemeteries, monasteries, and church buildings.

Grenfell and Hunt's choice of the ancient rubbish heap at Oxyrhynchus (now called El Bahnasa) was fortuitous, for it yielded the largest cache of papyri ever discovered. From the time they began digging in January 1897, they made new finds of papyrus fragments almost continuously—day after day and week after week—until they ceased operations in 1906.

### Significant Oxyrhynchus Papyrus Manuscripts

*𝔓¹ (P. Oxy. 2)* When Grenfell and Hunt went to Oxyrhynchus in search of ancient Christian documents, 𝔓¹ was discovered on the second day of the dig. (Papyri are denoted with the symbol 𝔓 and are numbered according to the order in which they were found.) At the time of this discovery, this was the earliest extant copy of any New Testament portion—at least one hundred years earlier than Codex Vaticanus. The copyist of 𝔓¹ seems to have faithfully followed a very reliable exemplar. This third-century manuscript contains Matthew 1:1-9, 12, 14-20.

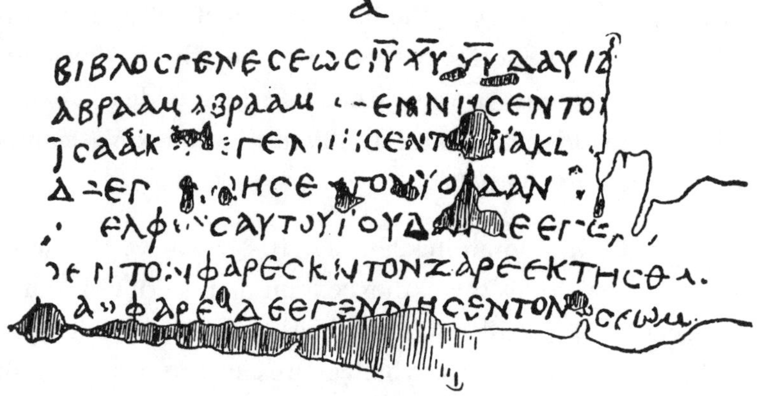

FIGURE **2.1**: Papyrus $\mathfrak{P}^{1}$. Third Century. Matthew 1:1-3.

*$\mathfrak{P}^{5}$ (P. Oxy. 208 and 1781)* Two separate portions of this manuscript (dated to the third century) were unearthed from Oxyrhynchus by Grenfell and Hunt, both from the same papyrus manuscript. The first portion contains John 1:23-31, 33-40 on one fragment and John 20:11-17 on another—probably on the first and last **quires** of a manuscript containing only the Gospel of John.

*$\mathfrak{P}^{13}$ (P. Oxy. 657 and PSI 1292)* This manuscript, dated to the third century, contains twelve columns from a roll preserving the text of Hebrews 2:14–5:5; 10:8-22; 10:29–11:13; 11:28–12:7. The text of Hebrews was written on the back of the papyrus containing the New Epitome of Livy. For this reason, some scholars think the manuscript was possibly brought to Egypt by a Roman official and left behind when he left his post. $\mathfrak{P}^{13}$ displays nearly the same text as $\mathfrak{P}^{46}$. Out of a total of eighty-eight variation-units, there are seventy-one agreements and only seventeen disagreements.

*$\mathfrak{P}^{20}$ (P. Oxy. 1171)* This manuscript, containing James 2:19–3:9, is the earliest extant manuscript of James 2–3 (early

third century). A study of the handwriting of $\mathfrak{P}^{20}$ and $\mathfrak{P}^{27}$ reveals that the same scribe probably produced both. However, these two fragments are not from the same codex because their dimensions are distinctly different. Codex Vaticanus basically concurs with $\mathfrak{P}^{20}$.

*$\mathfrak{P}^{23}$ (P. Oxy. 1229)* Containing James 1:10-12, 15-18, this fragment dated ca. 200 is the earliest extant manuscript of James 1. In general, $\mathfrak{P}^{23}$ agrees with Codices Sinaiticus, Vaticanus, and Ephraemi Rescriptus, which represent the best texts of the General Epistles.

*$\mathfrak{P}^{24}$ (P. Oxy. 1230)* This late-third-century papyrus is the earliest extant manuscript of Revelation 5–6 (5:5-8; 6:5-8). Codex Alexandrinus (an excellent witness in Revelation) generally agrees with the papyrus.

*$\mathfrak{P}^{30}$ (P. Oxy. 1598)* This manuscript, from the early third century, has 1 Thessalonians 4:12-13, 16-17; 5:3, 8-10, 12-18, 25-28; 2 Thessalonians 1:1-2. $\mathfrak{P}^{30}$ must originally have contained all of Paul's epistles, because two leaves show the page numbers 207 and 208.

*$\mathfrak{P}^{39}$ (P. Oxy. 1780)* This manuscript, showing John 8:14-22, was produced in the third century. The large letters and beautiful calligraphy show that this manuscript was probably produced by a professional scribe for church use. Codex Vaticanus agrees with $\mathfrak{P}^{39}$ verbatim.

*$\mathfrak{P}^{48}$ (PSI 1165)* This fragment preserves Acts 23:11-17, 23-29; it should be dated to the middle of the third century (the same time as $\mathfrak{P}^{13}$—the two manuscripts bear a close resemblance in handwriting). The remarkable feature about this manuscript is that it displays an early form of the D-text (see page 87).

*$\mathfrak{P}^{49}$ + $\mathfrak{P}^{65}$ (Yale Papyrus 415 + PSI 1373)* The first manuscript ($\mathfrak{P}^{49}$) contains Ephesians 4:16-29; 4:31–5:13; the second ($\mathfrak{P}^{65}$) contains 1 Thessalonians 1:3-10; 2:1, 6-13. These manuscripts, of the third century, were produced by the same scribe and probably belong to the same codex. This can be seen in a detailed analysis of the two hands, and in an analysis of the physical features of both manuscripts. $\mathfrak{P}^{49}$ + $\mathfrak{P}^{65}$ is the fifth early manuscript to display a Pauline codex. The others are $\mathfrak{P}^{13}$, $\mathfrak{P}^{30}$, $\mathfrak{P}^{46}$, and $\mathfrak{P}^{92}$.

*$\mathfrak{P}^{77}$ (P. Oxy. 2683 + 4405)* Dated to the late second century, this is one of the earliest manuscripts of Matthew (containing a small portion of Matt. 23). The manuscript, which is clearly a literary production, has the closest affinity with Codex Sinaiticus. $\mathfrak{P}^{103}$ may be part of the same manuscript as $\mathfrak{P}^{77}$.

*$\mathfrak{P}^{90}$ (P. Oxy. 3523)* This late-second-century manuscript contains John 18:36–19:7. The handwriting (an upright, rounded, elegant script) is much like that found in $\mathfrak{P}^{66}$. Furthermore, $\mathfrak{P}^{90}$ has more affinity with $\mathfrak{P}^{66}$ than with any other single manuscript, though it does not concur with $\mathfrak{P}^{66}$ in its entirety.

*$\mathfrak{P}^{104}$ (P. Oxy. 4404)* Containing Matthew 21:34-37, 43, 45, this manuscript could be the earliest extant manuscript of the New Testament. $\mathfrak{P}^{104}$ is a carefully executed manuscript in what could be called the rounded, decorated style. In this style, every vertical stroke finishes with a serif or decorated roundel. This style began during the Ptolemaic period (323 to 30 B.C.) and extended to the second century A.D. Whatever the date of $\mathfrak{P}^{104}$, it is textually pure and accurate. It does not include Matthew 21:44, thus making it the earliest witness to the exclusion of this verse.

*$\mathfrak{P}^{115}$ (P. Oxy. 4499)* This manuscript, dated ca. A.D. 300, contains many portions of Revelation 2–15 (with **lacunae**). It tends to agree with Codices Alexandrinus and Ephraemi Rescriptus, the best witnesses to Revelation. One remarkable reading is found in Revelation 13:18—$\mathfrak{P}^{115}$ has the number of the beast as "616" instead of "666."

### The Chester Beatty Papyri

In 1931 it was announced that twelve manuscripts were found in a **Coptic** graveyard in Egypt, stowed away in jars—eight books of the Old Testament and three of the New Testament. It is generally believed that the manuscripts came from the ruins of an ancient church or monastery—perhaps in Aphroditopolis (modern Atfih, Egypt). These manuscripts were likely hidden during the Diocletian persecution.

The three Greek New Testament manuscripts said to be found in the Coptic graveyard were the earliest manuscripts to contain large portions of the New Testament text. The first manuscript, $\mathfrak{P}^{45}$ (early third century), is a codex of the four Gospels and Acts; the second, $\mathfrak{P}^{46}$ (second century), is a codex of the Pauline Epistles; and the third, $\mathfrak{P}^{47}$ (third century), is a codex of Revelation. A dealer from Cairo sold the manuscripts in different batches to two different parties—Chester Beatty and the University of Michigan.

The ten leaves in the Beatty collection were first published in Fasciculus III of *The Chester Beatty Papyri* (1936). The thirty leaves in the Michigan collection were published in 1935 by H. A. Sanders in *A Third-Century Papyrus Codex of the Epistles of Paul.*

### Significant Chester Beatty Papyrus Manuscripts

*$\mathfrak{P}^{45}$ (Chester Beatty Papyrus I)* This codex has the four Gospels and Acts (Matt. 20:24-32; 21:13-19; 25:41–26:39; Mark 4:36–

9:31; 11:27–12:28; Luke 6:31–7:7; 9:26–14:33; John 4:51–5:2, 21-25; 10:7-25; 10:30–11:10, 18-36, 42-57; Acts 4:27–17:17). According to Frederic Kenyon, the order of books in the original intact manuscript was probably as follows: Matthew, John, Luke, Mark, Acts. This manuscript was dated by Kenyon to the early third century, a date which was confirmed by other **papyrologists**.

The scribe of $\mathfrak{P}^{45}$ was very free in making his copy of the text. Instead of copying the text verbatim, he reproduced the basic thought of the text. In short, he liked to paraphrase and edit as he went. He had a penchant for pruning and for harmonizing the gospels. The text of $\mathfrak{P}^{45}$ varies with each book. In Mark, $\mathfrak{P}^{45}$ shows a strong affinity with those manuscripts which used to be called Caesarean.[1] In Matthew, Luke, and John, $\mathfrak{P}^{45}$ stands midway between the "Alexandrian" manuscripts and so-called "Western" manuscripts (see page 87). In Acts, $\mathfrak{P}^{45}$ shows the greatest affinity with the Alexandrian uncials—as over against the manuscripts with a "Western" text.

$\mathfrak{P}^{46}$ *(Chester Beatty Papyrus II)* This codex has most of Paul's epistles (excluding the Pastorals) in this order: Rom. 5:17–6:14; 8:15–15:9; 15:11–16:27; Heb. 1:1–13:25; 1 Cor. 1:1–16:22; 2 Cor. 1:1–13:13; Eph. 1:1–6:24; Gal. 1:1–6:18; Phil. 1:1–4:23; Col. 1:1–4:18; 1 Thess. 1:1; 1:9–2:3; 5:5-9, 23-28 (with minor lacunae in each of the books).

Kenyon dated $\mathfrak{P}^{46}$ to the first half of the third century. Kenyon's dating was largely influenced by the handwriting of the **stichometrical notes** at the end of several of the epistles, which he dated to the early part of the third century.[2] Ulrich

---

[1] The supposed "Caesarean" family is represented by Θ, $f^1$, and the Armenian and Georgian versions. Textual scholars now doubt the existence of this text type as a coherent family of manuscripts.

[2] See introductory pages in Kenyon, *Chester Beatty Papyri* fasciculus III.

Wilcken thought $\mathfrak{P}^{46}$ belonged to the second century and said it could be dated safely to ca. A.D. 200.[1] Other papyrologists date it to the middle of the second century.[2]

The scribe who produced $\mathfrak{P}^{46}$ used an early, excellent exemplar. He was a professional scribe because there are **stichoi** notations at the end of several books (Romans, 2 Corinthians, Ephesians, and Philippians). The stichoi were used by professionals to note how many lines had been copied, for commensurate pay. Most likely, an official at the **scriptorium** paginated the codex and indicated the stichoi. The scribe himself made a few corrections as he went, and then several other readers made corrections here and there.

Codex Vaticanus shows strong affinities with $\mathfrak{P}^{46}$ (especially in Ephesians, Colossians, and Hebrews), and so does Codex Sinaiticus, to a lesser extent. $\mathfrak{P}^{46}$ is proto-Alexandrian. In Hebrews, $\mathfrak{P}^{46}$ displays nearly the same text as $\mathfrak{P}^{13}$.

*$\mathfrak{P}^{47}$ (Chester Beatty Papyrus III)* This third-century codex contains Revelation 9:10–17:2; it is the earliest manuscript preserving this portion of Revelation. Codex Sinaiticus frequently agrees with $\mathfrak{P}^{47}$.

### The Bodmer Papyri

The most significant discovery of biblical manuscripts since the Dead Sea Scrolls is that of the Dishna Papers, several of which are known as the Bodmer Biblical Papyri and a few of which are also in the Chester Beatty collection. Most of these manuscripts were purchased by Martin Bodmer (founder of the Bodmer Library of World Literature) from a dealer in Cairo, Egypt, in the 1950s and 1960s. The four important New Testament papyri in this collection are $\mathfrak{P}^{66}$ (ca. 150, containing almost all of

---

[1] Wilcken, *Archiv*, 113.

[2] See the full discussion in Comfort and Barrett, eds., *Earliest New Testament Manuscripts*, 193-197.

John); $\mathfrak{P}^{72}$ (third century, having all of 1 and 2 Peter and Jude); $\mathfrak{P}^{74}$ (ca. 600, containing Acts and the General Epistles); and $\mathfrak{P}^{75}$ (ca. 175–200, containing large parts of Luke 3—John 15).

James Robinson, an expert in **Nag Hammadi manuscripts**, was able to pinpoint the place of discovery while attempting to find out where the Nag Hammadi manuscripts came from. The Bodmer Biblical Papyri (or Dishna Papers) were discovered seven years after the Nag Hammadi codices in close proximity. They were found in the Dishna Plain, midway between Panopolis and Thebes, Egypt, east of the Nile River. In 1945 the Nag Hammadi manuscripts were found in Jabal Al-Tarif (just north of Chenoboskion—near Nag Hammadi, the city where the discovery was first reported). In 1952 the Bodmer Papyri were found in Jabal Abu Manna, which is also located just north of the Dishna Plain, twelve kilometers east of Jabal Al-Tarif.[1]

It is quite likely that all these manuscripts belonged to a library of a monastery started by Pachomius. Within a few kilometers of Jabal Abu Manna lie the ruins of the ancient basilica of Pachomius (in Faw Qibli). Pachomius (287–346) brought monasticism to this area around 320. By the time of his death, there were thousands of monks in eleven monasteries within a radius of sixty miles along the Nile River. A century later, there were nearly fifty thousand monks in the area. As part of their daily regimen, these monks read and memorized the Scriptures—especially the New Testament and Psalms. Pachomius himself took an active role in this practice in that he read the Scriptures aloud to his first congregation (i.e., he was the **lector**). As Pachomius knew both Coptic (Egyptian) and Greek (as did other monks in his

---

1 James Robinson, *Pachomian Monastic Library.*

monasteries), some of the monks he taught must have also read the Scriptures in both languages. Of course, more monks read Coptic than Greek, and with the passing of time (beginning in the fifth century) almost all read only Coptic. Because the library in the Pachomian monastery could not have started until after 320, all earlier manuscripts—especially the New Testament papyri—must have been produced in another scriptorium (probably in Alexandria) and given to the library.

### Significant Bodmer Papyrus Manuscripts

*𝔓⁶⁶ (Papyrus Bodmer II)* This manuscript contains most of John's Gospel (1:1–6:11; 6:35–14:26, 29-30; 15:2-26; 16:2-4, 6-7; 16:10–20:20, 22-23; 20:25–21:9). It does not include the pericope of the adulteress (7:53–8:11), making it the earliest witness not to include this passage that is now generally considered spurious. The manuscript is usually dated ca. 200, but the renowned paleographer Herbert Hunger has argued that 𝔓⁶⁶ should be dated to the first half, if not the first quarter, of the second century.[1]

With a practiced calligraphic hand, the scribe of 𝔓⁶⁶ wrote in larger print as he went along in order to fill out the codex. The large print throughout indicates that it was written to be read aloud. The scribe of 𝔓⁶⁶ was very likely a Christian. The text exhibits his knowledge of other portions of Scripture (he harmonized John 6:66 to Matt. 16:16 and John 21:6 to Luke 5:5), his use of standard **nomina sacra**, and his special use of *nomina sacra* for the words "cross" and "crucify."

The scribe of 𝔓⁶⁶ was quite free in his interaction with the text; he produced several **singular readings**, which reveal his independent interpretation of the text. While the numerous

---

[1] Hunger, "Zur Datierung."

scribal mistakes would seem to indicate that the scribe was inattentive, many of the singular readings—prior to correction—reveal that he was not detached from the narrative of the text. Rather, he became so absorbed in his reading that he often forgot the exact words he was copying. His task as a copyist was to duplicate the exemplar word for word, but this was subverted by the fact that he was reading the text in logical semantic chunks and often became a coproducer of a new text. As a result, he continually had to stop his reading and make many in-process corrections. But he left several places uncorrected, which were later corrected by the **diorthotes**. Many of these corrections bring the manuscript into line with a proto-Alexandrian type of text.[1]

*$\mathfrak{P}^{72}$ (Papyrus Bodmer VII-VIII)* This manuscript, dated ca. 300, has an interesting collection of writings in one codex: 1 Peter 1:1–5:14; 2 Pet. 1:1–3:18; Jude 1-25; the *Nativity of Mary*; the **apocryphal** correspondence of Paul to the Corinthians; the eleventh ode of Solomon; Melito's *Homily on the Passover*; a fragment of a hymn; the *Apology of Phileas*; and Psalms 33 and 34.

Scholars think four scribes produced the entire manuscript. 1 Peter has clear Alexandrian affinities—especially with B (Codex Vaticanus) and then with A (Codex Alexandrinus). The copies of 2 Peter and (especially) Jude in $\mathfrak{P}^{72}$ display more of an uncontrolled type text (usually associated with the "Western" text), with several independent readings.

*$\mathfrak{P}^{74}$ (Papyrus Bodmer XVII)* This seventh-century codex contains Acts and the General Epistles (with lacunae). Despite the late date, this manuscript is important because it presents an Alexandrian text and is an excellent witness for the book of Acts.

---

[1] Comfort and Barrett, *Earliest New Testament Manuscripts*, 371-378.

*𝔓75 (Papyrus Bodmer XIV-XV)* This codex contains most of Luke and John (Luke 3:18–4:2; 4:34–5:10; 5:37–18:18; 22:4–24:53; John 1:1–11:45, 48-57; 12:3–13:1, 8-9; 14:8-30; 15:7-8.) The manuscript does not include the pericope of the adulteress (John 7:53–8:11). 𝔓75 can be dated to the late second century (ca. 175–200).

The copyist of 𝔓75 was a literate scribe trained in making books. His craftsmanship shows through in his tight calligraphy and controlled copying. The scribe's Christianity shows in his abbreviations of the *nomina sacra*, as well as in his abbreviation of the word "cross." These are telltale signs of a scribe who belonged to the Christian community. Furthermore, the large typeface indicates that the manuscript was composed to be read aloud. The scribe even added a system of sectional divisions to aid any would-be lector. Thus, we have a manuscript written by a Christian for other Christians.

There are several indications of the scribe's Alexandrian orientation. First and foremost is his **scriptoral** acumen. He is the best of all the early Christian scribes, and his manuscript is an extremely accurate copy. 𝔓75 is the "result of a single force: namely the disciplined scribe who writes with the intention of being careful and accurate. There is no evidence of revision of his work by anyone else, or in fact of any real revision, or check. . . . The control had been drilled into the scribe before he started writing."[1]

Calvin Porter established the fact that 𝔓75 displays the kind of text that was used in making Codex Vaticanus. Porter demonstrated 87 percent agreement between 𝔓75 and Vaticanus.[2] In general, textual scholars have a high regard for the textual fidelity of 𝔓75.

---

[1] Colwell, "Scribal Habits," 119-121.

[2] Porter, "Papyrus Bodmer XV."

## Other Important Papyrus Manuscripts

*$\mathfrak{P}^{4}$ + $\mathfrak{P}^{64}$ + $\mathfrak{P}^{67}$ (fragments of the same codex)* $\mathfrak{P}^{4}$ was discovered in Coptos (modern Qift), Egypt, on the east bank of the Nile, by Fr. V. Scheil during his expedition to Upper Egypt in 1889. This codex, the work of an accomplished scribe, displays a text which was very much like the exemplar used for Codex Vaticanus.

$\mathfrak{P}^{64}$ was first purchased by Rev. Charles B. Huleatt in Luxor, Egypt, in 1901 and then given to the Magdalene College Library in Oxford, where it was examined by Colin Roberts, who then published it in 1953. A few years later, P. Roca-Puig published a papyrus fragment known as $\mathfrak{P}^{67}$. Colin Roberts realized that $\mathfrak{P}^{67}$ was from the same manuscript as $\mathfrak{P}^{64}$. Further analysis by various scholars has revealed that $\mathfrak{P}^{4}$, $\mathfrak{P}^{64}$, and $\mathfrak{P}^{67}$ all belong to the same codex, which can be dated to the mid-second century (ca. 150). Thus, this is one of the earliest Gospel codices. The textual character of this codex is clearly proto-Alexandrian. Where $\mathfrak{P}^{4}$ and $\mathfrak{P}^{75}$ overlap, there is great agreement.

$\mathfrak{P}^{4}$ contains portions of Luke (1:58-59; 1:62–2:1, 6-7; 3:8–4:2, 29-32, 34-35; 5:3-8; 5:30–6:16). $\mathfrak{P}^{64}$ and $\mathfrak{P}^{67}$ preserve small portions of Matthew (Matt. 3:9, 15; 5:20-22, 25-28; 26:7-8, 10, 14-15, 22-23, 31-33).

*$\mathfrak{P}^{32}$ (Papyrus Rylands 5)* This manuscript, preserving Titus 1:11-15; 2:3-8, is dated ca. 150–175, making it the earliest extant copy of any of the Pastoral Epistles. Codex Sinaiticus largely agrees with $\mathfrak{P}^{32}$.

*$\mathfrak{P}^{40}$ (Papyrus Heidelberg 645)* This third-century manuscript has portions of Romans (1:24-27; 1:31–2:3; 3:21–4:8; 6:2-5, 15-16; 9:16-17, 27). A previously unidentified fragment (Rom. 6:2-4a and 6:15) has been reconstructed by Comfort and Barrett.[1]* $\mathfrak{P}^{40}$ shows a proto-Alexandrian text type.

[1] Comfort and Barrett, *Earliest New Testament Manuscripts*, 140-144.

𝔓[52] *(Papyrus Rylands 457)* This fragment, containing John 18:31-34, 37-38, is noteworthy because of its date: ca. A.D. 110–125. Many scholars (Kenyon, H. I. Bell, Deissmann, and W. H. P. Hatch) have confirmed this dating. And remarkably, it resembles many manuscripts with dates around 90–120: P. Fayyum 110 (94), P. Egerton 2 (110–130), and P. London 2078 (reign of Domitian, ca. 81–96). 𝔓[52] came from Fayyum or from Oxyrhynchus. It was acquired in 1920 by Grenfell, but it remained unnoticed among hundreds of papyri until 1934, when C. H. Roberts recognized that this scrap preserves a few verses from John's Gospel.[1]

𝔓[87] *(P. Col theol. 12)* This small fragment preserves Philemon 13-15, 24-25. It has to be dated concurrently with 𝔓[46] (early second century), because the handwriting of the two manuscripts is virtually identical. 𝔓[87], therefore, is the earliest extant fragment of Philemon.

𝔓[98] *(P. IFAO inv. 237b, from Institut Francais d'Archeologie Orientale)* This fragment contains Rev. 1:13–2:1. Dated to the second century, it is the earliest fragment of Revelation.

## UNCIAL MANUSCRIPTS

The manuscripts typically classified as **uncial** (meaning written in capital letters) are so designated to differentiate them from papyrus manuscripts. This is actually a misnomer, because the real difference has to do, not with the kind of lettering used, but with the material they are written on—vellum or parchment (treated animal hide), rather than papyrus. The papyri were also written in uncials (capital letters), but the

[1] Roberts, *Unpublished Fragment.* This was republished with a few alterations in the *Bulletin of the John Rylands Library* XX (1936), 45-55; and then again in the *Catalogue of the Greek and Latin Papyri in the John Rylands Library* III (Manchester: 1938), 1-3. The last publication contains critical notes and bibliography of scholarly reviews.

term *uncial* typically describes the **majuscule** (capital) lettering that was prominent in fourth-century biblical texts written on parchment or vellum.

### Significant Uncial Manuscripts

*0189 (Parchment Berlin 11765)* This manuscript, containing Acts 5:3-21, is dated late second or early third century, making it the earliest parchment manuscript of the New Testament. The manuscript was produced by an experienced scribe, and the text nearly always agrees with the Alexandrian witnesses.

*Codex Sinaiticus (א or Aleph)* Codex Sinaiticus contains the entire Old Testament, and the entire New Testament in this order: Four Gospels, Pauline Epistles (including Hebrews), Acts, General Epistles, Revelation. It also includes the *Epistle of Barnabas* and the *Shepherd of Hermes*. The manuscript contains 346 leaves of fine parchment, written in four columns. The codex cannot be earlier than 340 (the year Eusebius died) because the Eusebian sections of the text are indicated in the margins of the Gospels by a contemporary hand. Most scholars date it ca. 350–375.

Codex Sinaiticus was discovered by Constantin von Tischendorf in St. Catherine's Monastery (situated at the foot of Mount Sinai). On a visit to the monastery in 1844, he noticed in

ΠΑΡΑΚΑΛΩΔΕΫΜΑϹ
ΑΔΕΛΦΟΙΑΝΕΧΕ
ϹΘΕΤΟΥΛΟΓΟΥΤΗϹ
ΠΑΡΑΚΛΗϹΕΩϹΚΑΙΓΑΡ
ΔΙΑΒΡΑΧΕΩΝΕΠΕ
ϹΤΙΛΑΫΜΙΝ

FIGURE 2.2: Codex Sinaiticus. Fourth Century. Hebrews 13:22.

a wastebasket some parchment leaves that were being used to light the lamps. He was allowed to take this wastepaper, which proved to be forty-three leaves from various parts of the Greek translation of the Old Testament. He was shown other sections of the Old Testament but was not allowed to have them.

In 1853 he made a second trip to the monastery and found nothing. In 1859, however, on his third trip, he found not only other parts of the Old Testament, but also the complete New Testament. He was finally able to persuade the monastery authorities to present the manuscript to the Czar, the great patron of the Greek Catholic Church, who placed it in the Imperial Library in St. Petersburg. The Czar gave great honors to the monastery and its authorities, and everybody seemed well pleased. Later, Tischendorf was charged with having stolen the manuscript from its lawful owners, but the better textual scholars do not accept that story.

The manuscript remained in the Imperial Library until 1933, when it was purchased by the British Museum for the huge sum of one hundred thousand pounds. Textual criticism made the headlines when one manuscript was bought for a half million dollars, raised largely by public subscription during the Great Depression. The manuscript is now on display in the manuscript room of the Museum, where it is considered one of the Museum's most prized possessions.[1]

The text of Sinaiticus is very closely related to that of Codex Vaticanus. They agree in presenting the purest type of text, usually called the **Neutral** (sometimes Alexandrian) type. Tischendorf greatly used the textual evidence of Codex Sinaiticus in preparing his critical editions of the Greek New

[1] Tischendorf issued an edition of this codex printed in facsimile type in 1862: *Codex Sinaiticus Petropolitanus.* Other important volumes on this manuscript are Scrivener, *Full Collation of Codex Sinaiticus;* Lake and Lake, *Codex Sinaiticus;* Milne and Skeat, *Scribes and Correctors of Codex Sinaiticus;* and Milne and Skeat, *Codex Sinaiticus and Codex Alexandrinus.*

Testament. Codex Sinaiticus provides a fairly reliable witness to the New Testament; however, the scribe was not as careful as the scribe of Vaticanus. He was more prone to error and to creative emendation.

*Codex Alexandrinus (A)* Codex Alexandrinus is one of the three most important codices preserving an early copy of the whole Bible in Greek (the other two being the Codex Vaticanus and Codex Sinaiticus). The name "Alexandrinus" comes from ancient records suggesting that it was copied in Alexandria, Egypt, during the early part of the fifth century A.D.

The early history of this manuscript and its Egyptian provenance is partially revealed by its flyleaves. A note by Cyril of Lucar (patriarch of Alexandria, and then of Constantinople in the 1620s) states that, according to tradition, it was written by Thecla, a noble lady of Egypt, shortly after the council of Nicea (325), and that her name was originally inscribed at the end of the volume, but the last page was lost due to mutilation. An Arabic note of the thirteenth or fourteenth century also says that the manuscript was written by "Thecla the martyr." Another Arabic note says that it was presented to the patriarchal cell of Alexandria (ca. 1098). Cyril of Lucar took the manuscript from Alexandria to Constantinople in 1621 and then gave it to Charles I of England in 1627, where it became part of the Royal Library, then later the British Museum.

Only 773 of the original estimated 820 pages still exist.

FIGURE 2.3: Codex Alexandrinus. Fifth Century. Acts 20:28.

The rest were lost as the book was passed down through the centuries. The surviving parts of Alexandrinus contain a Greek translation of the whole Old Testament, the Apocrypha (including four books of Maccabees and Psalm 151), most of the New Testament, and some early Christian writings (of which the First and Second Epistles of Clement to the Corinthians are the most important).

Evidently, the scribe(s) of this codex used exemplars of varying quality for various sections of the New Testament. The exemplar used for the Gospels was of poor quality, reflecting a Byzantine text type. Alexandrinus's testimony in the Epistles is much better, and in Revelation it provides the best witness to the original text.[1]

*Codex Vaticanus (B)* This manuscript has been in the Vatican's library since at least 1475, but it was only made available to scholars, such as Tischendorf and Tregelles, in the middle of the nineteenth century.

Certain textual evidence points to Egypt (and Alexandria) as the place of production. Vaticanus's order and inclusion of New Testament books completely coincides with that found in the description provided by Athanasius (bishop of Alexandria), as found in his *Festal Letter* (dated 367): Matthew, Mark, Luke, John, Acts, James, 1 and 2 Peter, 1—3 John, Jude, Romans, 1 and 2 Corinthians, Galatians, Ephesians, Philippians, Colossians, 1 and 2 Thessalonians, Hebrews, 1 and 2 Timothy, Titus, Philemon, and Revelation. Also, the titles of some of the books in Codex Vaticanus contain letters of distinctly Coptic character.

At one time, the codex originally contained the whole Greek

---

[1] E. M. Thompson published the *Facsimile of the Codex Alexandrinus.* See also Milne and Skeat, *Sinaiticus and Alexandrinus.*

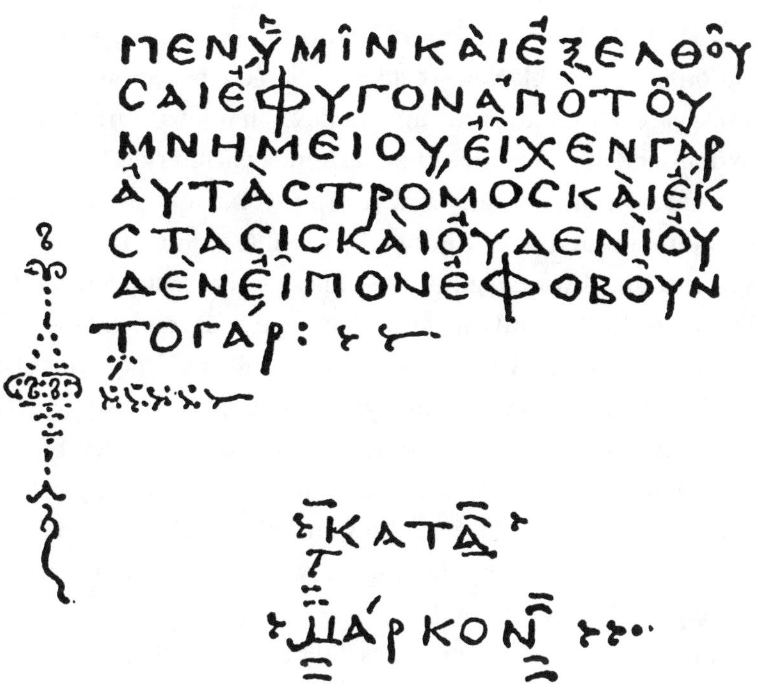
ΠΕΝΥΜΙΝΚΑΙΕΞΕΛΘΟΥ
ΣΑΙΕΦΥΓΟΝΑΠΟΤΟΥ
ΜΝΗΜΕΙΟΥΕΙΧΕΝΓΑΡ
ΑΥΤΑΣΤΡΟΜΟΣΚΑΙΕΚ
ΣΤΑΣΙΣΚΑΙΟΥΔΕΝΙΟΥ
ΔΕΝΕΙΠΟΝΕΦΟΒΟΥΝ
ΤΟΓΑΡ

ΚΑΤΑ
ΜΑΡΚΟΝ

FIGURE 2.4: Codex Vaticanus. Fourth Century. Mark 16:8.

Bible, including most of the books of the Apocrypha, but it has lost many of its leaves. Originally it must have had about 820 leaves (1,640 pages), but now it has 759 leaves—617 in the Old Testament and 142 in the New.[1]

The text of Codex Vaticanus is much like that of Codex Sinaiticus. These are generally recognized as the two finest examples of the Alexandrian type of Greek text of the New Testament. The Greek text of the Old Testament is very fine too, but it is not quite so important, as the original language of the Old Testament was Hebrew.

---

[1] Tischendorf published *Novum Testamentum Vaticanum.* A photographic edition was published by the Vatican Library authorities: *Bibliorum SS. Graecorum Codex Vaticanus* 1209. Milan: Vatican Library, 1904-1907.

In 1881, B. F. Westcott and A. J. Hort published their critical edition of the Greek New Testament, largely based on the evidence of Codex Vaticanus and Codex Sinaiticus. Virtually all textual scholars since that time have recognized this "Neutral" type of text as a very early and very pure text, an extremely accurate reproduction of what the original text must have been. Westcott and Hort called it a second century text accurate in 999 out of 1,000 words, so far as any matter of translatable difference is concerned. Codices Sinaiticus (א) and Vaticanus (B) are the finest examples of this type of text, but this text type is also found in a few other Greek uncial manuscripts, a few of the early translations (called **versions**), and in the writings of a few of the early church fathers. Westcott and Hort's theory has since been confirmed by the discovery of papyrus manuscripts, notably the Bodmer Papyri.

The scribe of Codex Vaticanus did his task with rote fidelity. This is underscored by Westcott and Hort's comments about this scribe's copying habits:

> The final impression produced by a review of all the trustworthy signs is of patient and rather dull or mechanical type of transcription, subject now and then to the ordinary lapses which come from flagging watchfulness, but happily guiltless of ingenuity or other untimely activity of brain, and indeed unaffected by mental influences except of the most limited and unconscious kind.[1]

*Codex Ephraemi Rescriptus (C)* This codex is a **palimpsest** (the original writing was erased and different words written on the same material). It originally contained the entire Bible, but now has only parts of six Old Testament books and portions of every

[1] Westcott and Hort, *Introduction*, 321.

ΜΑ : ΤΗΡΟΥΝΤΑΙ ΚΑΙΕΓΕΝΕΤΟΑΥΤΟΝ
ΕΝϹΑΒΒΑΤΩΔΕΥΤΕΡΟΠΡΩΤΩΔΙΑ
ΠΟΡΕΥΕϹΘΑΙΔΙΑΤΩΝϹΠΟΡΙΜΩΝ

FIGURE 2.5: Codex Bezae (Greek). Fifth Century. Luke 6:1.

New Testament book except 2 Thessalonians and 2 John. The single-column Bible text, written in the fifth century A.D., was erased in the twelfth century and replaced by a two-column text of a Greek translation of sermons or treatises by a certain Ephraem, a fourth-century Syrian church leader. Such practice was common in periods of economic depression or when parchment was scarce. Using chemicals and ultraviolet light, Tischendorf was able to read much of the erased documents.[1]

The text of this manuscript is mixed—it is compounded from all the major text types, agreeing frequently with the later Byzantine type, which most scholars regard as the least valuable type of New Testament text.

*Codex Bezae (D)* This is a Greek-Latin **diglot** containing Matthew—Acts and 3 John, with lacunae. Most scholars date it to the late fourth or early fifth century (ca. 400). Some scholars think this codex was produced in either Egypt or North Africa by a scribe whose mother tongue was Latin. D. C. Parker argues that it was copied in Beirut, a center of Latin legal studies during the fifth century, where both Latin and Greek were used. Evidently, it was produced by a scribe who knew Latin better than Greek, and then was corrected by several scribes.[2] The codex ended up in the hands of Theodore Beza, French scholar and successor to John Calvin. Beza gave it to the Cambridge University Library in 1581.

---

1 See Tischendorf, *Ephraemi Syri rescriptus*. See also Lyon, "Ephraemi Rescriptus." Lyon provides a list of corrections to Tischendorf's work.

2 See Parker, *Codex Bezae*.

This codex is probably the most controversial of the New Testament uncials because of its marked independence. Its many additions, omissions, and alterations (especially in Luke and Acts) are the work of a significant theologian. A few earlier manuscripts ($\mathfrak{P}^{29}$(?), $\mathfrak{P}^{38}$, $\mathfrak{P}^{48}$, and 0171) appear to be precursors to the type of text found in D, which is considered the principal witness of the Western, or D-type, text. (The fifth-century papyrus, $\mathfrak{P}^{112}$, also has a D-text.) Thus, Codex Bezae could be a copy of an earlier revised edition. The redactor must have been a scholar who had a propensity for adding historical, biographical, and geographical details. More than anything, he was intent on filling in gaps in the narrative by adding circumstantial details.

*Codex Freerianus or the Washington Codex of Paul's Epistles (I)* This fifth-century codex contains Paul's epistles and Hebrews (1 Cor.—Heb.). The manuscript, which was a blackened and decayed lump of parchment as hard and brittle on the exterior as glue, was in the hands of a Gizeh dealer, Sheikh Ali Abdel Hai el Arabi, in the autumn of 1906, according to Grenfell and Hunt. It was purchased in December of 1906 by Charles Freer, then carefully separated and examined by H. A. Sanders.[1] The manuscript is Alexandrian, showing more agreement with Codices Sinaiticus (א) and Alexandrinus (A) than with Codex Vaticanus (B).

*Codex Washingtonianus or The Freer Gospels—named after its owner, Charles Freer (W)* This codex, dated to ca. A.D. 400, has the four Gospels and Acts. The handwriting is quite similar to that found in a fifth-century fragment of the book of Enoch found at Akhmim in 1886.

Codex W was copied from a parent manuscript (exemplar) that had been pieced together from several different manu-

---

[1] See Sanders, *Freer Collection: Part II.*

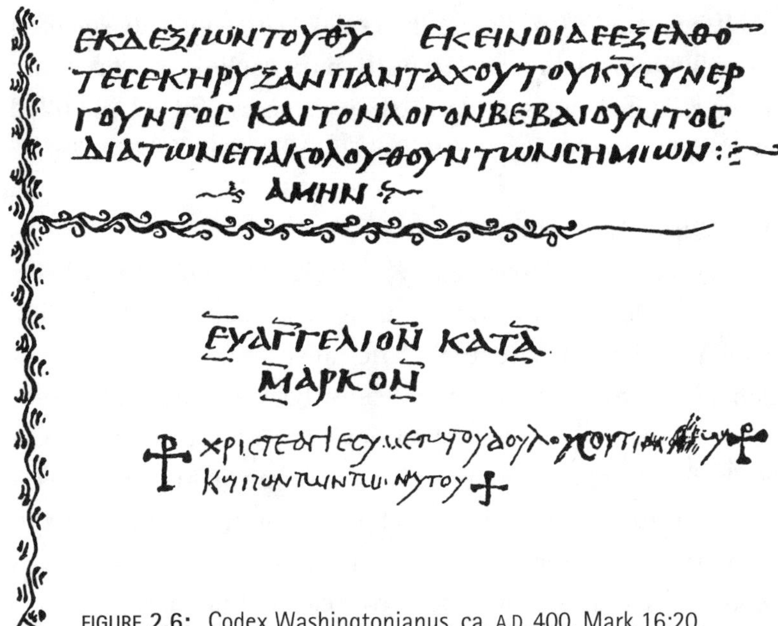


FIGURE 2.6: Codex Washingtonianus. ca. A.D. 400. Mark 16:20.

scripts. Sanders suggested that the parent manuscript was probably put together shortly after the Diocletian persecution, when manuscripts of the New Testament were scarce. The text came from North Africa (the "Western" text) for the first part of Mark, and the scribe of W used manuscripts from Antioch for Matthew and the second part of Luke to fill the gaps in the more ancient manuscript, which he was copying. Detailed textual analysis reveals the variegated textual stratifications of W, as follows: in Matthew the text is Byzantine; in Mark the text is first Western (1:1–5:30), then Caesarean in Mark 5:31–16:20 (akin to $\mathfrak{P}^{45}$); in Luke the text is first Alexandrian (1:1–8:12) then Byzantine. John is more complicated. This first section of John has a mixture of Alexandrian and Western readings, as does the rest of John.

The extreme textual variation in this manuscript reveals the tremendous liberties the scribes (of the exemplar and of W itself) exerted in producing the codex. They not only selected various exemplars of various portions of each Gospel (as many as seven different exemplars), they also harmonized and filled in textual gaps.[1]

## ASSESSING THE MANUSCRIPTS

Westcott and Hort, followed by Colwell,[2] urged that knowledge of documents must precede all decisions about textual variants. They insisted that a textual critic must know the scribal tendencies at work in each manuscript before using that manuscript to make a decision about a reading. For example, if the scribe for a particular manuscript was prone to prune phrases, a textual critic should be wary about citing this manuscript in support of a shorter reading as being original. Each scribe, as a reader of a manuscript, tended to treat that manuscript a particular way. Some scribes tended to lengthen a text with explanatory phrases. Other scribes tended to shorten a text by editing. Still others tended to make certain types of unintentional errors in the process of copying the manuscript. Clearly, knowledge about the particular scribal tendencies of the scribe who produced a particular manuscript must precede all decisions about readings. A textual critic can then take this knowledge and apply it to the task of textual criticism.[3]

In recent years, textual critics have been able to identify some of the very best manuscripts—with respect to textual purity. At the top of the list is $\mathfrak{P}^{75}$. It is well-known that the text produced by the scribe of $\mathfrak{P}^{75}$ is very pure. The scribe was a trained professional, who made very few errors and who refrained from making intentional changes. The text of $\mathfrak{P}^{75}$,

---

[1] See Sanders, *Freer Collection: Part I.*

[2] Westcott and Hort, *Introduction*, 17; Colwell, "Hort Redivivus," 152.

[3] For a complete development of this concept, see Comfort, *Scribe as Interpreter.*

when compared to other texts, is obviously superior; it represents the best of Alexandrian scribal workmanship.

It is also well-known that $\mathfrak{P}^{75}$ was the kind of manuscript used in formulating Codex Vaticanus (B)—the readings of $\mathfrak{P}^{75}$ and Vaticanus are remarkably similar. Prior to the discovery of $\mathfrak{P}^{75}$, certain scholars thought Codex Vaticanus was the work of a fourth-century **recension** (a purposely-created edition); others (chiefly Hort) thought it must trace back to a very early and accurate copy. Hort said that Codex Vaticanus preserves "not only a very ancient text, but a very pure line of a very ancient text."[1] $\mathfrak{P}^{75}$ (which was not discovered until after Hort) appears to have shown that Hort was right.

Prior to the discovery of $\mathfrak{P}^{75}$ in the late 1950s, many textual scholars were convinced that the second- and third-century papyri displayed a text in flux, a text characterized only by individual independence. The Chester Beatty Papyrus ($\mathfrak{P}^{45}$) and the Bodmer Papyri ($\mathfrak{P}^{66}$ and $\mathfrak{P}^{72}$ in 2 Peter and Jude) show this kind of independence. Scholars thought that scribes at Alexandria must have used several such texts to produce a good recension—as is exhibited in Codex Vaticanus.

But we now know that Codex Vaticanus was not the result of a scholarly recension, resulting from editorial selection across the various textual histories. Rather, it is now quite clear that Codex Vaticanus was simply a copy (with some modifications) of a manuscript much like $\mathfrak{P}^{75}$. Gordon Fee argued this very effectively in an article appropriately titled "$\mathfrak{P}^{76}$, $\mathfrak{P}^{66}$, and Origen: The Myth of Early Textual Recension in Alexandria," in which Fee showed that there was no Alexandrian recension before the time of $\mathfrak{P}^{75}$ (late second century) and Codex Vaticanus (early fourth) and that both these manuscripts

---

[1] Westcott and Hort, *Introduction*, 250-251.

"seem to represent a 'relatively pure' form of preservation of a 'relatively pure' line of descent from the original text."[1]

Some scholars may point out that this does not automatically mean that $\mathfrak{P}^{75}$ and Vaticanus represent the original text. What it does mean, they say, is that we have a second-century manuscript showing great affinity with a fourth-century manuscript whose quality has been highly esteemed. Other scholars, such as Eldon Epp,[2] have argued that the high esteem accredited to $\mathfrak{P}^{75}$ and to Vaticanus comes only from a subjective assessment of their relative purity in comparison to other manuscripts.

However, textual critics who have worked with many actual manuscripts, collating and doing textual analysis, and who have thereby seen firsthand the kind of errors, expansions, harmonizations, and interpolations that are present in other manuscripts, are convinced that manuscripts like $\mathfrak{P}^{75}$ and B represent the best of textual purity. This was Westcott's and Hort's assessment of B, after twenty years of study. This was Kurt Aland's assessment of $\mathfrak{P}^{75}$, after many years of study. Scores of other scholars have come to the same conclusion.

The current view about the early text is that certain scribes in Alexandria and/or scribes familiar with Alexandrian scriptoral practices (perhaps such as the scribes in Oxyrhynchus) were probably responsible for maintaining a relatively pure text throughout the second, third, and fourth centuries. The work of textual preservation was probably done here and there by various individual scribes or in small Christian **scriptoria** such as the one established by Pantaneus in Alexandria around 180.

Many manuscripts were produced in accordance with Alex-

[1] Gordon Fee, "$\mathfrak{P}^{75}$, $\mathfrak{P}^{66}$, and Origen."

[2] Epp, "Twentieth Century Interlude."

andrian scriptoral standards in the early centuries of the church. Other manuscripts, however, were produced with a great deal of freedom. One particular scribe/scholar in the late second century produced an edition of the Gospels and Acts that is now known as the D-text. This theologically-minded **redactor** (editor) created a **text type** (text family) that had short-lived popularity—reaching its culmination with Codex Bezae (denoted as D). Three third-century papyri—$\mathfrak{P}^{29}$, $\mathfrak{P}^{38}$, $\mathfrak{P}^{48}$, each containing a portion from the book of Acts—may be early copies of the D-type text in Acts. But there are other papyri containing portions of Acts that provide even earlier testimony to a purer form of Acts—namely, $\mathfrak{P}^{45}$ (early third century) and $\mathfrak{P}^{91}$ (ca. 200), thereby showing that the D-type text of Acts did not necessarily antedate the purer form.

Another kind of text seemed to have developed in the late second century. This is known as the "Western" text. The "Western" text was given its name because this type of text circulated in western countries like North Africa, Italy, and Gaul. However, "Western" is probably a misnomer inasmuch as manuscripts that have been classified "Western" are so named usually on the basis that they are non-Alexandrian. E. C. Colwell has said, "The so-called Western text or Delta type text is the uncontrolled, popular edition of the second century. It has no unity and should not be referred to as the 'Western text.'"[1]

Nonetheless, other scholars still speak of a Western text, and still argue that the "Western" form of text is as early as the Alexandrian, for it was used by Marcion, Irenaeus, Tertullian, and Cyprian—all of whom were alive in the second century. Unfortunately, we do not possess as many early "Western" manuscripts as those called "Alexandrian." (The climate of

---

[1] Colwell, "Hort Redivivus."

the western regions of the Mediterranean is hardly as good as that of Egypt for preserving ancient documents.) Though the "Western" text was early, it is characterized as being uncontrolled and interpolative. Westcott and Hort characterized the "Western" text as one in which the scribes had a "disposition to enrich the text at the cost of its purity by alterations or additions taken from traditional and perhaps from apocryphal and other non-biblical sources."[1]

Some scholars, such as Epp,[2] have argued that the negative assessment of the Western text is subjectively biased, in that the Western text is criticized by those who favor a shorter text, as is usually found in the Alexandrian manuscripts. However, the actual practice of textual criticism has convinced the majority of scholars that the Western text is notoriously expansive. Two of the leading textual critics of our time, Kurt Aland and Bruce Metzger, have affirmed this by their experience of trying to reconstruct the original text of the New Testament.[3] No one yet has convincingly argued that the original text was longer and then was trimmed by editors. Instead, the opposite is the rule of thumb with ancient manuscripts, as is recognized by textual scholars working with all kinds of ancient texts, not just the New Testament.

In the final analysis, the manuscripts that represent a pure preservation of the original text are usually those called "Alexandrian." Some scholars, such as Metzger, have called the earlier manuscripts **proto-Alexandrian**, for they (or manuscripts like them) are thought of as being used to compose an Alexandrian type text. However, this is looking at things backwards—from the perspective of the fourth century. We should look at

[1] Westcott and Hort, *New Testament in the Original Greek*, 134.

[2] Epp, op. cit.

[3] See Aland and Aland, *Text of the New Testament;* and Metzger, *Text of the New Testament.*

things forwardly—from the second century onward—and then compare fourth century manuscripts to those of the second. The second-century manuscripts could still be called "Alexandrian" in the sense that they were produced under Alexandrian influences. Perhaps a distinguishing terminology could be "early Alexandrian" (pre-Constantine) and "later Alexandrian" (post-Constantine). Manuscripts designated as "early Alexandrian" would generally be purer, less editorialized. Manuscripts designated "later Alexandrian" would display editorialization, as well as the influence of other textual traditions. Generally speaking, the "Western" text is not as trustworthy as the Alexandrian text type. But because the later Alexandrian text is known as a polished text, the "Western" or popular text sometimes preserves the original wording. When a variant reading has the support of "Western" texts *and* early Alexandrian texts, it could very likely be original; but when the two are divided, the Alexandrian witnesses more often preserve the original wording.

The "early Alexandrian" text is reflected in many second- and third-century manuscripts. As has been mentioned previously, on the top of the list is $\mathfrak{P}^{75}$ (ca. 175–200), the work of a competent and careful scribe. Not far behind in quality is $\mathfrak{P}^{4}$ + $\mathfrak{P}^{64}$ + $\mathfrak{P}^{67}$ (ca. 150), the work of an excellent copyist. Other extremely good copies are $\mathfrak{P}^{1}$ (third c.), $\mathfrak{P}^{20}$ (early third c.), $\mathfrak{P}^{23}$ (ca. 200), $\mathfrak{P}^{27}$ (third c.), $\mathfrak{P}^{28}$ (third c.), $\mathfrak{P}^{32}$ (ca. 150), $\mathfrak{P}^{39}$ (third c.), $\mathfrak{P}^{46}$ (ca. 125), $\mathfrak{P}^{65}$ (third c.), $\mathfrak{P}^{66}$ (in its corrected form—$\mathfrak{P}66^{c}$; ca. 150), $\mathfrak{P}^{70}$ (third c.), $\mathfrak{P}^{77}$ (ca. 150), $\mathfrak{P}^{87}$ (ca. 125), $\mathfrak{P}^{90}$ (ca. 175), $\mathfrak{P}^{91}$ (ca. 200), $\mathfrak{P}^{100}$ (third c.), $\mathfrak{P}^{104}$ (ca. 150). The "later Alexandrian" text, which displays editorial polishing, is exhibited in a few manuscripts, such as A (fourth century), T (fifth century), Ψ (seventh century), L (eighth century), 33 (ninth century), 1739 (a tenth-century manuscript copied from a fourth-century Alexandrian manuscript much like $\mathfrak{P}^{46}$), and 579 (thirteenth century).

In addition to the "Western," Alexandrian, and D-text types, many manuscripts fall into the Byzantine text type. The Byzantine text likely traces back to the work of Lucian of Antioch (in Syria). According to Jerome, Lucian compared different readings of the New Testament with those with which he was acquainted and produced a revised form of the text. This revised text soon became very popular, not only at Antioch, where Lucian worked, but also at Constantinople and eventually all over the Mediterranean area. From what can be judged in later manuscripts bearing a "Lucianic" text, Lucian's work was the first major recension of the Greek New Testament. This recension involved a great deal of harmonization (especially in the Gospels), emendation, and some interpolation.

From the fourth century onward, Lucian's recension became the most prevailing type of text throughout the Greek-speaking world. In fact, it became (with minor modifications) the received text of the Greek Orthodox Church. From the fourth until the eighth century, the Byzantine text was revised even further until it was nearly standardized. From then on, almost all Greek manuscripts followed the Byzantine text, including those manuscripts that were used by Erasmus in compiling his edition of the Greek New Testament (which became the basis of the English King James Version, discussed in later chapters).

Beginning in the fifth century, Byzantine-type manuscripts began to make their influence in Egypt. Some manuscripts dated around 400 that came from Egypt clearly reflect this influence. Codex Alexandrinus (A), in the Gospels, is probably the best example. Other Egyptian manuscripts of this era, such as Codex Sinaiticus (א) and Codex Washingtonianus (W) display large-scale harmonization in the Gospels, which cannot be directly linked to any kind of recension.

## NEW TESTAMENT TEXTUAL CRITICISM

The primary task of the textual critic is to examine the evidence of the **extant manuscripts** in an effort to determine—among all the **variant readings**—what the original wording was. The task of textual criticism (resulting in the creation of new editions of the Greek New Testament) has been going on intensely for the past three hundred years.

I do not think there is any way to be certain of recovering the original wording of the autographs. But I do think the wording of the originally "published" texts of the New Testament can be recovered through the disciplines of textual criticism. This is a position I made clear in the very first page of *The Quest for the Original Text of the New Testament*:

> When I speak of the original text, I am referring to the "published" text—that is, the text as it was in its final edited form and released for circulation in the Christian community. For some books of the New Testament, there is little difference between the original composition and the published text. After the author wrote or dictated his work, he (or an associate) made the final editorial corrections and then released it for distribution. As is the case for books published in modern times, so in ancient times—the original writing of the author is not always the same as what is published, due to the editorial process. Nonetheless, the author is credited with the final edited text, and the published book is attributed to the author and considered the autograph. This autograph is the original published text.[1]

---

[1] Comfort, *Quest for the Original Text.*

When we speak of recovering the text of the New Testament, we need to go about that task on a book-by-book basis, because each book (or group of books—such as the Pauline Epistles) had its own unique history of textual transmission. The earliest extant copy of an entire New Testament text is the one preserved in Codex Sinaiticus (written about 375). Codex Vaticanus (written about 350) contains most of the New Testament but lacks the Pastoral Epistles and Revelation. Prior to the fourth century, the New Testament was circulated in its various parts as a single book or a group of books (such as the four Gospels or the Pauline Epistles). Manuscripts from the second century to the third century have been found with individual books, such as Matthew ($\mathfrak{P}^{1}$, $\mathfrak{P}^{77}$), Mark ($\mathfrak{P}^{88}$), Luke ($\mathfrak{P}^{69}$), John ($\mathfrak{P}^{5, 22, 52, 66, 90}$), Acts ($\mathfrak{P}^{91}$), Revelation ($\mathfrak{P}^{18, 47, 98, 115}$). Manuscripts have also been found containing groups of books, such as the four Gospels with Acts ($\mathfrak{P}^{45}$), the Pauline Epistles ($\mathfrak{P}^{30}$, $\mathfrak{P}^{46}$, $\mathfrak{P}^{92}$), or Peter's epistles and Jude ($\mathfrak{P}^{72}$). Each of the books of the New Testament has had its own textual history and has been preserved with varying degrees of accuracy. Nonetheless, all of the books were altered from their original state due to the process of manual copying decade after decade and century after century. So the text of each of the books, individually, needs to be recovered.

Since none of the autographs for any of the New Testament books are extant, scholars have to rely on copies to recover or reconstruct the original wording. Some scholars think it is impossible to recover the original text of the Greek New Testament because they have not been able to reconstruct the early history of textual transmission. Other modern scholars are less pessimistic but still guarded in affirming the possibility. And yet others are optimistic because we possess many early manuscripts of excellent quality and because our view of the early period of textual transmission has been getting clearer and clearer.

## THE CANONS OF CRITICISM

Most modern textual critics use one rule of thumb or **canon** as they go about doing the task of recovering the original wording of the text. They try to abide by the rule that *the reading that is most likely original is the one that best explains the variants*. This canon is actually a development of Bengel's maxim (1855:xiii), *proclivi scriptoni praestat ardua* ("the harder reading is to be preferred"), a maxim he formulated in responding to his own question as to which variant reading is likely to have arisen out of the others.

This overarching canon for **internal criticism** involves several criteria, which various scholars have posited and implemented during the past three hundred years of New Testament textual criticism. Having made a thorough historical survey of the development of canons for internal criticism, Eldon Epp summarized all the criteria as follows:

1. A variant's status as the shorter or shortest reading.
2. A variant's status as the harder or hardest reading.
3. A variant's fitness to account for the origin, development, or presence of all other readings.
4. A variant's conformity to the author's style and vocabulary.
5. A variant's conformity to the author's theology or ideology.
6. A variant's conformity to koiné (rather than Attic) Greek.
7. A variant's conformity to Semitic forms of expression.

8. A variant's lack of conformity to parallel passages or to extraneous items in its context generally.
9. A variant's lack of conformity to Old Testament passages.
10. A variant's lack of conformity to liturgical forms and usages.
11. A variant's lack of conformity to extrinsic doctrinal views.[1]

It should be admitted that some of these criteria are problematic when implemented. Two textual critics, using the same principle to examine the same variant, will not always agree. For example, with respect to the fourth canon, one critic will argue that a particular variant was produced by a copyist attempting to emulate the author's style; the other critic will claim the same variant has to be original because it accords with the author's style. And with respect to the fifth canon, one will argue that one variant was produced by an orthodox scribe attempting to rid the text of a reading that could be used to promote heterodoxy or heresy; another will claim that the same variant has to be original because it is orthodox and accords with Christian doctrine (thus a heterodox or heretical scribe must have changed it).

Furthermore, internal criticism allows for the possibility that the reading selected for the text can be taken from any manuscript of any date. This produces subjective eclecticism. Those who advocate "thoroughgoing eclecticism," such as Kilpatrick and Boismard, have argued for the legitimacy of certain variant readings on the basis of internal criticism alone. The readings they favor do have some manuscript support, but often those readings come from one Latin version (versus all

[1] Epp, "Eclectic Method," 243.

Greek witnesses), or a late minuscule, or the testimony of some church father.

Modern textual scholars try to temper the subjectivism of purely internal criticism by employing a method called "reasoned eclecticism." According to Michael Holmes,

> Reasoned eclecticism applies a combination of internal and external considerations, evaluating the character of the variants in light of the manuscript evidence and vice versa in order to obtain a balanced view of the matter and as a check upon purely subjective tendencies.[1]

Kurt Aland favors the same kind of approach, calling it the **local-genealogical method**, which is defined as follows (italics mine):

> It is impossible to proceed from the assumption of a **manuscript stemma**, and on the basis of a full review and analysis of the relationships obtaining among the variety of interrelated branches in the manuscript tradition, to undertake a **recensio** of the data as one would do with other Greek texts. Decisions must be made one by one, instance by instance. This method has been characterized as eclecticism, but wrongly so. After carefully establishing the variety of readings offered in a passage and the possibilities of their interpretation, it must always then be determined afresh on the basis of external and internal criteria which of these readings (and frequently they are quite numerous) is the original, from which the others may

[1] Holmes, "New Testament Textual Criticism," 53.

> be regarded as derivative. From the perspective of our present knowledge, this local-genealogical method (if it must be given a name) is the only one which meets the requirements of the New Testament textual tradition.[1]

The local-genealogical method assumes that for any given **variation unit**, any manuscript (or manuscripts) may have preserved the original text.

The danger of doing textual criticism on the basis of the local-genealogical method is that the editors must decide on a word-by-word basis what the authors most likely wrote. This, of course, verges on claiming knowledge of the author's original intentions. But no one can do this with any degree of certainty. Those who say they can, run the risk of falling prey to the well-known **intentional fallacy,** as postulated by Wimsatt and Beardsley.[2]

The other problem with the local-genealogical method is that it produces an uneven documentary presentation of the text. For the first half of a verse, the evidence of Codex Vaticanus is followed; for the second half, Vaticanus is rejected in favor of Beza. And so on.

## EDITIONS OF THE GREEK NEW TESTAMENT USED TODAY

Most scholars and translators today use one of two modern critical editions of the Greek New Testament: the Nestle-Aland *Novum Testamentum Graece* and/or the United Bible Societies' *Greek New Testament*. These editions are described as **critical editions** because the text they contain is not a copy of any one manuscript; instead, the text is the result of modern textual scholarship.

---

[1] Aland *et al.*, *Novum Testamentum Graece* (26th ed.), 43.

[2] Wimsatt and Beardsley, "The Intentional Fallacy."

It must be remembered that the modern critical editions of the Greek New Testament were never read by any ancient reader. Nonetheless, these are the two critical editions of the Greek New Testament that scholars and translators use today because most modern scholars, endorsing the eclectic method, believe that these editions most accurately represent the original text of the New Testament.

At the beginning of the twentieth century, Eberhard Nestle used the best editions of the Greek New Testament produced in the nineteenth century to compile a text that represented the majority consensus. The work of making new editions was carried on by his son for several years, and then came under the care of Kurt Aland. The latest edition (the 27th) of Nestle-Aland's *Novum Testamentum Graece* appeared in 1993. The same Greek text appears in another popular volume published by the United Bible Societies, called the *Greek New Testament* (fourth revised edition, 1993). These two volumes, which have the same text but differ as to punctuation and textual notes, represent the best in modern textual scholarship.

Aland has argued that the Nestle-Aland text, 27th edition (denoted as $NA^{27}$), comes closer to the original text of the New Testament than did Tischendorf or Westcott and Hort. And in several writings he intimates that $NA^{27}$ may very well be the original text. Though few, if any, scholars would agree with this, the twenty-seventh edition of the Nestle-Aland text is regarded by many as representing the latest and best in textual scholarship. One can be assured that most of the wording in the text is what the writers of the New Testament actually wrote; and if the editors got it wrong, the correct reading can be found in the critical apparatus. Though many modern English translators use these texts, none does so slavishly. The translators usually apply their own eclecticism in adopting or rejecting what is printed in these critical editions. Marginal notes usually inform the attentive reader about variant readings in other manuscripts.

CHAPTER THREE

# The Theory and Practice of Bible Translation

## WHAT A BIBLE TRANSLATION IS AND IS NOT

There is a distinct difference between the manuscripts of the Bible, which are written in Hebrew and Greek, and translations of the Bible. I hear people talk about a translation as if it were the original Bible, and I hear people talk about manuscripts as if they were the original writings. This all needs to be made clear, so that people can have an accurate understanding of Bible translations. That is the point of the first two chapters of this book.

When we speak of "the originals" (the **autographs**), we are speaking of the actual writings of the Old Testament prophets and the New Testament apostles. None of these originals exist any longer. When we speak of **manuscripts** we are usually speaking of Hebrew and Greek copies, of which there are thousands in existence. (There are, of course, "manuscripts" of ancient translations of the Bible in languages such as Latin, Syriac, Coptic, etc., but these belong to a separate category called ancient **versions**.) When we speak of "translations," we are referring to translations of the Hebrew and Greek texts into any number of languages.

The Old Testament was originally written in Hebrew, with a few sections of Daniel penned in Aramaic. Copies of the Hebrew text are called Old Testament manuscripts. Translations of the Hebrew text are called Old Testament versions. As far as we know, all translations were made from Hebrew copies or from editions compiled from various copies, not from the original texts (the autographs).

The New Testament was originally written in Greek. Copies of the Greek text are called New Testament manuscripts. Translations of the Greek text are called New Testament versions. As far as we know, all translations of the New Testament were made from Greek manuscripts or from editions compiled from various Greek manuscripts, not from the original texts themselves.

The English Bible we hold in our hands (in whatever translation) has gone through quite a process. Let us imagine that we are reading the Gospel of Luke. The physician Luke wrote this Gospel in Greek, his native tongue, around A.D. 60. Luke's original (the autograph) no longer exists. Copies (manuscripts) of Luke's Gospel must have been made shortly after he produced his original work, and copies were made for hundreds of years thereafter. We have hundreds and hundreds of manuscript copies of the Gospel of Luke; a few of them date to a hundred or so years after the time he wrote the original. Such manuscripts are $\mathfrak{P}^{4}$, $\mathfrak{P}^{45}$, and $\mathfrak{P}^{75}$. There are many more from the third century, even more from the fourth century, and so on. In due course, scholars have studied these manuscripts, decided which ones were the best, and then compiled editions of the Greek text. Most English Bible translators use these editions to make their English translations, but some have translated straight from a particular Greek manuscript or used only a limited number of Greek manuscripts.

As we read the Gospel of Luke in English, we should realize that we are reading a translation of a copy (or copies) of the original text. Several people have been at work to make that original text accessible to us: (1) Luke, the writer who produced the autograph; (2) scribes who produced copies upon copies of this work; (3) archaeologists who discovered these copies; (4) paleographers who provided transcriptions of these copies; (5) textual critics who compared the copies and compiled critical editions of the Greek text; and (6) translators who produced English renderings of the Greek text.

Having this knowledge, one should realize that translators are working with copies of the original text—or editions made from various copies. Translators cannot alter the original text (by making additions to it or deletions from it) because they do not have the original texts and they are not the textual critics who have reconstructed those texts. Often, critics of Bible translators like to "spook" them with the admonition found at the end of the book of Revelation: "If anyone adds anything to what is written here, God will add to that person the plagues described in this book. And if anyone removes any of the words of this prophetic book, God will remove that person's share in the tree of life and in the holy city that are described in this book" (Rev. 22:18-19, NLT). But this doesn't apply to modern translators (at least not in the way this interpretation is usually intended); it applies to those attempting to alter the Greek text of the book of Revelation.

Interestingly, it is the **Textus Receptus** (the Greek text behind the King James Version) that has the most alterations to the book of Revelation. The man behind the Textus Receptus was Erasmus, who created the first printed edition of the

Greek New Testament (1516). Erasmus was not able to find a complete manuscript of the New Testament, nor anything earlier than the twelfth century. So he had to use several manuscripts for various parts of the New Testament. For most of his work, he relied upon two inferior manuscripts from the twelfth century (Codex $1^{eap}$ and Codex 2). For the book of Revelation, he used another twelfth-century manuscript, which lacked the last leaf containing the last section of Revelation 22 (Codex $1^{r}$). For this section, as well as for others throughout Revelation where the manuscript was difficult to read, Erasmus used the Latin Vulgate and translated it back into Greek! Consequently, the Textus Receptus and KJV have erroneous verses at the end of Revelation. For example, in Revelation 22:14, the KJV reads, "Blessed are they who *do his commandments* that they may have right to the tree of life." Superior manuscript evidence, followed by all modern versions, supports the reading, "Blessed are they who *wash their robes,* that they may have right to the tree of life." The difference is very significant! The KJV tells us that works will get us eternal life; the better text tells us that we need our robes washed (i.e., we need to be cleansed by Jesus' blood) to have eternal life. In Revelation 22:19 (quoted above), which is the very verse that warns against changing the text, Erasmus changed "tree of life" to "book of life." This alteration still appears in the KJV and NKJV. These are the kind of textual alterations that critics should take notice of!

Those who choose to criticize a translation must look at the original language and then make a judgment about whether or not a translation faithfully renders the meaning of the best text found in the best manuscripts. Various scribes making copies of the Hebrew Scriptures or Greek Scriptures made many alterations to the text—especially the monks in the Middle

Ages! It has been the job of textual critics, ever since, to sort through these changes and provide translators with a reconstructed text.

## DEFINING TRANSLATION

There are two basic theories and/or methodologies of Bible translation. The first is called **formal equivalence**. According to this theory, the translator attempts to render the exact words (hence the word *formal,* meaning "form-for-form") of the original language into the receptor language. This kind of translation is commonly known as a "literal" translation; others call it a "word-for-word" translation.

The second kind of translation has been called **dynamic equivalence** or **functional equivalence** by the eminent translation theorist, Eugene Nida. He has defined the ideal of translation as "the reproduction in a receptor language [i.e., English] of the closest natural equivalent of the source language [i.e., Hebrew or Greek] message, first in terms of meaning, and second in terms of style."[1] Nida, therefore, believes that a translation should have the same dynamic impact upon modern readers as the original had upon its audience. He elaborates on this as follows:

> Dynamic equivalence is therefore to be defined in terms of the degree to which the receptors of the message in the receptor language respond to it in substantially the same manner as the receptors in the source language. This response can never be identical, for the cultural and historical settings are too different, but there should be a high degree of equivalence of response, or the translation will have failed to accomplish its purpose.[2]

[1] Nida and Taber, *Theory and Practice*, 210.

[2] Ibid., 24.

Nida's theory of dynamic equivalence has become a standard or ideal that many modern translators have attempted to attain. Goodspeed expressed this desire about his *American Translation* when he said, "I wanted my translation to make on the reader something of the impression the New Testament must have made on its earliest readers."[1]

Another way of speaking about a functionally-equivalent translation is to call it a *thought-for-thought* translation (as opposed to a word-for-word translation). Of course, to translate the thought of the original language requires that the text be interpreted accurately and then rendered in understandable idiom. Thus, the goal of any functionally-equivalent translation is for it to be exegetically accurate and idiomatically powerful.

A good translation must be reliable and readable—that is, it must reliably replicate the meaning of the text without sacrificing its readability. At various points in the Scriptures, there is evidence that the biblical documents were written to be read aloud, usually in public worship (see Neh. 8; Luke 4:16-17; 1 Tim. 4:13; Rev. 1:3). Undoubtedly, those ancient hearers of the Word understood the message as it was delivered to them. Any translation should be just as fluent and intelligible to a modern audience. This, of course, does not mean that translation can replace interpretation of difficult passages—as in the case of the eunuch who needed Philip's interpretation of Isaiah 53 (see Acts 8:28-35); but a good rendering minimizes the need for unnecessary interpretation (or **exegesis**, a technical term that means "drawing out the meaning of the text").

Ever since the time of Jerome (fourth century A.D.), who produced the translation known as the Latin Vulgate, there

[1] Goodspeed, *New Chapters*, 113.

has been debate over what is the best method to translate the Bible: the word-for-word approach or the thought-for-thought or sense-for-sense. In a letter to a person called Pammachius, Jerome exhibited this tension when he wrote:

> I myself not only admit but freely proclaim that, in translating from the Greek (except in the case of the holy Scriptures where even the order of the words is a mystery), I render sense for sense and not word for word.[1]

When it came to translating the Scriptures, Jerome, contrary to his normal practice, felt the compulsion to render word for word; but he did not always do so in the Vulgate. Yet very few would now demand it of him because most agree that strict literalism can greatly distort the original meaning.

Martin Luther, the great Reformer and translator of the German Bible, believed that a translator's paramount task was to reproduce the spirit of the author; at times this could only be accomplished by an idiomatic rendering, though when the original required it, word-for-word was to be used.[2] Other translators have preferred to be very literal because they have feared that in translating on a thought-for-thought basis they might alter the text according to their own subjective interpretation. Indeed, it is true that a word-for-word rendering can be executed more easily than a thought-for-thought one; in doing the latter, the translator must enter into the same thought as the author—and who can always know with certainty what the author's original, intended meaning was? Therefore, a functionally-equivalent or thought-for-thought translation should

---

[1] Schaff and Wace, eds., *St. Jerome*, 113.

[2] Schwarz, *Principles and Problems*, 205–206.

be done by a group of scholars (to guard against personal subjectivism), who employ the best exegetical tools. In this regard, Beekman and Callow give excellent advice:

> Translating faithfully involves knowing what Scripture means. This is fundamental to all idiomatic translation, and it is at this point that exegesis comes in. Toussaint, in an article in *Notes on Translation,* defines exegesis as follows: "Exegesis is a critical study of the Bible according to hermeneutical principles with the immediate purpose of interpreting the text." In other words, its immediate purpose is to ascertain, as accurately as possible, using all the means available, just what the original writer, "moved by the Holy Spirit," meant as he dictated or penned his words, phrases, and sentences. Exegesis thus lies at the heart of all translation work, for if the translator does not know what the original means, then it is impossible for him to translate faithfully.[1]

The analysis in chapter 7 of the modern translations of the prologue to John's Gospel will demonstrate how important exegesis is to translation. Major differences in translation come from major differences in interpretation.

In the final analysis, we must admit that there is no perfect translation of the Bible. There has never been one and there never will be, because it is impossible to convey in a translated language all that is contained in the original languages. There is an old saying that "Every translator is a traitor" (Latin, *translator traducor*) for not having done it just right. I don't

[1] Beekman and Callow, *Translating,* 34–35.

think any translator would disagree, for everyone who has translated the Bible has felt the pull of two forces: the desire to accurately render the original text and the desire to do so in a way that communicates the message to modern readers. This cannot always be done. My own experience as the New Testament coordinator of the New Living Translation taught me again and again how daunting a task it is to produce a perfect translation. English was not created to do justice to Greek!

Let me give an example. John 1:14a literally reads, "And the Word became flesh, and tabernacled among us, and we saw his glory." To those versed in Scriptures, this literal rendering is quite rich. But to most modern readers it is obscure. Assuming that the reader has begun with verse 1 of John's Gospel, he or she will probably realize that the Word is God. The reader might also realize that "became flesh" means "became human" (as in the NLT). Thus, they would probably understand that God became human.

But what does it mean that he "tabernacled among us"? Therefore, English translators attempt to render this in more communicable terms, using a verb such as "dwell" (RSV, NIV, NASB, NEB) or "live" (NRSV, NLT). While these renderings help English readers understand the basic meaning, they obscure a word that was pregnant with meaning to the original readers. The ancient reader of this Gospel, when hearing or reading the Greek word *eskenosen* ("he pitched tent" or "he tabernacled"), would associate it with the Old Testament tabernacle. In the Old Testament account, God lived among his people Israel by "tabernacling" among them in a tabernacle, or tent. His presence and glory filled that tabernacle; and wherever that tabernacle went in the journeys of Israel, God also went (see Exod. 40). With this image in view, the writer, John, must have intended his readers to see the connection between the Old

Testament tabernacle and Jesus, who is the new dwelling place of God. God lived in Jesus; those who realized it saw God's glory in him (as the next clause states— "we saw his glory"). The point is this: not one English translation can do perfect justice to John 1:14. A translator can either win on the side of literalism or win on the side of trying to communicate, but not both at once.

## LANGUAGE CHANGES

Another challenge that translators face is that language constantly changes. Many statements in the KJV translation (published in 1611) no longer make any sense—or, worse still, communicate the wrong idea to modern readers. Let us look at some examples. According to the KJV, James talks about someone coming into a church who "weareth the gay clothing" (James 2:3). You know what that communicates to modern readers! 1 Samuel 18:4 says that Jonathan "stripped himself . . . to his girdle." Such language doesn't make it in the twenty-first century. These translations made perfectly good sense to contemporary readers, at the time when the KJV was translated. But the times have changed, and so has our language. "Gay clothing" communicates today something about the person's sexual orientation; "stripped to his girdle" communicates today that the man is a cross-dresser! Fortunately, modern versions, including the New King James Version, have made changes in these verses to accommodate modern ideas about sexuality.

Other verses in the KJV exhibit dated, male-oriented language, when such is not warranted by the text. For example, Paul tells the Corinthians, "In malice be ye children, but in understanding be men" (1 Cor. 14:20). Modern readers, accustomed to male-female equality, would take exception to this rendering. And well they should. According to the Greek, Paul was encouraging his readers to "be mature"; it has nothing to do with maleness or manliness.

In another instance, Paul tells his readers, "Quit you like men" (1 Cor. 16:13, KJV). According to a modern, yet literal, translation, this would be "act like men" (see NASB). But the real thought here is simply an encouragement to bravery. Thus, many modern versions say "be brave" (NKJV, NJB, TEV) or "be courageous" (NLT). Some critics would say these modern renderings show that the translators caved in to feminist pressures. Interestingly, the Greek word (*andrizomai*) in ancient Greek literature wasn't applied to men alone; women were also encouraged to *andrizomai.*[1] Thus, a male-originated word had become an idiom for bravery many centuries before the New Testament was written. How anachronistic to translate it as if bravery was only a male virtue!

Bible translators need to stay current with shifts in modern English language if they want to communicate the message of the Bible to modern men and women. In the 1970s, the Modern Language Association (the primary association for English professors worldwide) began to issue statements encouraging writers and teachers of writing to avoid using the masculine pronoun wherever possible because this would help relieve English from an unnecessary, long-standing, male-dominated orientation. This position made sense to many English professors, who promoted this in the colleges. This position was also adopted by grammar schools and in educational textbooks. By the 1980s it had become established in the American educational system. Writers had to find ways to avoid using the masculine pronoun to refer generically to any person. Writers also

---

[1] Bauer *et al.*, *Greek-English Lexicon*, 64.

had to find synonyms for the word "man" when speaking of a human being.

Of course, Bible translators can choose to ignore this shift in English language, and they can justify their use of the third person singular "he/his/him" by saying that they are being true to the original languages. But the fact is, failure to cope with this shift in language signals failure in communication. American readers under the age of thirty will misunderstand many passages of Scripture. Furthermore, a persistent use of the third person singular "he" or "man" may not even be an accurate translation.

The Greek language has two words that can be translated "man." The first is *anthropos;* the second is *aner.* The word *anthropos* primarily designates a human being, regardless of sex. It can also be used of a male individual—as in John 1:6, which says "there was a man sent from God named John." The context makes it clear whether the word is referring to people in general or males. There are hundreds of verses in the Bible where the reference is to human beings in general, not to males. The KJV and other literal translations (RSV, NASB, NKJV) use the words "man" or "men" in these verses. To many modern readers, who understand "man" or "men" as referring to males only, these verses are very exclusive. Let us look at some examples from the KJV:

> "Man shall not live by bread alone, but by every word that proceedeth out of the mouth of God" (Matt. 4:4).
>
> "In him was life; and the life was the light of men" (John 1:4).
>
> "For there is none other name under heaven given among men, whereby we must be saved" (Acts 4:12).

> "We trust in the living God, who is the Saviour of all men" (1 Tim. 4:10).

Clearly, the intent of these passages is that God has some wonderful things (his word, life, and salvation) to offer to all human beings, not just males. Therefore, to translate this in current times as "men" fails to deliver the message of the text. Not only are modern sensibilities against doing this, it is unnecessary to use the term "man" when the words "people" or "human beings" communicate the same idea and are intelligible to all readers.

The other Greek word for "man" is *aner.* It designates a male person (as opposed to a female), an adult, or a husband. It is also used to specify certain people groups. In most instances, it should be translated as "man" or "husband" or "the people of such and such a place."

The notion of gender inclusiveness carries over to the term "brother" (Greek *adelphos*), a term frequently used by Paul. In a literal translation, the word is simply rendered as "brother." But many scholars understand the meaning of this term, in context, to refer to all the believers, male and female. In other words, when the writers of the New Testament Epistles addressed their readers as "brothers," they were not speaking only to the male believers.

In the early church, it is apparent that both male and female believers gathered together for fellowship (see Acts 1:14; 12:12-13; 16:13; 17:12; 1 Cor. 11; Col. 4:15). During these gatherings the Epistles would be read to them. It is also clear from a close reading of the Epistles that Paul was speaking to both the men and women in the church (see, for example, 1 Cor. 7; 11; 14; Philem. 1:1-2). At certain points in his letters, he would give specific admonitions to husbands or to wives, separately—indicating that he expected both to be in the audience (Eph. 5:22; Col. 3:18). Peter did the same (see 1 Pet. 3:1, 7). This indicates that both men and women were included in Paul's audience, as well as in Peter's. At other times, Paul would make direct appeals in his writing to certain female believers, such as Euodia and Syntyche (Phil. 4:2), or he would pass along his greetings to various female Christians, such as Priscilla, Junia, and Julia (see Rom. 16:3, 7, 15).

Given this context, it seems right to translate "brothers" as "brothers and sisters" if we are trying to communicate accurately the historical situation of the early church to modern readers. This translation effectively communicates what Paul meant when he addressed his readers as "brothers." Surely, he was including male and female believers.

The same could be said of the term "sons." In most New Testament verses the term for God's children is "sons." Since God's "sons" are *all* of his children, whether male or female, it could be misleading to only use the word "sons" in a Bible translation that seeks to communicate the biblical message effectively. The question for translators is this: Did the writers use this to mean male believers only, or did they use it to speak of all believers who now share a special life-relationship with God?

During the past twenty-five years I have preached and taught Paul's epistles quite frequently. In four instances Paul uses the word "sons" to describe all believers (see Rom. 8:14, 19; Gal. 4:6-7). Whenever I read these passages, I found myself explaining to the females in the audience that "sons" was an inclusive term. I told them that they were not excluded from passages that extolled the spiritual benefits of being "sons." I think Paul would concur. In fact, Paul had told the Galatians that there is no longer "male or female" when it comes to understanding our new position in Christ and in the church (Gal. 3:28). In the NLT, for example, the word used in all the above-mentioned verses is "children," not "sons." This translates the meaning of the text, not the literal words.

Furthermore, the NLT corrects the traditional mistranslation of "sons" found in several verses in the KJV. The Greek word for "sons" is *huioi;* another Greek term, *teknoi,* means "children." Because the period in which the KJV was translated was one in which male-dominated language ruled, the term "sons of God" appears in John 1:12, Phil. 2:15, and 1 John 3:1-2, when it should be "children [*teknoi*] of God."

Finally, let's look at a more sensitive issue: the translation of the titles "God the Father" and "God the Son." In recent years, some radical feminists have demanded that God not be presented in patriarchal terms in translations of the Bible. This means they think that expressions such as "God our Father" should be changed to "God our Parent," and that Jesus should be called "the Child of God," not "the Son of God." But these kinds of translations violate the original intent of the Scriptures, which is to present God as "Father" and "Son." Modern versions, including the NRSV and NLT, respect this revelation and translate accordingly. Throughout these versions, Jesus is called the "Son of God" or "Son of Man," never the "Child of God" or "Child of Humanity." And "the Father" is a consistent rendering of *ho patros.*

As would be expected, there has been some resistance against modern versions that incorporate gender-neutral language. Some individuals, such as Wayne Grudem (President of the Council on Biblical Manhood and Womanhood), have strongly criticized certain modern versions of the Bible for bowing to feminist pressures. Quite specifically, the *New International Version: Inclusive Language Edition* was the target of the criticism because it was believed by its critics to have mistranslated the Bible in the interest of making it gender-inclusive.[1]

Grudem insists that a translation must be literal in order to be accurate. He glories in his literalism—but only a certain kind of literalism—that which fits his agenda of being faithful to male-oriented language. But Grudem gets caught in his own trap. In one of his articles, Grudem uses the pronoun "he" when referring to the Holy Spirit. He says, "It is terribly presumptuous of translators to think they can be sure they are able to foresee all the possible implications and subtle nuances that the Holy Spirit intended when he caused Scripture to be written exactly as it was."[2]

Surely, Grudem knows that "the Spirit" in Greek (*to pneuma*) is neuter, not masculine. Shouldn't a literalist insist that we use the pronoun "it" when referring to the Spirit? After all, Grudem just told us in his article that every single word must be translated just as it is. Why, then, does Grudem use "he," not "it," when referring to the Holy Spirit? Because "he" has been deemed the appropriate pronoun in English to communicate the personhood of the Spirit. If translators talked about the Spirit as an "it"—though this would be literally accurate—this would not convey the right message to readers. The point is this: translators must not only know the meaning of the text, they must also know how to communicate that meaning in the receptor language, which is constantly changing.[3]

This last point is well worth emphasizing: translations must change as the language changes. There is nothing sacrosanct

---

[1] Grudem, "Battle for the Bible."

[2] Ibid.

[3] For more on this issue, see the printed debate between Grudem and Osborne: "Do Inclusive-Language Bibles Distort Scripture?" See also Carson, *Inclusive Language Debate.*

about a translation—it is changeable and fluid. By contrast, the text underlying the translation should not be changed because it is sacred and inviolable. Unfortunately, the Hebrew and Greek texts of the Bible were altered by various scribes throughout the ages, but textual critics have worked hard and long to recover the original wording as much as possible. Readers need to keep these distinctions in mind.

All too often these distinctions are blurred by people who want to warn translators against making changes in the Bible. Those who make such warnings often confuse the notion of "original documents" with "translations." For example, when it comes to assessing textual inviolability, people must not compare a Bible *translation* to a document like the Declaration of Independence or the Gettysburg Address. Lincoln's Gettysburg Address is an *original* document written in English; as an historical document, it should not be altered or modernized. Likewise, the Hebrew and Greek Scriptures, also historical documents, should not be changed. But this "inviolability" cannot be applied to *translations* of the Scriptures. They have to change—in order to keep up with the changes that happen in any and all languages. These changes do not alter the original text; rather, they make the original text clearer to modern readers.

By way of concluding this section, as well as this chapter, let me use the Gettysburg Address as an example of what the difference is between doing the work of textual criticism and doing a translation of the text. Most people don't know that there are five different versions of the Gettysburg Address. In the first version, Lincoln wrote, "This nation shall have a new birth of freedom." In the fifth and final version, Lincoln wrote, "This nation, under God, shall have a new birth of freedom." The task of a textual critic is to discover when the phrase "under God" appeared in the text. Was it in the first edition and then dropped out? Or was it added later—by Lincoln or someone else? Textual scholars of the Gettysburg Address are certain that it was added later—in this case, by Abraham Lincoln himself.

The task of translating the Gettysburg Address is a different one. A translator needs to choose which version of the address he or she is going to translate and then give a faithful rendering in current language. If the Gettysburg Address was being translated into Spanish, the translation would not have a literal rendering of "Four score and seven years ago." It would simply contain the modern Spanish expression for "eighty seven years." And a modern Spanish translation would not give a literal, male-oriented rendering of the phrase "all men are created equal." Rather, it would contain the modern, Spanish way of saying "all people are created equal."

Anyone who has tried to translate the Bible will honestly admit how difficult a task it is. Those who stand on the sidelines and criticize the efforts of those who have been engaged in Bible translation work need to try their own hands at it. They themselves will inevitably be criticized for not rendering a certain Hebrew or Greek phrase accurately—or, when having done so (they think), for doing it in an unintelligible manner. Translators will be criticized by lexical purists for not having produced a literal translation or by modern readers for failing to communicate. Most criticism would abate if people took the time to understand the methodology at work behind each translation.

CHAPTER FOUR

# Early Versions of the Bible

Not everyone can read Hebrew or Greek, the original languages of the Bible. Therefore, throughout the ages, scholars who could read Hebrew and/or Greek translated these biblical languages into a multitude of other languages so that others could read the Bible in their native tongue.

The Hebrew Bible was translated into Greek, Aramaic, and Syriac before the era of Christ. Thereafter, it was translated into hundreds of languages. Shortly after the era of Christ, the Greek Bible was translated into Latin, Coptic, Syriac, Armenian, and Gothic—to name a few. Thereafter, the Greek New Testament has been translated into hundreds of languages. Bible translation work has gone on for centuries. Today, most language populations on earth have either the entire Bible or some part of it translated into their own language. Several small language populations still await the work of translators.

The purpose of this chapter is to provide a sketch of the most significant, early translations of the Hebrew Bible and Greek New Testament, and then to narrow our survey to the history of the English Bible leading up to William Tyndale's monumental version of 1526, as well as other important versions of the sixteenth century. The following chapters will focus on the King James Version, important revisions of the King James Version, and modern translations—in that order.

## TRANSLATIONS OF THE HEBREW SCRIPTURES

For hundreds of years, the Jewish nation was consolidated in the area of Palestine. In due course, however, many Jews were dispersed from their own country. Four great dispersions (or **diaspora**) occurred in the early history of the Jews—one from the northern kingdom and another three from the southern kingdom.

After Solomon's death, his kingdom broke in two. The northern kingdom of Israel sunk deep into idolatry and immorality (2 Kings 17:14-18). Assyria conquered the northern kingdom in 722 B.C. and took more than twenty-seven thousand Israelites into exile, as had been predicted (2 Kings 17:23). They were settled in cities along the tributaries of the Euphrates River and in Media. Assyrians from cities around Babylon, in turn, colonized Israel (2 Kings 17:6, 24), intermarrying with remaining Jews and thereby creating a mixed race, many of whom were later known as "Samaritans" (see discussion below).

The southern kingdom of Judah suffered exile to the east in Babylonia and to the south in Egypt. The Babylonian king Nebuchadnezzar captured Judeans in several expeditions from 605 B.C. to the fall of Jerusalem in 586 B.C. All but the very poorest people were carried away captive (2 Kings 25:8-21; Jer. 52:12-16).

Shishak, king of Egypt, deported exiles from Judah as early as the tenth century B.C. (1 Kings 14:25-26; 2 Chron. 12:9). About four hundred years later, Johanan, a Judean, thought he could escape from Nebuchadnezzar by fleeing to Egypt. Johanan forced Jeremiah and a group of other Jews to go with him; they settled at Migdol, Tahpanhes, and Memphis. The Babylonians pursued them, took control of Egypt, and executed many of the Jews there (Jer. 43:5–44:30). A few surviving exiles established permanent colonies in Egypt (Isa. 19:18-19).

All these dispersions to different countries meant that the Jews had to learn different languages in order to survive in a new culture. In time, the younger generations did not have the ability to read or write in Hebrew, in which the Old Testament was written. Hence, they needed translations. This is made evident in the book of Nehemiah, when the Levites read the Old Testament Scriptures to the Jews who had returned from Babylon to Jerusalem. After reading the Scriptures in Hebrew, the Levites had to explain what had been read because the peoples' knowledge of Hebrew was limited. Evidently, this explanation involved both translation and interpretation (Neh. 8:8).

## THE SAMARITAN PENTATEUCH

The region of Samaria was a province allotted to Ephraim and half the tribe of Manasseh in the days of Joshua. After the death of Solomon and the revolt of the ten northern tribes, the inhabitants of Samaria followed the idolatry introduced by Jeroboam, refusing to go to Jerusalem to worship at the temple. Years later, after the ten tribes had been carried away into captivity, the king of Assyria put into this province a colony from various nations, which soon intermingled and intermarried with the original people, causing a strange medley of religion. 2 Kings 17:33 says "they feared the Lord and served their own gods" (NASB). This conglomerate of people became known as "Samaritans."

When a remnant of Jews returned from the Babylonian captivity, they refused the Samaritans any participation in rebuilding the temple or the city of Jerusalem, even though the Samaritans claimed to have the same God as the Jews. This refusal led to a bitter animosity between the two groups, which continued to the time of Christ and was succinctly summed up by John: "Jews have no dealings with Samaritans" (John 4:9, NASB).[1]

At some point in their history, the Samaritans adopted the books of Moses (the *Pentateuch*) as their Scriptures, and they set up a place to worship on Mount Gerizim (see Deut. 11:26-29; 27:11-13). A copy of the Samaritan Pentateuch came to the attention of scholars in 1616. This text differs from the Masoretic Text in some six thousand instances. At first, many scholars thought this to be the result of sectarian differences between Samaritans and Jews. Some scholars simply viewed it as a sectarian revision of the Masoretic Text. But after further assessment, it became clear that the Samaritan Pentateuch represented a text of much earlier origin than the Masoretic Text. And although a few of the distinctions of the Samaritan Pentateuch were clearly the result of sectarian concerns, most of the differences were neutral in this respect. The fact that the Samaritan Pentateuch had much in common with the Septuagint and some of the Dead Sea Scrolls revealed that most of its differences with the Masoretic Text were not due to sectarian differences. More likely, they were due to the use of a different textual base, which was probably in wide use in the ancient Near East until well after the time of Christ.

## THE SEPTUAGINT (LXX)

The story behind the making of the Septuagint is told in "The Letter of Aristeas" (written around 150–100 B.C.). Aristeas was

---

[1] Comfort and Hawley, *Gospel of John*, 65.

an official of Egypt's Ptolemy Philadelphus (285–247 B.C.). According to this story, Ptolemy was attempting to gather all of the world's books into his great Alexandrian library. The Old Testament was not available in a Greek translation, so Ptolemy sent to the high priest in Jerusalem for texts and scholars. Texts and six elders of each tribe were sent. After being royally entertained by Ptolemy, these seventy-two elders were cloistered and in exactly seventy-two days produced the full Greek translation of the Old Testament, called Septuagint ("Seventy") and usually abbreviated LXX in Roman numerals. According to the story, all seventy-two translations agreed to the letter.

So goes the folklore. The truth of the matter is that the Septuagint was produced over an extended period of time. The Septuagint is a translation done for hellenized (Greek-speaking) Jews of the diaspora who, no longer understanding Hebrew, wished to hear and teach the Bible in their own language. Scholars argue over the date of the translation, placing portions as early as 250 B.C. and other parts as late as 100 B.C. Most concur that it was translated in segments by many translators over several centuries and then was gathered together into one library of scrolls or one codex. The Septuagint follows a different order from English Bibles and usually includes up to fifteen apocryphal or noncanonical books.

Thus, the Septuagint is not a single version but a collection of versions made by various authors, who differed greatly in their methods and their knowledge of Hebrew. The translations of the individual books are in no way uniform. Many books are translated almost literally, while others like Job and Daniel are quite dynamic. The books translated literally are clearly more helpful in making comparisons with the Masoretic Text than the more dynamic ones.

The content of some books is significantly different when comparing the Septuagint and the Masoretic Text. For example, in the Septuagint, Jeremiah is missing significant portions that are found in the Masoretic Text, and the order of the text is different as well. What these differences actually mean is difficult to know with certainty. It has been conjectured that the Septuagint is simply a poor translation and is therefore missing portions of the original Hebrew. But these same differences could also indicate that editorial additions and changes worked their way into the Masoretic Text during its long history of development. It is also possible that there were a number of textual traditions at that time, one followed by the Septuagint, and another followed by the Masoretic Text.

The Septuagint was the standard Old Testament text used by the early Christian church. The expanding Gentile church needed a translation in the common language of the time—Greek. By the time of Christ, even among the Jews, a majority of the people spoke Aramaic and Greek, not Hebrew. The New Testament writers demonstrated their preference for the Septuagint over the Hebrew Bible by using the Septuagint when quoting the Old Testament.

The Septuagint has been preserved in many manuscripts. Portions of it are extant in several papyrus manuscripts of the first century to the fourth century A.D., especially in the Chester Beatty Papyri. The entire Septuagint Old Testament is contained in the famous biblical codices: Codex Sinaiticus, Codex Vaticanus, and Codex Alexandrinus. These same manuscripts contain the Greek New Testament. These copies have been studied intensely because they bear a Greek witness to Hebrew texts far earlier than the Masoretic Text.

## THE GREEK VERSIONS OF AQUILA, SYMMACHUS, AND THEODOTIAN

Because of the broad acceptance and use of the Septuagint among Christians, the Jews renounced it in favor of other Greek versions. Aquila, a proselyte and disciple of Rabbi Akiba, produced a new translation around 130. In the spirit of his teacher, Aquila wrote an extremely literal translation, often to the point of communicating poorly in Greek. This literal approach, however, gained this version wide acceptance among Jews. Only fragments of this version have survived.

Symmachus produced a new version around 170 designed not only for accuracy, but also to communicate the Greek language idiomatically. His version has survived only in a few *Hexapla* fragments (the *Hexapla* is discussed below).

A third Greek version came from Theodotian, a Jewish proselyte from the end of the second century A.D. His version was apparently a revision of an earlier Greek version, possibly the Septuagint. This version has only survived in quotations in a few early Christian writings, though it was once widely used.

## ORIGEN'S HEXAPLA

The Christian theologian Origen (ca. 185–255) arranged the Old Testament with six parallel versions for comparison in his **Hexapla**. In his effort to find the best text of the Old Testament, Origen wrote out the Old Testament in six parallel columns: (1) the Hebrew, (2) the Hebrew transliterated into Greek characters, (3) the text of Aquila, (4) the text of Symmachus, (5) Origen's own corrected Septuagint text, and (6) the text of Theodotian.

Jerome used this great Bible at Caesarea in his work on the Latin Vulgate (see page 125). Almost four centuries after

Origen's death, a Mesopotamian Bishop, Paul of Tella, also used the Hexapla in the library at Caesarea (616–617) to make a translation into Syriac of Origen's fifth column, the corrected Septuagint. Then in 638 the Islamic hordes swept through Caesarea and the Hexapla disappeared. Other than a few surviving fragments, only Bishop Paul's Syriac translation of Origen's fifth column remains. An eighth-century copy of this is extant in a Milan museum.

## THE ARAMAIC TARGUMS

The Aramaic Targums were Aramaic translations of the Hebrew Old Testament. Since the common language of the Jews during the post-exilic period (i.e., the period after their exile into Babylon) was Aramaic and not Hebrew, a need for Aramaic translations of the Hebrew Bible arose. Hebrew remained the language of scholarly religious circles, and translations for the common people were often spurned by the religious leadership. But over time, the reading of the Scriptures and commentaries in Aramaic became an accepted practice in the synagogues.

The purpose of the Targums was to communicate the message of the Scriptures to the people. Thus, the translations were extremely interpretive. The translators paraphrased, added explanatory glosses, and often reinterpreted the text according to the theological biases of their time. They sought to relate the Bible text to contemporary life and culture.

## THE SYRIAC VERSION

Another version worthy of note is the Syriac Version. This version was in common use in the Syriac (eastern Aramaic) church, which designated it the **Peshitta**, meaning "simple or plain." What they intended by this designation is difficult to discern. It may indicate that it was intended for popular use, or that it avoided adding explanatory glosses and other additions, or perhaps that it was not an annotated text, as was the annotated Syro-Hexapla then in use by the same community.

Though the history of the Syriac Version is not known, it must have been complex. Some scholars have identified it as the reworking of an Aramaic Targum in Syriac, while others claim it has a more independent origin. Some connect it to the conversion of the leaders of Adiabene (east of the Tigris River) to the Jewish faith during the first century A.D. Their need for an Old Testament could have brought about the development of a version in their common tongue, Syriac.[1]

## EARLY NON-ENGLISH VERSIONS OF THE NEW TESTAMENT AND THE ENTIRE BIBLE

We now step into the era just after Jesus Christ was on earth. As the gospel spread and churches multiplied in the early centuries of the Christian era, Christians in various countries wanted to read the Bible in their own language. As a result, many translations of the New Testament (as well as the Old Testament) were made in different languages. For example, translations were done in Coptic for the Egyptians, in Syriac for those whose language was Aramaic, in Armenian for the Armenians, in Gothic for the Germanic people called the Goths, and in Latin for the Romans and Carthaginians. The most famous Latin translation was done by Jerome around 400. This translation, known as the Latin Vulgate (*vulgate* means "common"—the Latin text for the common man), was

[1] A few portions of this section were adapted from V. Walter, "Versions of the Bible" in Comfort, *Origin of the Bible*, 291-306.

used extensively in the Roman Catholic church for centuries and centuries. As far as we know, the first English versions were based on the Latin Vulgate.

## COPTIC VERSIONS

**Coptic**, an Egyptian language, was the primary language of the native populations who lived along the Nile River. Coptic script is composed of twenty-five Greek uncials and seven cursives taken over from Egyptian writing to express sounds not in the Greek. Through the centuries it developed at least five main dialects: Achmimic, sub-Achmimic (also called Memphitic), Sahidic, Fayyumic, and Bohairic. Fragments of biblical material have been found in all five dialects. Three of the dialects faded out of use until—by the eleventh century—only Bohairic and Sahidic remained. In time, these two dialects became strictly religious languages used only in Coptic churches.

The earliest translation was in Sahidic in Upper Egypt (i.e., southern Egypt), where Greek was less universally understood. The Sahidic Old and New Testaments were probably completed around 200. Greek was so much more dominant in the Delta that the translation of the Scriptures into Bohairic probably was not completed until somewhat later. Since Bohairic was the language of the Delta, however, it was also the language of the Coptic Patriarch in Alexandria.

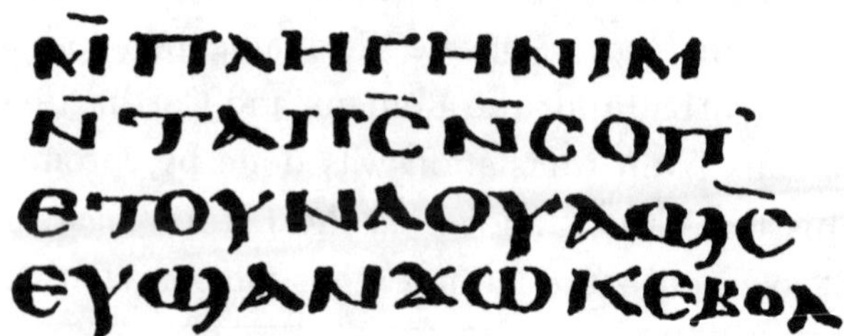

FIGURE 4.1: Sahidic Version. Fifth Century. Revelation 11:6.

When the Patriarchate moved from Alexandria to Cairo in the eleventh century, the Bohairic texts went along. Bohairic gradually became the major religious language of the Coptic church.

The three most prominent dialects of Coptic preserved in biblical manuscripts are Bohairic (designated $cop^{bo}$) in northern Egypt, Fayyumic ($cop^{fay}$) in central Egypt, and Sahidic (designated $cop^{sa}$) in southern Egypt. We have several extant translations of the New Testament into Coptic, some dated as early as the fourth century. Some extant manuscripts, such as $\mathfrak{P}^{6}$ (a fourth-century papyrus copy of the Gospel of John), are **diglots**, presenting the text both in Coptic and in Greek.

## THE SYRIAC NEW TESTAMENT

Syriac was the predominant tongue of the region of Edessa and western Mesopotamia. The version known today as the Peshitta Bible (still the official Bible of Christians of the old Assyrian area churches) developed through several stages. One of the most famous and widely-used translations in the early church was the Syriac Diatessaron, done in about 170 by Tatian, a man who had been a disciple of Justin Martyr at Rome. The Diatessaron (meaning "through the four") was a work that wove all four Gospels into one account. The Diatessaron was very popular among Syriac-speaking Christians. Syrian bishops had an uphill battle getting Christians to use "The Gospel of the Separated Ones" (meaning the text in which the four Gospels were separated from one another rather than blended) in their churches.

Other portions of the Bible were also put into Old Syriac. Quotations from the church fathers indicate that some type of second-century Old Syriac text existed along with the

Diatessaron. In fact, the Syriac Old Testament may have been a Jewish translation into Syriac that Syrian Christians made their own, just as Greek Christians had done with the Septuagint. It then underwent a more or less official revision around the end of the fourth century, emerging as the Peshitta text. Tradition indicates that the New Testament portion of that version may have been made at the instigation of Rabbula, bishop of Edessa (411–435).

Two important Syriac New Testament manuscripts are the Syriac Curetonian (syr$^{c}$) and the Syriac Sinaiticus (syr$^{s}$). Syriac Curetonian (named after its discoverer, William Cureton) is a fifth-century manuscript. Syriac Sinaiticus was discovered by Agnes Smith Lewis and Margaret Dunlop Gibson in the monastery of St. Catherine's in 1892. This manuscript, dated in the fourth century, is the earliest extant document of the Old Syriac translation.

Old Syriac translations began to be made in the early fourth century. The Syriac Sinaiticus represents an early stage in this process, and the Syriac Curetonian probably represents the next stage inasmuch as it is a revision. Both manuscripts are generally regarded as "Western."

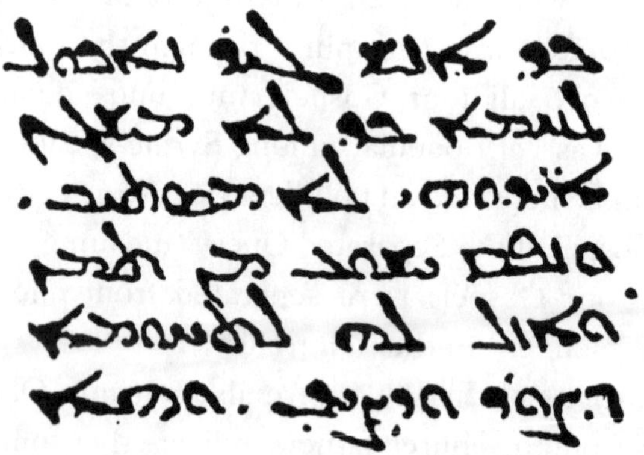

FIGURE 4.2: Syriac Curetonian. Fifth Century. Matthew 15:20.

## THE ARMENIAN VERSION

Christians from Syria carried their faith to their Armenian neighbors in eastern Asia Minor. As early as the third century, Armenia became a Christian kingdom—the first such in history. Sometime during the fifth century an Armenian alphabet was created so that the Bible could be translated into the language of these new believers. The Armenian translation is considered one of the most beautiful and accurate of the ancient versions. An old tradition says that the New Testament was the work of Mesrop (a bishop in Armenia, 390–439), who is credited with inventing both the Armenian and Georgian alphabets. The first translations of the New Testament into Armenian were probably based on Old Syriac versions. Later translations, which have the reputation for being quite accurate, were based on Greek manuscripts of the Byzantine text type.

## THE GEORGIAN VERSION

According to tradition, the Georgian New Testament was also the work of Mesrop, credited with inventing the Armenian and Georgian alphabets. The same tradition credits an Armenian slave woman as being the first missionary to bring the gospel to Georgian-speaking people.

The earliest extant manuscript for the Georgian Scriptures is from the ninth century and is called the Adysh manuscript of 897 (designated $geo^1$; two other manuscripts of the tenth century are designated $geo^2$). The Georgian translation shows traces of Syriac and Armenian influence. There is an entire manuscript copy of the Georgian Bible in two volumes in the Iberian Monastery on Mount Athos.

## THE GOTHIC TRANSLATION OF ULFILAS

Ulfilas grew up in Constantinople, the Roman Empire's eastern capital. Here he received his education and began his life of service to the church. In 341, Eusebius of Nicomedia, bishop of Constantinople, consecrated Ulfilas as bishop. Soon afterward the young bishop proceeded to Dacia (north of the Danube River), and for his remaining years he served as the church's principal missionary to the western Goths in this region. The many converts he made indicate that Ulfilas's efforts to spread the gospel had extensive results. Persecution eventually forced Ulfilas out of Dacia, and his work thereafter originated from a residence in Moesia (south of the Danube), an area within the empire's borders.

Ulfilas's move to Moesia prompted the beginnings of the project for which he is best remembered. This was his translation of the Old and New Testaments into the Goths' vernacular language. Toward this end, Ulfilas first had to reduce Gothic speech to writing, a task involving the invention of an alphabet based on Greek. Ulfilas appears to have translated the whole New Testament. This translation, as reflected in later editions, appears to be quite literal and dependent on the early Byzantine text. He also translated most of the Old Testament, except for 1 and 2 Samuel, and 1 and 2 Kings. It is supposed that he purposely omitted these sections for fear that they would only encourage the aggressive Goths.

Surviving remnants of this translation, as copied in the early Middle Ages, represent the earliest extant examples of Gothic literature. Portions of a beautiful copy of the Gothic Bible have been preserved at the University of Uppsala, Sweden. Early sources of information about Ulfilas exist mainly in works by fifth-century church historians, primarily Philostorgius, Socrates, and Sozomen. Scattered fragments of his Old Testament translation survive, and only about half of the gospels are preserved in the Codex Argenteus (a manuscript of Bohemian origin of the fifth or sixth century), now at Uppsala.

## LATIN VERSIONS

In the early days of the Roman Empire and of the church, Greek was the language of Christians. Even the first leaders of the church in Rome wrote and preached in Greek. As empire and church aged, Latin began to win out, especially in the West. It was natural that the Christians began to translate the Greek New Testament and Septuagint into Latin. The initial Latin version is called the Old Latin Bible. No complete manuscript of it survives. Much of the Old Testament and most of the New, however, can be reconstructed from quotations of the early church fathers. For example, around A.D. 160 Tertullian apparently used a Latin version of the Scriptures. Not long after this, the Old Latin text seems to have been in circulation, evidenced by Cyprian's use of it before his death in 258. Consequently, scholars think an Old Latin Bible was in circulation in Carthage in North Africa as early as 250. From the surviving fragments and quotations there seem to have been two types of Old Latin text, the African and the European.

Around the third century A.D., Latin began to replace Greek as the language of learning in the larger Roman world. A uniform, reliable text was needed for theological and liturgical uses. To fill this need, Pope Damasus I (336–384) commissioned Jerome, an eminent scholar in Latin, Greek, and Hebrew, to undertake the translation.

Jerome completed the Gospels in 383; Acts and the rest of

SERUANTUR ETFACTUMESTEUM
INSABBATOSECUNDOPRIMO
ABIRE PERSEGETES

FIGURE 4.3: Codex Bezae (Latin). Fifth Century. Luke 6:1.

the New Testament evidently followed. The Gospels were a thorough and painstaking retranslation based on the European Old Latin and an Alexandrian Greek text. The rest of the New Testament, however, was a much more limited effort—with the Old Latin remaining dominant unless the Greek text demanded change. No one is sure if the rest of the New Testament was the work of Jerome himself.

Before Damasus died (and Jerome lost his patronage), Jerome completed the Psalms. Then from a monastery in Bethlehem, Jerome continued his translation work—often against strong opposition. Using the *Hexapla* of Origen, Jerome had access to the Septuagint, the Greek translation of the Old Testament. From that he translated into Latin the books of Job, 1 and 2 Chronicles, Proverbs, Ecclesiastes, and the Song of Songs. He also translated the Psalms again. This version of the Psalms came to be known as the *Gallican Psalter,* an important part of Roman Catholic liturgy and breviary. Later, around 389, Jerome stopped using the Greek Old Testament and began translating from the original Hebrew texts; he completed his Latin version of the Old Testament in 405.

Jerome did nearly all of his work by private initiative, so his translation was slow to be accepted by the church. The Old Latin version was extremely familiar and was not easily abandoned. In addition, the Greek church leaders held the Septuagint to be divinely inspired, so some leaders thought that the Vulgate would sever ties between the Latin and the Greek churches. Jerome was stubborn, however, and held out against all his critics. In time the Vulgate was vindicated, and by the middle of the sixth century a complete Bible within a single cover was in use. This contained Jerome's Old Testament, his *Gallican Psalter,* his translations of Tobit and Judith, and his revision of the Gospels. Older Latin versions completed his New Testament. These may also have been revised by Jerome.

Evidence seems to indicate that the compiling of all of Jerome's work into one book may have been done by Cassiodorus (died ca. 580) in his monastery at Scylacium in Italy. The earliest extant manuscript containing Jerome's Bible in its entirety is the Codex Amiatinus, written in the monastery at Jarrow, Northumbria, England, around 715. The old texts of the Vulgate are second only to the Septuagint in importance for Hebrew textual study, for Jerome was working from Hebrew texts that antedate the now-extant work of the Jewish Masoretes.

Only very gradually did the Vulgate supplant the Old Latin Bible. It took a thousand years before the Vulgate was made the official Roman Catholic Bible (by the Council of Trent in 1546). That council also authorized an official, corrected edition, which was first issued by Pope Sixtus V (1585–1590) in 1590 in three volumes. It proved unpopular, however, and Pope Clement VIII (1592–1605) recalled it and issued a new official Vulgate in 1592, which has been the standard edition to recent times.[1]

Our printed Bibles today contain chapter and verse divisions that go back to the Latin versions. Chapter divisions began in the Latin Vulgate and are variously credited to Lanfranc, Archbishop of Canterbury (died 1089); to Stephen Langton, Archbishop of Canterbury (died 1228); or to Hugo de Sancto Caro of the thirteenth century. Verse numbers first appeared in the fourth edition of the Greek New Testament issued at Geneva in 1551 by Robert Estienne (Stephanus) and in the Athias Hebrew Old Testament of 1559–1561.

---

[1] For further reading on the early versions of the New Testament, see Metzger, *Early Versions.*

## EARLY ENGLISH VERSIONS

The gospel was brought to London, England, sometime before the end of the second century. It is possible that sometime shortly thereafter the Greek Scriptures were translated into the local language. But we have no history of this. We know that missionaries from Rome, from the fifth century and thereafter, brought the Latin Vulgate to England. The Christians living in England at that time depended on monks for any kind of instruction from the Bible. The monks read and taught the Latin Bible. After a few centuries, when more monasteries were founded, the need arose for translations of the Bible in English.

### EARLY ENGLISH TRANSLATIONS: CAEDMON'S, BEDE'S, ALFRED THE GREAT'S

The earliest English translation, as far as we know, is one done by a seventh-century monk named Caedmon, who made a metrical version of parts of the Old and New Testaments. Another English churchman, named Bede, is said to have translated the Gospels into English. Tradition has it that he was translating the Gospel of John on his deathbed in 735. Another translator was Alfred the Great (reigned 871–899), who was regarded as a very literate king. He included in his laws parts of the Ten Commandments translated into English, and he also translated the Psalms.

### OTHER EARLY VERSIONS: LINDISFARNE GOSPELS, SHOREHAM'S PSALMS, ROLLE'S PSALMS

All translations of the English Bible prior to Tyndale's version were done from the Latin text. Some Latin versions of the Gospels called interlinear translations, with word-for-word

English translations written between the lines, survive from the tenth century. The most famous translation of this period is called the Lindisfarne Gospels (ca. 950).[1] In the late tenth century, Aelfric (ca. 955–1020), abbot of Eynsham, made idiomatic translations of various parts of the Bible. Two of these translations still exist. Later, in the 1300s, William of Shoreham translated the Psalms into English, and so did Richard Rolle, whose editions of the Psalms included a verse-by-verse commentary. Both of these translations, which were metrical and therefore called Psalters, were popular when John Wycliffe was a young man.

## WYCLIFFE'S VERSION (LATE 1300s)

John Wycliffe (ca. 1329–1384), the most eminent Oxford theologian of his day, and his associates were the first to translate the entire Bible from Latin into English. Wycliffe has been called the "Morning Star of the Reformation" because he boldly questioned papal authority, criticized the sale of indulgences (which were supposed to release a person from punishment in purgatory), denied transubstantiation (the doctrine that the bread and wine are changed into Jesus Christ's body and blood during Communion), and spoke out against church hierarchies. The pope reproved Wycliffe for his heretical teachings and asked that Oxford University dismiss him. But Oxford and many government leaders stood with Wycliffe, so he was able to survive the pope's assaults.

Wycliffe believed that the way to prevail in his struggle with the church's abusive authority was to make the Bible available to the people in their own language. Then they could read for themselves about how each one of them could have a personal

---

1 The Lindisfarne Gospels are also known as the Book of Durham or The Gospels of St. Cuthbert. The original manuscript has been kept at the Bodleian Library in Oxford.

relationship with God through Christ Jesus—apart from any ecclesiastical authority. Wycliffe, with his associates, completed the New Testament around 1380 and the Old Testament in 1382. Wycliffe concentrated his labors on the New Testament, while an associate, Nicholas of Hereford, did a major part of the Old Testament. Wycliffe and his coworkers, unfamiliar with the original Hebrew and Greek, translated the Latin text into English.

After Wycliffe finished the translation work, he organized a group of poor parishioners, known as Lollards, to go throughout England preaching Christian truths and reading the Scriptures in their mother tongue to all who would hear God's word. As a result, the word of God, through Wycliffe's translation, became available to many Englishmen.

He was loved by the people yet hated by the religious leaders. His ecclesiastical enemies did not forget his opposition to their power or his successful efforts in making the Scriptures available to all. Several decades after he died, they condemned him for heresy, dug up his body, burned it, and threw his ashes into the Swift River.

One of Wycliffe's close associates, John Purvey (ca. 1353–1428), continued Wycliffe's work by producing a revision of his translation in 1388. Purvey was an excellent scholar; his work was very well received by his generation and following generations. Within less than a century, Purvey's revision had replaced the original Wycliffe Bible.[1]

## TYNDALE'S VERSION, 1525

Latin was the dominant language of learning in Europe for nearly a thousand years—from 400 to 1400. As learning was en-

[1] There are about 170 extant manuscripts of the Wycliffe Bible; about 25 of these manuscripts come from the original work of 1382. The oldest known manuscript of Purvey's revision is dated 1408.

The xiij. Chapter.

The same daye wentt Jesus mar. iiij. Luc. viij.
out of the housse/and satt by the see syde/and mo=
che people resorted vnto him/so gretly that he wēt
and sat in a shyppe/and all the people stode on the
shore. And he spake many thyngs to them in similitudes/ sa=
yinge: beholde/the sower went forth to sowe/and as he so=
wed/some fell by the wayes syde/& the fowlls cā/and devow=
red it uppe. Some fell apon stony grounde where it had nott
moche erth/and a non it spronge uppe/because it had no de=
pht of erth: and when the son was vppe/hit cauth heet/and
for lake of rotynge wyddred awaye. Some fell amonge thor=
nes/and the thornes arose/and chooked it. Parte fell in
goode grounde/and broght forth good frute: some an hun=
dred fold/some fyfty fold/some thyrty folde. Whosoever hath
eares to heare/let him heare.
¶ And hys disciples cam/and sayde to him: Why speakest
thou to them in parables: he answered and saide vnto them:
Hit is geven vnto you to knowe the secretts of the kyngdo=
me of heven/but to them it is nott geven. For whosomever
hath/to him shall hit be geven: and he shall have aboundan= mat. xxv
nce: But whosoever hath nott: from him shalbe takyn a
waye evē that same that he hath. Therfore speake I to them

FIGURE 4.4: Tyndale's English Version. Matthew 13:1-13.

joyed only by the wealthy nobility and by churchmen of high rank, and as the Roman Catholic hierarchy—headed by the pope—claimed a firm grip on Western Christendom, the Bible was removed from the hands of the laity. At the same time, Latin came to be considered almost a sacred language; so translations of the Bible into the vernacular were viewed with suspicion. Pope Gregory VII (1073–1085) voiced such suspicions when, only two hundred years after Adrian II and John VIII had called for a Slavonic translation, Gregory attempted to stop its circulation. He wrote to King Vratislaus of Bohemia in 1079:

> For it is clear to those who reflect upon it that not without reason has it pleased Almighty God that holy scripture should be a secret in certain places lest, if it were plainly apparent to all men, perchance it would be little esteemed and be subject to disrespect; or it might be falsely understood by those of mediocre learning, and lead to error.[1]

This attitude was about to change, for with the coming of the Renaissance came the resurgence of the study of the classics—and with it the resurgence of the study of Greek, as well as Hebrew. Thus, for the first time in nearly a thousand years, scholars began to read the New Testament in its original language, Greek. By 1500, Greek was being taught at Oxford.

William Tyndale was born in the age of the Renaissance. He graduated in 1515 from Oxford, where he had studied the Scriptures in Greek and in Hebrew. By the time he was thirty, Tyndale had committed his life to translating the Bible from the original languages into English. His heart's desire is exemplified in a statement he made to a clergyman when refuting the view that only the clergy were qualified to read and correctly interpret the Scriptures: "If God spare my life, ere many years, I will cause a boy that driveth the plough to know more of the Scripture than thou dost."[2]

In 1523, Tyndale went to London seeking a place to work on his translation. When the bishop of London would not give him hospitality, he was provided a place by Humphrey Monmouth, a cloth merchant. Then, in 1524, Tyndale left England for Germany because the English church, which was still under the papal authority of Rome, strongly op-

---

[1] Cited by Walter, "Versions of the Bible" in Comfort, *Origin of the Bible*, 291.

[2] Edwards, *God's Outlaw*, 61.

posed putting the Bible into the hands of the laity. Tyndale settled in Hamburg, Germany. Quite possibly, he met Luther in Wittenberg soon thereafter. Even so, Tyndale was well acquainted with Luther's writings and Luther's German translation of the New Testament (published in 1522). Throughout his lifetime, Tyndale was harassed for propagating Luther's ideas. Both Luther and Tyndale used the same Greek text (one compiled by Erasmus in 1516) in making their translations.

Tyndale completed his translation of the New Testament in 1525. Fifteen thousand copies, in six editions, were smuggled into England between the years 1525 and 1530. Church authorities did their best to confiscate copies of Tyndale's translation and burn them, but they couldn't stop the flow of Bibles from Germany into England. Tyndale himself could not return to England because his life was in danger since his translation had been banned. However, he continued to work abroad—correcting, revising, and reissuing his translation until his final revision appeared in 1535. Shortly thereafter, in May of 1535, Tyndale was arrested and carried off to a castle near Brussels. After being in prison for over a year, he was tried and condemned to death. He was strangled and burnt at the stake on October 6, 1536. His final words were so very poignant: "Lord, open the king of England's eyes."[1]

After finishing the New Testament, Tyndale had begun work on a translation of the Hebrew Old Testament, but he did not live long enough to complete his task. He had, however, translated the Pentateuch (the first five books of the Old Testament), Jonah, and some historical books. While Tyndale was in prison, an associate of his named Miles Coverdale (1488–

---

[1] Ibid., 168.

1569) brought to completion an entire Bible in English—based largely on Tyndale's translation of the New Testament and other Old Testament books. In other words, Coverdale finished what Tyndale had begun.

## COVERDALE'S VERSION, 1537

Miles Coverdale was a Cambridge graduate who, like Tyndale, was forced to flee England because he had been strongly influenced by Luther to the extent that he was boldly preaching against Roman Catholic doctrine. While he was abroad, Coverdale met Tyndale and then served as an assistant—especially helping Tyndale translate the Pentateuch. By the time Coverdale produced a complete translation (1537), the king of England, Henry VIII, had broken all ties with the pope and was ready to see the appearance of an English Bible.[1] Perhaps Tyndale's prayer had been answered—with a very ironic twist. The king gave his royal approval to Coverdale's translation, which was based on the work done by Tyndale, whom Henry VIII had earlier condemned.

## THOMAS MATTHEW'S VERSION: THE GREAT BIBLE, 1537

In the same year that Coverdale's Bible was endorsed by the king (1537), another Bible was published in England. This was the work of one called Thomas Matthew, a pseudonym for John Rogers (ca. 1500–1555), a friend of Tyndale. Evidently, Rogers used Tyndale's unpublished translation of the Old Testament historical books, other parts of Tyndale's translation, and still other parts of Coverdale's translation, to form an entire Bible. This Bible also received the king's approval. Matthew's Bible was revised in 1538 and printed for distribution in the churches throughout England. This Bible, called the Great

---

[1] The Coverdale Bible was the first English Bible to be printed in England.

Bible because of its size and costliness, became the first English Bible authorized for public use.

Many editions of the Great Bible were printed in the early 1540s. However, its distribution was limited. Furthermore, King Henry's attitude about the new translation changed. As a result, the English Parliament passed a law in 1543 restricting the use of any English translation. It was a crime for any unlicensed person to read or explain the Scriptures in public. Many copies of Tyndale's New Testament and Coverdale's Bible were burned in London.

Greater repression was to follow. After a short period of leniency (during the reign of Edward VI, 1547–1553), severe persecution came from the hands of Mary Tudor. She was a Roman Catholic who was determined to restore Catholicism to England and repress Protestantism. Many Protestants were executed, including John Rogers, the Bible translator. Coverdale was arrested, then released. He fled to Geneva, a sanctuary for English Protestants.

### THE GENEVA BIBLE, 1550

When Coverdale arrived at Geneva, he discovered that the English exiles in Geneva had chosen William Whittingham (ca. 1524–1579) to make an English translation of the New Testament for them. Whittingham used Theodore Beza's Latin translation and consulted the Greek text. This Bible (published in 1550), dubbed the Geneva Bible, became very popular because it was small and moderately priced. For nearly two hundred years, it was the most popular English Bible—until it was superseded by the popularity of the King James Version in the mid-1700s. The first English Bible to be brought to America was the Geneva Bible; some of the Puritan passengers on the Mayflower (1620) owned copies of this version.

The preface to the Geneva Bible and its many annotations were affected by a strong evangelical influence, as well as by the teachings of John Calvin. Calvin was one of the greatest thinkers of the Reformation, a renowned biblical commentator, and the principal leader in Geneva during those days.

## THE BISHOPS' BIBLE, 1568

While the Geneva Bible was popular among many English men and women, it was not acceptable among many leaders in the Church of England because of its Calvinistic notes. These leaders, recognizing that the Great Bible was inferior to the Geneva Bible in style and scholarship, initiated a revision of the Great Bible. This revised Bible, published in 1568, became known as the Bishops' Bible; it continued in use until it, too, was superseded by the King James Version of 1611.

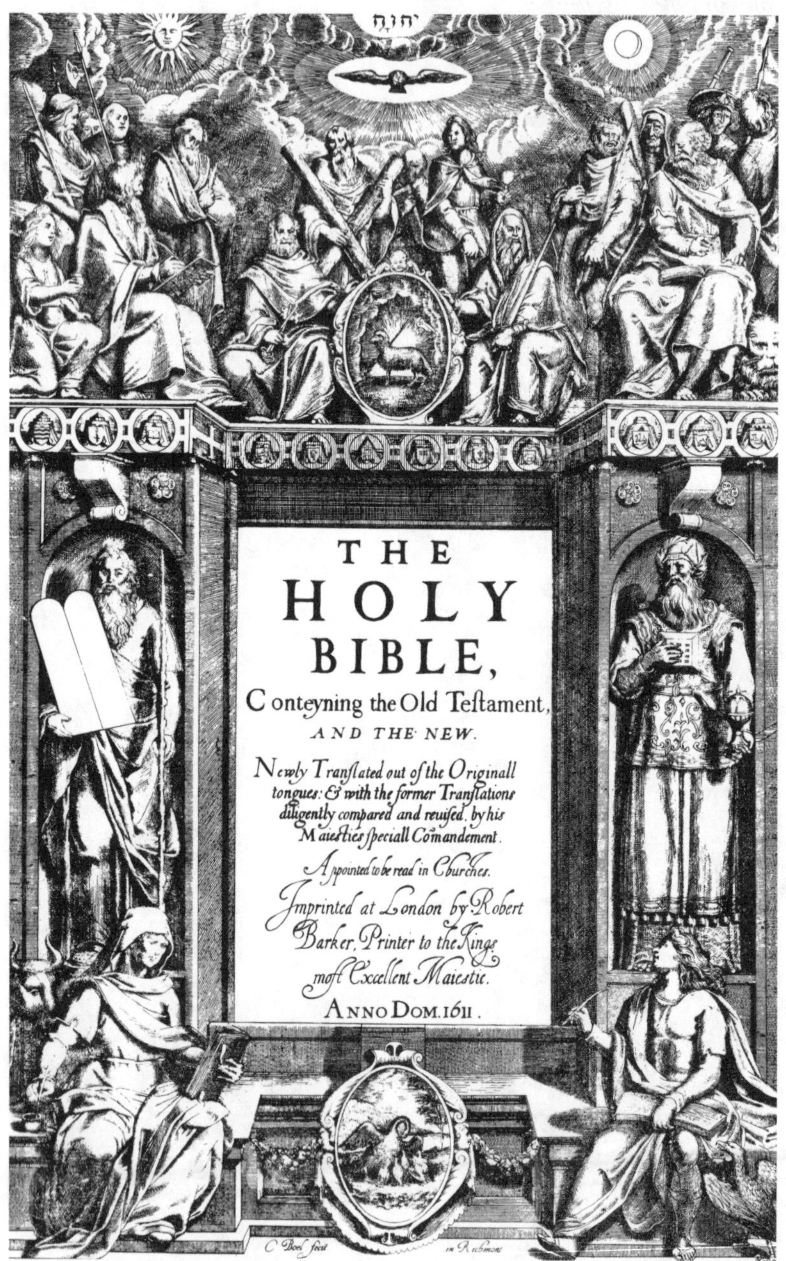

יהוה

THE
HOLY
BIBLE,
Conteyning the Old Teſtament,
AND THE NEW.

Newly Tranſlated out of the Originall tongues: & with the former Tranſlations diligently compared and reuiſed, by his Maieſties ſpeciall Comandement.

Appointed to be read in Churches.

Imprinted at London by Robert Barker, Printer to the Kings moſt Excellent Maieſtie.

ANNO DOM. 1611.

C Boel fecit in Richmont

FIGURE 5.1: The King James Version. A.D. 1611. Title page.

CHAPTER FIVE

# The Authorized Versions: From the King James Version to the New Revised Standard Version

## THE KING JAMES VERSION (KJV), 1611

### HISTORICAL OVERVIEW OF THE KING JAMES VERSION

After James VI of Scotland became the king of England (known as James I), he invited several clergymen from Puritan and Anglican factions to meet together with the hope that differences could be reconciled. The meeting did not achieve this. However, during the meeting one of the Puritan leaders, John Reynolds, president of Corpus Christi College, Oxford, asked the king to authorize a new translation because Reynolds wanted to see one that was more accurate than previous translations.

King James liked this idea because the Bishops' Bible had not been successful, and because he considered the notes in the Geneva Bible to be seditious. The king initiated the work and took an active part in planning the new translation. He suggested that university professors work on the translation to assure the best scholarship, and he strongly urged that they should not have any marginal notes besides those pertaining to literal renderings from the Hebrew and Greek. The absence of interpretive notes would help the translation be accepted by all the churches in England.

More than fifty scholars, trained in Hebrew and Greek, began the work in 1607. The translation went through several committees before it was finalized. The scholars were instructed to follow the Bishops' Bible as the basic version, as long as it adhered to the original text, and to consult the translations of Tyndale, Matthew, and Coverdale, as well as the Great Bible and the Geneva Bible when they appeared to contain more accurate renderings of the original languages. This dependence on other versions is expressed by the translators of the King James Version: "Truly, good Christian reader, we never thought from the beginning that we should need to make a new translation, nor yet to make of a bad one a good one . . . but to make a good one better, or out of many good ones one principal good one."[1]

The King James Version, known in England as the Authorized Version because it was authorized by the king, captured the best of all the preceding English translations and exceeded all of them. It was the culmination of all the previous English Bible translations; it united high scholarship with Christian devotion and piety. Furthermore, it came into being at a time when the English language was vigorous and beautiful—the age of Elizabethan English and Shakespearean English. This version has justifiably been called "the noblest monument of English prose." Indeed, the King James Version has become an enduring monument of English prose because of its gracious style, majestic language, and poetic rhythms. No other book has had such a tremendous influence on English literature, and no other translation has touched the lives of so many English-speaking people for centuries and centuries.

---

[1] Preface to the Authorized King James Version.

## DEFICIENCIES OF THE KING JAMES VERSION

The King James Version became the most popular English translation in the seventeenth and eighteenth centuries. As such, it acquired the stature of becoming the standard English Bible. But the King James Version had deficiencies that did not go unnoticed by scholars in subsequent years. First, knowledge of Hebrew was inadequate in the early seventeenth century. The Hebrew text they used (i.e., the Masoretic Text) was adequate, but their understanding of the Hebrew vocabulary was insufficient. It would take many more years of linguistic studies to enrich and sharpen understanding of the Hebrew vocabulary. Second, the Greek text underlying the New Testament of the King James Version is an inferior text. The King James translators basically used a Greek text known as the "received text" (the *Textus Receptus*—commonly abbreviated as TR), which came from the work of Erasmus, who compiled the first Greek text to be produced on a printing press. When Erasmus compiled this text, he used five or six very late manuscripts dating from the tenth to the thirteenth centuries. These manuscripts were far inferior to earlier manuscripts.

Allow me to go back into history a little bit, and to repeat a few things explained in previous chapters. This is important for understanding the vast difference between the Greek text used for the King James Version and the text used by modern versions.

The Textus Receptus (TR) has its roots in the fourth century. According to Jerome, Lucian of Antioch produced an edited version of the Greek New Testament. Lucian's text was a definite **recension** (i.e., a purposely created edition).[1] The Lucianic text is characterized by smoothness of language, which is

---

[1] Jerome, *Patrologia Latina* 29, col. 527.

achieved by the removal of obscurities and awkward grammatical constructions, by harmonization, and by the conflation of variant readings.

Lucian's text was produced prior to the Diocletian persecution (ca. 303), during which time many copies of the New Testament were confiscated and destroyed. Not long after this period of devastation, Constantine came to power and then recognized Christianity as the state religion. There was, of course, a great need for copies of the New Testament to be made and distributed to churches throughout the Mediterranean world. It was at this time that Lucian's text began to be propagated by bishops going out from the school at Antioch to churches throughout the east, taking the text with them. Lucian's text soon became the standard text of the Eastern church, and formed the basis for the Byzantine text.

For century after century—from the sixth to the fourteenth—the great majority of New Testament manuscripts were produced in Byzantium, all bearing the same kind of text. When the first Greek New Testament was printed (ca. 1516), it was based on a Greek text that Erasmus had compiled, using a few late Byzantine manuscripts.

Both Luther and Tyndale used the same Greek text in making their translations. Luther completed his work in the 1520s. Tyndale completed his translation of the New Testament in 1525. Thus, Erasmus's text served two very important translations—the first English and first German versions to be based on the Greek.

Erasmus's text then went though a few more revisions by Robert Stephanaus and then Theodore Beza. Beza's text was then published by the Elzevir brothers in 1624, with a second edition in 1633. In this edition they announced that their edition contained "the text which is now received by all, in which we give nothing changed or corrupted." As such, the name "received text" (Latin, *textus receptus*) became a descriptor of this form of the Greek New Testament text.

The New Testament of the King James Version was based on the Textus Receptus. In time, the KJV superseded all English translations, including William Tyndale's version, even though the KJV largely reproduces Tyndale's masterpiece.

But after the King James Version was published, earlier manuscripts were discovered, which began to show deficiencies with the TR. Around 1630, Codex Alexandrinus (dated ca. 400) was brought to England. Two hundred years later, a German scholar named Constantin von Tischendorf discovered Codex Sinaiticus in St. Catherine's Monastery located near Mount Sinai. Codex Sinaiticus, dated 350, is one of the two oldest vellum manuscripts of the Greek New Testament. The earliest vellum manuscript, Codex Vaticanus, had been in the Vatican's library since at least 1481, but it was not made available to scholars until the middle of the nineteenth century. Codex Vaticanus, dated slightly earlier (ca. 325) than Codex Sinaiticus, has both the Old and New Testaments in Greek.

As the various manuscripts were discovered and made public, scholars labored to compile a Greek text that would more closely represent the original text than did the TR. Around 1700 John Mill produced an improved TR, and in the 1730s Johannes Albert Bengel published a text of the TR with appended notes displaying superior readings. In the 1800s, scholars began to abandon the TR. Karl Lachman, a classical philologist, produced a fresh text in 1831 that represented the fourth-century manuscripts. Samuel Tregelles published a Greek text (1852–1872), in which he sought "to exhibit the text of the New Testament in the very words in which it has been transmitted on the evidence of ancient authority."[1] During this same era, Constantin von Tischendorf discovered Codex Sinaiticus, deciphered the palimpsest Codex Ephraemi Rescriptus, collated countless manuscripts, and produced several editions of the Greek New Testament (the eighth edition is the best).

All these men worked to produce a text that was much closer to the original than what was printed in the TR. Of course, some scholars strongly resisted this movement to return to earlier manuscripts because they considered it an attack on a text that had become "the standard" in the Christian church. Dean Burgon criticized Codex Vaticanus and Codex Sinaiticus and those who upheld their value.[2] Scrivener (a scholar who published the transcription of twenty manuscripts, produced a list of all extant manuscripts, and created a system for classifying manuscripts) was an enthusiastic supporter of the Textus Receptus. He opposed the text produced by Westcott and Hort but did not gain a following among biblical scholars.[3]

The unfavorable opinion toward the TR was solidified by the work of two British scholars, Brooke Westcott and Fenton Hort, who produced a volume entitled *The New Testament in the Original Greek* (1881). Along with this publication, they made known their theory that Codex Vaticanus and Codex Sinaiticus, along with a few other early manuscripts, represent a text that most closely replicates the original writings. They called this text the **Neutral Text**. (The Neutral Text described certain manuscripts that had the least amount of textual corruption.) In the twentieth century, many second-

---

[1] Prolegomena to Samuel Tregelles' *Greek New Testament.*

[2] Burgon, *Revision Revised.*

[3] Scrivener, *Plain Introduction.*

and third-century papyrus manuscripts of the New Testament have been discovered. Several of these (such as $\mathfrak{P}^{75}$) have a text that is very similar to Codex Vaticanus, and others (such as $\mathfrak{P}^{4}$ + $\mathfrak{P}^{64}$ + $\mathfrak{P}^{67}$) have a text that is quite similar to Codex Sinaiticus.

One of the most noteworthy papyrus manuscripts is $\mathfrak{P}^{75}$, dated ca. 175-200. It is universally recognized as a very accurate manuscript, and it bears extremely close resemblance to Codex Vaticanus. Prior to the discovery of $\mathfrak{P}^{75}$, certain scholars thought Codex Vaticanus was the work of a fourth-century recension; others (chiefly Hort) thought it must trace back to a very early and accurate copy. Hort said that Codex Vaticanus preserves "not only a very ancient text, but a very pure line of a very ancient text."[1] $\mathfrak{P}^{75}$ proves that Hort was right—because of $\mathfrak{P}^{75}$, we are certain that a pure line of textual transmission was preserved from the middle of the second century to the fourth century. This knowledge furthers the cause against the reliability of the TR.

## TWO DIFFERENT TEXTS

The New Testament of the King James Version is slightly bigger than most modern versions of the Bible. I am not speaking of the trim size or a larger black leather cover. I am speaking of the content. The New Testament of the King James Version has fifty more verses than do most modern versions. This is because the King James Version is based on an edition of the Greek New Testament known as the Textus Receptus, which has about fifty more verses than do other modern critical editions of the Greek New Testament, such as the text of Westcott and Hort, or the Nestle-Aland text.

The way it stands today is that there are two distinctly

---

1 Westcott and Hort, *Introduction*, 250-251.

different texts of the Greek New Testament—that printed in the Textus Receptus (followed by the KJV and NKJV) and that printed in modern versions such as Westcott and Hort's or the Nestle-Aland. The text of the TR has about one thousand more words than that of Westcott and Hort, and about fifty more verses. (These extra verses are discussed in chapter 8.) Several of these verses have become so much a part of the biblical tradition and church liturgy that it has been excruciatingly painful for modern translators to wrench them from the text and place them in a marginal note, even when scholars have known that they were not originally in the text. The pain comes from knowing that most people expect to see these words in their Bible.

Taking the Nestle-Aland text as a starting point, the extra verses in the KJV and NKJV are as follows:

Matthew 5:44b; 6:13b; 16:2b-3; 17:21; 18:11; 20:16b; 20:22-23; 23:14; 27:35b
Mark 7:16; 9:44, 46; 11:26; 15:28; 16:8-20
Luke 4:4b; 9:54c-56; 11:2; 17:36; 22:43-44; 23:17, 34
John 5:3b-4; 7:53–8:11
Acts 8:37; 15:34; 24:6b-8a; 28:16b, 29
Romans 16:24
1 John 5:6b-8a

## THE MAJORITY TEXT

Since the time of Westcott and Hort, very few scholars have upheld the textual purity of the Textus Receptus. Those who have done so in recent years call it by a different name—the **Majority Text**—insofar as the majority of manuscripts, being Byzantine, usually support the TR, which was based on a few Byzantine manuscripts. The Majority Text is nearly the same as the Textus Receptus in that the TR was composed from manuscripts belonging to the Majority Text. But the two are not completely synonymous because the TR does not consistently display a Majority Text type throughout. The Majority Text is synonymous with the Byzantine Text because it was in Byzantium (and surrounding areas) that the Lucian text was copied again and again until it was standardized in thousands of manuscripts.

Modern advocates of the superiority of the Majority Text over other text types include Zane Hodges and Arthur Farstad, who produced *The Greek New Testament According to the Majority Text.* At the core, those who advocate the Majority Text do so more for theological reasons than for textual ones. They reason that God would not have allowed a corrupt or inferior text to be found in the majority of manuscripts, while permitting a superior text to be hidden away in a few early manuscripts somewhere in the sands of Egypt. Further, they reason that the church's adoption of the Majority Text was a vindication of its correctness, while the obscurity of the Egyptian text was a sign of its rejection.[1] But most textual scholars today recognize this as an erroneous view because the early church fathers (second to third century) did not quote a text anything like the TR, and because most of the early manuscripts are vastly different from the TR in significant ways[2] (which suggests that the originals were different from the TR as well).

Most contemporary scholars contend that a minority of manuscripts—primarily the earliest ones—preserve the earliest, most authentic wording of the text. Those who defend the TR and KJV would have to prove that earlier manuscripts or the originals themselves must have had these words and that the earlier manuscripts are textually corrupt. However, not

---

1 For an excellent discussion on this whole issue, see Wallace, "Majority Text Theory."

2 See Kurt Aland's defense in "The Text of the Church?"

one scholar has shown that there was any kind of major recension of the New Testament text in the late first or early second century. Certainly, there were some minor changes here and there, but most of the major editorial changes were introduced later in the course of textual transmission.

For those who refuse to accept that God would have allowed the text to have been tampered with, I offer another theological perspective. God is a God of recovery. He is a God who allows things—his people, his nation, and even his word—to be lost and then found. This is the principle of recovery. The entire theology of redemption is one of recovering what had been lost. Some of Jesus' parables refer to this. Luke 15 has three such parables—about the lost sheep, the lost coin, and the lost son. All are recovered, and the recovery brings great joy.

Believe it or not, the Bible had been lost for nearly sixty years—during the reigns of Manasseh and Amon (697–642 B.C.). At that time, the Bible consisted of the first five books of the Old Testament, called the Pentateuch or the law of Moses. During the reign of the evil kings Manasseh and Amon, the Temple was destitute and the Scriptures totally neglected—to the extent they must have been hidden in a **genizah** somewhere. Then Josiah became king, and the high priest, Hilkiah, recovered the scroll of Moses' laws in the Temple. Shaphan read the scroll to Josiah, who then realized why God's people had been suffering so greatly—they had grossly violated the laws of their God. This recovery of God's word brought significant revival to Judea just prior to the Babylonian captivity (see 2 Kings 22:8–23:30). Thereafter, the Old Testament Scriptures were treasured and were even taken into Babylon when the Jews were made captives (see Dan. 9:1-2).

Thus, God's providential care of the Scriptures can be seen in his protecting them from total ruin and then guiding Hilkiah to recover what was lost. In similar fashion, the New Testament text went through a period of tremendous textual corruption—which was a great loss. However, under God's providence, many early manuscripts have been recovered, thereby enabling scholars to reconstruct the original wording of the Greek New Testament. Among these manuscripts, it is apparent that some were produced with great acumen. Many scribes copied the text faithfully and reverently—they recognized that they were copying a sacred text.

The formalization of canonization did not *ascribe* this sacredness to the text. Canonization came about as the result of common, historical *recognition* of the sacredness of various New Testament books. Some New Testament books, such as the four Gospels, Acts, and Paul's epistles, were from the onset considered to be inspired literature. As such, most scribes copied them with fidelity. This is evident in early manuscripts of the second and third centuries (mentioned before), as well as in two fourth-century manuscripts, Codex Vaticanus (B) and Codex Sinaiticus (א). Other manuscripts in the following centuries also preserve a very pure text, including Codex Borgianus (T) of the fifth century, Codex Dublinensis (Z) of the sixth century, $\mathfrak{P}^{74}$ of the seventh century, Codex Regius (L) of the eighth century, and 1739 of the tenth century. Ironically, these manuscripts, which are not the majority, are the manuscripts that appear to best preserve the original wording of the Greek New Testament. God has preserved his written word, and finding the earlier manuscripts has represented part of the recovery of what God has preserved.

## THEOLOGICAL DIFFERENCES

The Nestle-Aland edition is a far better representation of the original text than is the TR or the Majority Text. This does not mean, however, that those who read the TR and/or KJV are receiving a "different gospel" or a different theology than what is found in the Nestle-Aland text. What it does mean is that they are reading a text that—for the most part—was not read in the first three centuries of the church. They are reading a text that is heavily edited with interpolations and harmonizations, and they are reading a text that is somewhat misrepresentative in Christology (see below).

Most of the significant theological differences between the TR and modern critical editions of the Greek text pertain to issues of Christology, especially as reflected in titles or descriptions of Christ. Several significant examples demonstrate this, as the following verses show. (The first reading is that found in the TR/KJV/NKJV; the second, in the Nestle-Aland text.)

### Matthew 24:36

TR: of that day and hour, no one knows, not even the angels of heaven, but my Father only

NA: of that day and hour, no one knows, not even the angels of heaven nor the Son, but my Father only

The TR and KJV don't include "the Son" to avoid indicating that Jesus didn't know the timing of the last days.

### Luke 9:35

TR: This is my beloved Son

NA: This is my Son, the Chosen One

Harmonization to Mark 9:7 robs KJV readers of the double title, "My Son, the Chosen One."

### John 1:18

TR: the only begotten Son

NA: only begotten, God

Harmonization to the more usual expression "the only begotten Son" eliminates a wonderful title of Christ: "only begotten, God."

### John 6:69

TR: You are the Christ, the Son of the living God
NA: You are the Holy One of God

The TR shows harmonization to Matthew 16:16; hence, KJV readers miss a unique expression coming from the lips of Peter: "You are the Holy One of God."

### Acts 3:20

TR: Jesus Christ, who was preached to you before
NA: Christ Jesus, who was ordained for you before

The better textual evidence speaks of God's eternal purpose to send Christ for the salvation of the world.

### Acts 16:7

TR: the Spirit did not permit them
NA: the Spirit of Jesus did not permit them

The TR and KJV miss out on a unique title that unites Jesus and the Spirit: "the Spirit of Jesus."

### Colossians 2:2

TR: the mystery of God, both of the Father and of Christ
NA: the mystery of God, Christ

The TR and KJV obscure the fact that Christ is God's mystery revealed.

### 1 Timothy 3:16

TR: Great is the mystery of godliness: God was manifest in the flesh

NA: Great is the mystery of godliness, who [i.e., Christ] was manifest in the flesh

The TR and KJV obscure the truth that the incarnate Christ is the mystery of godliness.

### 1 Peter 3:15

TR: Sanctify the Lord God in your hearts
NA: Sanctify Christ in your hearts

The TR and KJV obscure the indwelling of Christ—that is, it is Christ who lives in each believer.

### Jude 4

TR: deny the only Lord God and our Lord Jesus Christ
NA: deny our only Master and Lord, Jesus Christ

The TR and KJV miss the point that Jesus Christ is our "only Master and Lord."

Readers of the TR and KJV miss out on some significant statements about Christ: He is "the Chosen One"; "the only begotten, God"; "the Holy One of God"; the One "preordained for us"; "the mystery of God"; "the mystery of godliness"; the One whom we sanctify in our hearts; and "our only Master and Lord." There are far more examples than these, but these are enough to show that the difference between the two texts is theologically significant. I must emphasize, however, this does not mean that the TR and KJV are theologically "wrong." This text presents the same basic truth about the Trinity as do modern versions, which are based on better Greek texts. What is problematic about the TR and KJV is that they obscure some significant titles of Christ.

## AN APPEAL FOR UNITY

The church has had enough issues over the past two millennia to divide it, let alone the issue of which Bible translation to use. Unfortunately, many devotees to the KJV have been declaring war on modern versions for the past several decades, thereby causing divisions in the church. This is senseless. No Christian should be a follower of a Bible translation; we are followers of Christ. No single translation can claim to be *the* God-inspired text. Instead, the original texts are sacred and God-inspired. Translations of the original texts will always be short of perfection—and in need of revision. This is why the KJV has been revised so much—beginning with the English Revised Version (ERV), and on to the American Standard Version (ASV), the Revised Standard Version (RSV), the New American Standard Bible (NASB), and the New Revised Standard Version (NRSV). All these versions trace their origin to the KJV, but all present significant revisions. These translators were following the pattern set by the KJV translators themselves, who were simply trying to improve upon the versions of their time.

Strong adherence to "the KJV only" is based on traditional sentimentality. To many people, the KJV sounds like the Bible because it is different than our modern English. It is old and therefore seems to be authoritative. It is the Bible they heard in church, read on the porch, and memorized time and again. For these people, the KJV is part of their tradition and constitutes their religious culture. Any other Bible just doesn't sound right. I think it is pointless to try to convince them to use another version. But I would appeal to them to understand why so many other people use modern versions. The primary reason is that people in the twenty-first century just don't understand the KJV. Its language is five hundred years old. Is it any wonder, then, that most Bible translators today, working all over the world, do not use the KJV in their translation work? And why not? Because they are at war against the KJV? No, most Bible translators greatly respect the KJV for what it is and what it was. But the KJV can't be used in modern translation work for the simple reason that its language and its text are out of date.

## REVISIONS OF THE KING JAMES VERSION

The King James Version is an all-time publishing phenomenon. No book has ever sold as many copies or has been read by as many English-speaking people. Nearly five hundred years after its publication, it is still one of the most popular Bible translations. Its popularity, however, does not mean that it hasn't needed revision.

In the 1800s, scholars recognized that its language was dated and its textual basis—especially for the New Testament—was marred. The need for revising the KJV is aptly expressed as follows:

> The King James Version has with good reason been termed "the noblest monument of English prose." Its revisers in 1881 expressed admiration for "its simplicity, its dignity, its power, its happy turns of expression . . . the music of its cadences, and the felicities of its rhythm." It entered, as no other book has, into the making of the personal character and the public institutions of the English-speaking peoples. We owe to it an incalculable debt.
>
> Yet the King James Version has grave defects. By the middle of the nineteenth century, the development of

> biblical studies and the discovery of many manuscripts more ancient than those upon which the King James Version was based, made it manifest that these defects are so many and so serious as to call for revision of the English translation.[1]

Thus began a series of revisions—beginning with the English Revised Version of 1885 and continuing with the American Standard Version of 1901, the Revised Standard Version of 1952, the New American Standard Version of 1971, and the New Revised Standard Version of 1990.

### THE ENGLISH REVISED VERSION (ERV), 1885 AND THE AMERICAN STANDARD VERSION (ASV), 1901

By the latter part of the nineteenth century, the Christian community had been given three very good Greek New Testament texts: Tregelles's text, Tischendorf's text, and Westcott and Hort's text. These texts were very different from the Textus Receptus. And, as was mentioned earlier, the scholarly community had accumulated more knowledge about the meaning of various Hebrew words and Greek words. Therefore, there was a great need for a new English translation based upon a better text—and with more accurate renderings of the original languages.

A few individuals attempted to meet this need. In 1871, John Nelson Darby, leader of the Plymouth Brethren movement, produced a translation called the *New Translation,* which was largely based on Codex Vaticanus and Codex Sinaiticus. In 1872, J. B. Rotherham published a translation of Tregelles's text, in which he attempted to reflect the emphasis inherent in the Greek text. This translation is still being published under

[1] From the Preface to the *Holy Bible,* Revised Standard Version.

the title *The Emphasized Bible.* And in 1875, Samuel Davidson produced a New Testament translation of Tischendorf's text.

The first major *corporate* effort was initiated in 1870 by the Convocation of Canterbury, which decided to sponsor a major revision of the King James Version. Sixty-five British scholars, working in various committees, made significant changes in the King James Version. The Old Testament scholars corrected mistranslations of Hebrew words and reformatted poetic passages into poetic form. The New Testament scholars made thousands of changes based upon better textual evidence. Their goal was to make the New Testament revision reflect not the Textus Receptus but the texts of Tregelles, Tischendorf, and Westcott and Hort. When the complete English Revised Version (ERV) appeared in 1885, it was received with great enthusiasm. Over 3 million copies sold in the first year of its publication. Unfortunately, its popularity was not long lasting because most people continued to prefer the King James Version over all other translations.

Several American scholars had been invited to join the revision work, with the understanding that any of their suggestions not accepted by the British scholars would appear in an appendix. Furthermore, the American scholars had to agree not to publish their own American revision until after fourteen years.

When, in 1901, the fourteen years had passed, the American Standard Version (ASV) was published by several surviving members of the original American committee of the ERV. This translation, generally regarded as superior to the English Revised Version, is an accurate, literal rendering of very trustworthy texts both in the Old Testament and the New.

From a textual perspective, the ASV made great advances

beyond the KJV. The text of the ASV New Testament reflects the evidence of the earlier, superior manuscripts. Several examples illustrate this: the appended conclusion to the Lord's Prayer ("For thine is the kingdom, and the power, and the glory, for ever. Amen."), not found in Codex Sinaiticus or Codex Vaticanus, was relegated to the margin of Matthew 6:13. Many other verses, not found in the earliest witnesses, were omitted from the ASV text and then usually noted in the margin. They are as follows: Matthew 17:21; 18:1; 23:14; 27:35b; Mark 7:16; 9:44, 46; 11:26; 15:28; Luke 9:54c-56; 17:36; 23:17; John 5:3b-4; Acts 8:37; 15:34; 24:6b-8a; 28:16b, 29; Romans 16:24; 1 John 5:6b-8a.

To exclude these verses from the text was a bold and correct move. It engendered the praise of Bible scholars who knew that these passages did not have good textual support, but it also provoked the wrath of critics who exclaimed that the ASV translators had taken verses out of the Bible! The curse was called down upon them: "If anyone takes away from the words of the book of this prophecy, God shall take away his part from the tree of life" (Rev. 22:19, NASB). But the ASV translators had not taken anything away from the text; to the contrary, they were merely attempting to faithfully render the best Greek text. If anyone had a cause for casting blame, the ASV translators could cry out against the KJV translators, "If anyone adds to these things, God will add to him the plagues that are written in this book" (Rev. 22:18, NKJV). But the problem with the added verses in the KJV did not originate with the translators, but with the Greek text they used. Hence, no translators are to blame for adding anything or taking anything away from the Bible. The fault goes back to some scribes and/or previous editors of the Greek manuscripts.

The point is this: the ASV translators were simply fixing the ills of the KJV. They could have done more fixing, but they showed some restraint on such verses as Luke 22:43-44; 23:34; John 7:53–8:11, which they included in the text, with notes indicating their omission from many early witnesses.

Two significant changes were implemented in the ASV Old Testament: (1) the Old Testament poetic books were set in poetic format, and (2) the personal name of God (*Yahweh*) was translated as "Jehovah" instead of the traditional LORD. For the second change, the ASV revisers explained their case as follows:

> The American Revisers, after a careful consideration, were brought to the unanimous conviction that a Jewish superstition, which regarded the Divine Name as too sacred to be uttered, ought no longer dominate in the English or any other version of the Old Testament. . . . This Memorial Name, explained in Exodus 3:14-15, and emphasized as such over and over in the original text of the Old Testament, designates God as the personal God. . . . This personal name, with its wealth of sacred associations, is now restored to the place in the sacred text to which it has an unquestionable claim.[1]

Unfortunately, "Jehovah" was not as good a choice as the more phonologically accurate "Yahweh." Nonetheless, the change was adventuresome. But the public did not receive it well, and subsequent authorized revisions went back to LORD.

Looking on the good side, the change to poetic format in the poetic books paved the way for future revisions and translations to cast even more of the Old Testament text into poetic format—especially in the poetical sections of the Prophets.

---

[1] From the Preface to the *Holy Bible*, American Standard Version.

To this day, the ERV and ASV are excellent study Bibles. They are full of helpful textual notes and lexical notes, which demonstrate the best of nineteenth-century biblical scholarship. However, both of these revisions have their shortcomings.

The first problem has to do with the restraints placed on the revisers before they began their task. Kubo and Specht explain:

> The committees were instructed to make as few changes as possible in the text of the KJV, consistent with faithfulness to the original. A two-thirds vote was required before a change could be made. And the wording of such changes was to be limited as far as possible to the language of the KJV and earlier versions. This meant that the language was not modernized.[1]

The second problem with the ERV and the ASV was that the translators tried to maintain lexical consistency in their work—in the sense that they rendered a given Hebrew word or Greek word by the same English word regardless of the context. As any translator knows, this produces some very unnatural renderings. The revisers also attempted to translate definite articles (such as "the") and verb tenses precisely; this, also, strains idiomatic English. Furthermore, the translators frequently followed the same word order as in the Hebrew or Greek. The result of these kinds of mechanical efforts is that the translation is quite mechanical. In short, the ERV and ASV are not good Bibles for extended reading.

## THE REVISED STANDARD VERSION (RSV), 1952

The English Revised Version and the American Standard Version had gained a reputation of being accurate study texts but

---

[1] Kubo and Specht, *So Many Versions?*, 41.

very "wooden" in their construction. These versions were good for scholars but not for general Bible readers. Consequently, there was need for revision.

The organization that held the copyright to the American Standard Version, called the International Council of Religious Education, authorized a new revision in 1937. The principles of the revision were specified by the translators:

> The Revised Standard Version is not a new translation in the language of today. It is not a paraphrase which aims at striking idioms. It is a revision which seeks to preserve all that is best in the English Bible as it has been known and used throughout the years.[1]

The New Testament was published in 1946, and the entire Bible with the Old Testament, in 1952.

### The Texts Behind the RSV

The demand for revision was strengthened by the fact that several important biblical manuscripts had been discovered in the 1930s and 1940s—namely, the Dead Sea Scrolls for the Old Testament and the Chester Beatty Papyri for the New Testament. It was felt that the fresh evidence displayed in these documents should be reflected in a revision.

The Old Testament translators generally followed the Masoretic Text. At the same time, they introduced a few different readings based on the famous Dead Sea Scroll of Isaiah (1QIsa[a], known as "the Isaiah Scroll"). The New Testament translators generally followed the seventeenth edition of the Nestle text (1941), but were far more eclectic in their selection of other readings. One of the New Testament translators, F. C. Grant, explained:

---

[1] From the Preface to the *Holy Bible*, Revised Standard Version.

> With the best will in the world, the New Testament translator or reviser of today is forced to adopt the eclectic principle: each variant reading must be studied on its merits, and cannot be adopted or rejected by some rule of thumb, or by adherence to such a theory as that of the "Neutral Text." It is the eclectic principle that has guided us in the present Revision. The Greek text of this Revision is not that of Westcott-Hort, or Nestle, or Souter; though the readings we have adopted will as a rule, be found either in the text or margin of the new (17th) edition of Nestle (Stuttgart, 1941).[1]

One of the primary motivations for adopting an eclectic method for the New Testament revision was the fact that several early New Testament papyri had just been discovered and therefore were consulted independently of the Nestle text. These are the Chester Beatty Papyri (discovered in the 1930s), designated as $\mathfrak{P}^{45}$, $\mathfrak{P}^{46}$, and $\mathfrak{P}^{47}$. Concerning these manuscripts, the revisers wrote:

> We now possess many more ancient MSS of the New Testament, and are far better equipped to seek to recover the original wording of the Greek text. . . . The revisers in the 1870s had most of the evidence that we now have for the Greek text, though the most ancient of all extant manuscripts of the Greek New Testament were not discovered until 1931.[2]

The revisers relied upon the evidence of the Chester Beatty Papyri in making several significant changes to the ASV.[3]

---

[1] Grant, *Introduction to the Revised Standard Version*, 41.

[2] From the Preface to the *Holy Bible*, Revised Standard Version.

[3] A detailed analysis of the results are recorded in Comfort, *Early Manuscripts and Modern Translations of the New Testament*, (second edition, pp. 189–193).

### Reactions to the Publication of the RSV

This revision was well received by many Protestant churches and soon became their "standard" text. The Revised Standard Version was later published with the Apocrypha of the Old Testament (1957), in a Catholic Edition (1965), and in what is called the *Common Bible,* which includes the Old Testament, the New Testament, the Apocrypha, and the **deuterocanonical books**, with international endorsements by Protestants, Greek Orthodox, and Roman Catholics.

Evangelical and fundamental Christians, however, did not receive the Revised Standard Version very well—primarily because of one verse, Isaiah 7:14, which reads, "Therefore the Lord himself will give you a sign. Behold, a young woman shall conceive and bear a son, and shall call his name Immanu-el" (RSV). Evangelicals and fundamentalists contend that the text should read "virgin," not "young woman," because Matthew 1:22-23 expressly states that this was fulfilled in Jesus' birth from a virgin (Greek, *parthenon*).

The term in the original Hebrew is ambiguous. The Hebrew *'almah* refers generally to a young girl who has passed puberty and thus is of marriageable age; this could be a virgin or just a young woman (the English term "maiden" is somewhat parallel in meaning). Another Hebrew word (*bethulah*) specifies a woman who is a virgin. The Septuagint translators, nevertheless, translated *'almah* as *parthenos,* which denotes a virgin. Matthew concurs with the Septuagint.

Those who argue for the rendering "young woman" in Isaiah 7:14 say that the woman was Isaiah's wife and the son was Maher-shalal-hashbaz. The definite article with *'almah* seems to indicate that "the woman" was known to Isaiah and Ahaz. Furthermore, Isaiah 7:15-16 seems to indicate that the prophecy was to be fulfilled in Isaiah's time. The difficulty here is that Isaiah's wife already had a son and so she could not be called *'almah.*

Others argue that the prophecy is purely messianic. This is the traditional evangelical position, based on the name of the child Immanuel, "God with us," and the references in Isaiah 9:6-7 and 11:1-5, which point to a divine person. Those who hold this view insist that the rendering in Isaiah should be "virgin."

A mediating position is that Isaiah 7:14 has double fulfillment: in Isaiah's day and in Mary's day. This view takes into account the historical fulfillment intended in verses 15-16, while seeing the future as being fulfilled through the virgin birth of Jesus, as indicated in Matthew 1:22-23.

Nowadays, many evangelicals (and perhaps some fundamentalists) will accept this mediating position. But it was not so when the RSV was first published. On account of Isaiah 7:14, the Revised Standard Version was banned by many evangelical and fundamental Christians. It was even burned! Yes, there were many RSV Bible burnings.

Some fundamentalists accused the RSV translators of removing "the blood of Jesus" from the text. They pointed to Colossians 1:13-14, which reads in the KJV as "his dear Son: In whom we have redemption through his blood, *even* the forgiveness of sins," in contrast to the RSV which reads, "his beloved Son, in whom we have redemption, the forgiveness of sins." Yes, the RSV does not have the words "through his blood," but that is because the phrase is lacking in *all* the ancient manuscripts. The KJV, following the TR, adds the phrase based on a few late manuscripts, whose scribes borrowed it from Ephesians 1:7, a parallel text. In all other places, where there should be a reference to Jesus' blood shed for redemption, the word "blood" appears in the RSV.

There were other passages in the RSV that troubled Bible readers. The story of the woman caught in adultery (John 7:53–8:11) was not included in the text but was put in the margin because none of the early manuscripts contain this story. Acting in good conscience to the textual evidence, which shows that John had not written this passage, the translators placed the story in the margin with a note saying this portion is not found in the most ancient manuscripts. When the RSV was first published, the outcry of protest was so great that in the second printing, the story was inserted back into the text, with a marginal note saying it is not included in the most ancient manuscripts.

The ending to Mark (16:9-20) was not included in the text because it is not found in the two earliest manuscripts, Codex Vaticanus and Codex Sinaiticus. Instead, the RSV translators concluded Mark at 16:8, and then placed the traditional longer ending to Mark (16:9-20) in a footnote, followed by the shorter ending that is found in a few manuscripts ("But they reported briefly to Peter and those with him all that they had been told. And after this, Jesus sent out by means of them, from east to west, the sacred and imperishable proclamation of eternal salvation."). This treatment of the text, though accurately reflecting the ancient manuscripts, was considered too liberal by most readers. Hence, in subsequent versions the translators included the traditional, longer ending as part of the conclusion to Mark.

But no matter what the RSV translators did to remove these "stumbling blocks" for the sake of the reading public, it had left a bad mark in the minds of conservative Christians, who happen to be the majority of Bible readers. The unfortunate consequence was that the RSV was disregarded by many Christians.

## THE *NEW AMERICAN STANDARD BIBLE* (NASB), 1971

Realizing that the RSV was not read by conservative Christians, a group of evangelical scholars decided to make their own revision of the American Standard Version, which would have a much better chance of being accepted by evangelicals and fundamentalists alike. This group worked under the auspices of the Lockman Foundation, a nonprofit Christian corporation committed to evangelism.

The Lockman Foundation promoted this revision of the American Standard Version because "the producers of this translation were imbued with the conviction that interest in the American Standard Version 1901 should be renewed and increased."[1] Indeed, the American Standard Version was a monumental work of scholarship and a very accurate translation. However, its popularity was waning, and it was fast disappearing from the scene. Therefore, the Lockman Foundation organized a team of thirty-two scholars to prepare a new revision. These scholars, all committed to the inspiration of Scripture, strove to produce a literal translation of the Bible in the belief that such a translation "brings the contemporary reader as close as possible to the actual wording and grammatical structure of the original writers."[2]

The translators of the *New American Standard Bible* were instructed by the Lockman Foundation to adhere to the original languages of the Holy Scriptures as closely as possible and at the same time to obtain a fluent and readable style according to current English usage. After the *New American Standard Bible* was published (1963 for the New Testament and 1971 for the entire Bible), it received a mixed response. Some critics applauded its literal accuracy, while others sharply

---

[1] From the Preface to the *New American Standard Bible.*

[2] Ibid.

criticized its language for neither being contemporary nor modern.

On the whole, the *New American Standard Bible* became respected as a good study Bible that accurately reflects the wording of the original languages. Yet it is not a good translation for Bible reading. Furthermore, it must be said that this translation is now nearly thirty years behind in terms of textual fidelity—especially the New Testament, which, though it was originally supposed to follow the twenty-third edition of the Nestle text, tends to reflect the Textus Receptus.

Indeed, many of the spurious verses eliminated in the ASV and RSV are now back in the text of the NASB. The reader of the NASB will see Matthew 17:21; 18:11; 23:14; Mark 7:16; 9:44, 46; 11:26; 15:28; 16:9-20; Luke 9:54c-56; 17:36; 22:43-44; 23:17, 34; John 5:3b-4; 7:53–8:11; Acts 8:37; 15:34; 24:6b-8a; 28:29; and Romans 16:24. Though all these verses are bracketed and noted, they are still included in the text. Such inclusion obviously caters to a conservative audience, but it does not accurately reflect the best Greek text. Interestingly, the New Testament translators originally omitted the verses from Luke 24 (verses 12, 36, 40, 51, 52) on the basis of Westcott and Hort's theory of "Western non-interpolations." In future editions, these verses were inserted into the text.

The NASB translators did not fully reflect the manuscript evidence of some very important discoveries in the decades prior to their work. The Dead Sea Scrolls were hardly influential in their work. And it seemed that they didn't take much notice of the Chester Beatty and Bodmer papyri for the New Testament.[1]

---

[1] This is fully documented in Comfort, *Early Manuscripts*, 193-196.

## THE NEW KING JAMES VERSION (NKJV), 1982

The New King James Version, published in 1982, is a revision of the King James Version, which is itself a literal translation. As such, the New King James Version follows the historic precedent of the King James Version in maintaining a literal approach to translation. The revisers have called this method of translation "complete equivalence." This means that the revisers sought to provide a complete representation of all the information in the original text with respect to the history of usage and etymology of words in their contexts.[1] Of course, achieving "complete equivalence" when translating from one language to another is an ideal that can never be completely achieved.

The most distinctive feature of the NKJV is its underlying original text. The revisers of the NKJV New Testament chose to use the Textus Receptus rather than modern critical editions, including the Majority Text and the Nestle-Aland text. By way of concession, they have footnoted any significant textual variation from the Majority Text and modern critical editions. The Majority Text, which is the text supported by the majority of all known New Testament manuscripts, hardly differs from the Textus Receptus; thus, there are few significant differences noted (as the "M" text). But there are well over a thousand differences footnoted regarding the $NA^{26}/UBS^{3}$ text (noted as the "NU" text). The reader, therefore, can note how many significant differences there are between the two texts.

Though exhibiting an antiquated text, the language of the NKJV is basically modern. All the Elizabethan English of the original King James Version has been replaced with contemporary American English. Though much of the sentence

---

1 From the Preface to the *Holy Bible,* New King James Version, iv.

structure of the NKJV is still dated and stilted, contemporary readers who favor the spirit of the King James Version but can't understand much of its archaic language will appreciate this revision.

## THE NEW REVISED STANDARD VERSION (NRSV), 1990

In due course, the time came for yet another revision of the authorized version. In the preface to this revision, Bruce Metzger, chair of the revision committee, wrote:

> The New Revised Standard Version of the Bible is an authorized revision of the Revised Standard Version, published in 1952, which was a revision of the American Standard Version, published in 1901, which, in turn, embodied earlier revisions of the King James Version, published in 1611.
>
> The need for issuing a revision of the Revised Standard Version of the Bible arises from three circumstances: (a) the acquisition of still older biblical manuscripts, (b) further investigation of linguistic features of the text, and (c) changes in preferred English usage.[1]

Metzger's three reasons for producing the New Revised Standard Version are essentially the same reasons behind all revisions of Bible translations. But the NRSV does present significant revision, especially with respect to the first and third of these issues: the acquisition of older biblical manuscripts and changes in preferred English usage.

### The Texts behind the NRSV

In the preface to the NRSV, the translators state that the discovery of additional Dead Sea Scrolls, not available to the RSV

[1] From the Preface to the *Holy Bible*, New Revised Standard Version, i.

committee, significantly contributed to the revision. Thus, while using the *Biblia Hebraica Stuttgartensia* (1977; ed. sec. emendata, 1983) as their primary text, the Old Testament Committee departed from it when the evidence of the Qumran manuscripts and/or other early versions (in Greek, Old Latin, and Syriac) warranted departure.

The departure from the MT is most manifest in 1 and 2 Samuel. One look at 1 Samuel 1–2 is quite telling. As Scanlin says, "These chapters contain the account of the birth and early life of Samuel. The NRSV contains twenty-seven textual notes in these two chapters; the translation departs from the MT in all cases, with Qumran support for seventeen departures from the MT."[1] The NRSV, departing from the MT, adopts the longer text of the Old Greek in 1 Samuel 4:1; 13:15; 14:23-24; and 29:10. These and other examples reveal that the increase in the number of MT departures indicates that text-critical considerations have increased in recent years.

Of all the modern translations, the NRSV most closely follows the text of $NA^{26}$/$UBS^{3}$. No doubt, this is due to Bruce Metzger's involvement in both editorial committees—a leading member of the $NA^{26}$/$UBS^{3}$ committee and the chair for the NRSV committee. As such, this translation reflects the most up-to-date textual studies for the New Testament. Many readings never before accepted in a Bible translation were included in the NRSV. For example, the NRSV adopts the reading "Jesus Barabbas" as the name of the rebel who was released by Pilate instead of Jesus of Nazareth (Matt. 27:16). And in Hebrews 4:2, the NRSV has the following rendering:

> For indeed the good news came to us just as to them;
> but the message they heard did not benefit them,

---

[1] Scanlin, *Dead Sea Scrolls*, 115-116.

> because they were not united by faith with those who listened.

Most other translations follow a reading in which the *message* "did not meet with faith in those who listened" (NRSV margin).

### Gender-Inclusive Language

Perhaps the most notable feature of the NRSV is its attention to gender-inclusive language. While respecting the historicity of the ancient texts, the NRSV translators attempted to make this new revision more palatable to readers who prefer gender-inclusive language. They did this by avoiding unnecessarily masculine renderings wherever possible. For example, in the New Testament Epistles, the believers are referred to with a word that is traditionally rendered "brothers" (*adelphoi*), yet it is clear that these epistles were addressed to all the believers—both male and female. Thus, the NRSV translators have used such phrases as "brothers and sisters" or "friends" (always with a footnote saying "Greek, brothers") in order to represent the historical situation while remaining sensitive to modern readers.

Metzger and the other translators were careful, however, not to overemphasize the gender-inclusiveness principle. Some readers had been hoping for a more radical revision regarding gender-inclusiveness. Many of these readers were hoping that the revision would incorporate this principle with language about God—changing such phrases as "God our Father" to "God our Parent." But the NRSV revisers, under the leadership of Metzger, decided against this approach, considering it an inaccurate reflection of the original text's intended meaning.

CHAPTER SIX

# Translations of the Twentieth Century

## TRANSLATIONS OF THE FIRST HALF OF THE TWENTIETH CENTURY (1900–1950)

The thousands and thousands of papyri that were discovered in Egypt around the turn of the twentieth century displayed a form of Greek called "koiné" Greek. **Koiné Greek** was everyman's Greek; it was the common language of almost everyone living in the Greco-Roman world from the second century B.C. to the third century A.D. In other words, it was the "lingua franca" of the Mediterranean world. Every educated person in that world could speak, read, and write in Greek. (In much the same way, English is becoming an international language, not the province of any one nation or culture, but the lingua franca of the contemporary world.) Koiné Greek was not literary Greek (i.e., the kind of Greek written by the Greek poets and tragedians). Instead, it was the kind of Greek used in personal letters, legal documents, and other nonliterary texts.

After the recovery of so many koiné Greek papyri, New Testament scholars began to discover that most of the New Testament was written in koiné Greek—the language of the people. As a result, there began to be a strong prompting for translators to translate the New Testament into the language of the people. Translators began to separate themselves from traditional Elizabethan English, as found in the King James Version (and even in the English Revised Version and the American Standard Version), and to produce fresh renderings of Scripture in the common idiom.

## THE TWENTIETH CENTURY NEW TESTAMENT, 1902

The first of the new, free-speech translations was *The Twentieth Century New Testament.* According to the translators,

> *The Twentieth Century New Testament* is a smooth-flowing, accurate, easy-to-read translation that captivates its readers from start to finish. Born out of a desire to make the Bible readable and understandable, it is the product of the labors of a committee of twenty men and women who worked together over many years to construct, we believe under divine surveillance, this beautifully simple rendition of the word of God.[1]

## THE NEW TESTAMENT IN MODERN SPEECH, 1903

A year after the publication of *The Twentieth Century New Testament,* Richard Weymouth published *The New Testament in Modern Speech* (1903). Weymouth, who had received the first Doctor of Literature degree from the University of London, was headmaster of a private school in London. During his life, he spent time producing an edition of the Greek text (published in 1862) that was more accurate than the Textus Receptus, and then he labored to produce an English translation of this Greek text (called *The Resultant Greek Testament*) in a modern speech version. His translation was very well received; it has gone through several editions and many printings.

---

[1] From the Preface to the new edition of the *Twentieth Century New Testament.*

## THE NEW TESTAMENT: A NEW TRANSLATION, 1913

Another new and fresh translation to appear in the early years of this century was one written by James Moffatt, a brilliant Scottish scholar. In 1913 he published his first edition of *The New Testament: A New Translation.* This was actually his second translation of the New Testament; his first was done in 1901, called *The Historical New Testament.* In his *New Translation,* Moffatt's goal was "to translate the New Testament exactly as one would render any piece of contemporary Hellenistic prose."[1] His work displays brilliance and marked independence from other versions; unfortunately it was based on Hermann von Soden's Greek New Testament, which, as all scholars now know, is quite defective.

## THE HOLY SCRIPTURES ACCORDING TO THE MASORETIC TEXT, 1917

The Jewish Publication Society created a translation of the Hebrew Scriptures called *The Holy Scriptures According to the Masoretic Text, A New Translation* (published in 1917). The translators explained their goals in making this translation:

> It aims to combine the spirit of Jewish tradition with the results of biblical scholarship, ancient, medieval and modern. It gives to the Jewish world a translation of the Scriptures done by men imbued with the Jewish consciousness, while the non-Jewish world, it is hoped, will welcome a translation that presents many passages from the Jewish traditional point of view.[2]

---

1 From the Preface to *The New Testament: A New Translation.*

2 From the Preface to *The Holy Scriptures According to the Masoretic Text: A New Translation.*

## THE COMPLETE BIBLE: AN AMERICAN TRANSLATION, 1923 AND 1935

The earliest American "modern speech" translation was produced by Edgar J. Goodspeed, a professor of New Testament at the University of Chicago. He criticized *The Twentieth Century New Testament,* Weymouth's version, and Moffatt's translation and said that he could make a better translation than any of them. As a consequence, he was challenged by some other scholars to do just that. He took up the challenge and in 1923 published *The New Testament: An American Translation.* When he made this translation he said that he wanted to give his "version something of the force and freshness that reside in the original Greek." He said, "I wanted my translation to make on the reader something of the impression the New Testament must have made on its earliest readers, and to invite the continuous reading of the whole book at a time."[1] His translation was a success—so much so that an Old Testament translation followed, produced by J. M. Powis Smith and three other scholars.

## THE HOLY BIBLE: A CATHOLIC VERSION BY R. KNOX, 1944, 1950

In 1943 Pope Pius XII issued the famous encyclical encouraging Roman Catholics to read and study the Scriptures. At the same time, the pope recommended that the Scriptures should be translated from the original languages. Previously, all Catholic translations were based on the Latin Vulgate.

Rolland Knox was encouraged by bishops in England to make a fresh translation of the Scriptures, still based on the Latin Vulgate, but revised in light of the Hebrew and Greek originals. Knox had converted from Anglicanism to the Roman Catholic Church and was ordained a priest in 1917. He taught

[1] Goodspeed, *New Chapters,* 113.

at St. Edmund's College, Ware, before becoming the chaplain to Roman Catholic students at Oxford University in 1926. He remained at Oxford until 1939. Knox then began his longtime ambition: the translation of the Bible into modern English.[1] The New Testament was published in 1944 and the Old Testament in 1950. It was very popular among English-speaking Roman Catholics.

## TRANSLATIONS OF THE SECOND HALF OF THE TWENTIETH CENTURY (1951–1999)

The second half of the twentieth century saw an immense proliferation of new Bible translations. These were fresh translations that were not at all connected with the standard versions and revisions discussed in the previous chapter. Two of these new versions had enormous success: *The Living Bible,* a paraphrase with nearly fifty million copies in print; and the New International Version, which is the first translation in history to outsell the King James Version. These two versions, along with several others, have provided God's Word in fresh new ways to millions of people over the past fifty years.

### NEW JEWISH VERSION (NJV), 1962, 1973

In 1955, the Jewish Publication Society appointed a new committee of seven eminent Jewish scholars to make a new Jewish translation of the Hebrew Scriptures. The translation called the New Jewish Version was published in 1962. A second, improved edition was published in 1973. This work is not a revision of *The Holy Scriptures According to the Masoretic Text;* it is a completely new translation in modern English. The NJV offers a translation of the "traditional text" of Judaism, i.e., the

[1] Knox's experiences as a translator are elaborated in his book, *Trials of a Translator.*

Masoretic Text. The translators attempted to produce a version that would carry the same message to modern man as the original did to the world of ancient times.

### *THE NEW ENGLISH BIBLE* (NEB), 1961, 1970

In the year that the New Testament of the Revised Standard Version was published (1946), the Church of Scotland proposed to other churches in Great Britain that it was time for a completely new translation of the Bible to be done. Those who initiated this work asked the translators to produce a fresh translation of the original languages in modern idiom; this was not to be a revision of any foregoing translation, nor was it to be a literal translation. The translators, under the direction of C. H. Dodd, were called upon to translate the meaning of the text into modern English. The preface to the New Testament (published in 1961), written by Dodd, explains this more fully:

> The older translators, on the whole, considered that fidelity to the original demanded that they should reproduce, as far as possible, characteristic features of the language in which it was written, such as the syntactical order of words, the structure and division of sentences, and even such irregularities of grammar as were indeed natural enough to authors writing in the easy idiom of popular Hellenistic Greek, but less natural when turned into English. The present translators were enjoined to replace Greek constructions and idioms by those of contemporary English.
>
> This meant a different theory and practice of translation, and one which laid a heavier burden on the translators. Fidelity in translation was not to mean keeping the general framework of the original intact while

> replacing Greek words by English words more or less equivalent. . . . Thus we have not felt obliged (as did the Revisers of 1881) to make an effort to render the same Greek word everywhere by the same English word. We have in this respect returned to the wholesome practice of King James's men, who (as they expressly state in their preface) recognized no such obligation. We have conceived our task to be that of understanding the original as precisely as we could (using all available aids), and then saying again in our own native idiom what we believed the author to be saying in his.[1]

The entire *New English Bible* was published in 1970; it was well received in Great Britain and in the United States (even though its idiom is extremely British) and was especially praised for its good literary style. The translators were very experimental, producing renderings never before printed in an English version and adopting certain readings from various Hebrew and Greek manuscripts never before adopted. As a result, *The New English Bible* was both highly praised for its ingenuity and severely criticized for its liberty.

Indeed, the text of the New Testament was extremely eclectic—so much so that the Greek text for *The New English Bible* was produced by R. V. G. Tasker *after* the English translation came out, in order to reflect the underlying text decided upon by the translation committee (on a verse by verse basis). To say the least, the resultant text is very uneven and yet very interesting. The translators adopted readings never before adopted by English translators.

The same kind of adventuresome spirit was at work in the making of the Old Testament. The translators, basically

---

[1] From the Preface to *The New English Bible.*

distrusting the Masoretic Text, were prone to make textual modifications in pursuit of what they considered to be the original text. They explain their approach as follows:

> The text . . . is not infrequently uncertain and its meaning obscure. . . . The earliest surviving form of the Hebrew text is perhaps that found in the Samaritan Pentateuch. . . . The Hebrew text as thus handed down [by the Masoretes] is full of errors of every kind due to defective archetypes and successive copyists' errors, confusion of letters, omissions and insertions, displacements of words and even whole sentences or paragraphs; and copyists' unhappy attempts to rectify mistakes have only increased the confusion. . . . When the problem before the translators was that of correcting errors in the Hebrew text in order to make sense, they had recourse, first of all, to the ancient versions. . . . These ancient versions, especially when they agree, contribute in varying degrees to the restoration of the Hebrew text when incapable of translation as it stands. . . . In the last resort the scholar may be driven to conjectural emendation of the Hebrew text.[1]

### THE LIVING BIBLE (TLB), 1966, 1971

In 1962, Kenneth Taylor published a paraphrase of the New Testament Epistles in a volume called *Living Letters.* This new, dynamic paraphrase, written in common vernacular, became well received and widely acclaimed—especially for its ability to communicate the message of God's word to the common man. In the beginning its circulation was greatly enhanced by the endorsement of the Billy Graham Evangelistic Association,

[1] Ibid.

which did much to publicize the book and distributed thousands of free copies. Taylor continued to paraphrase other portions of the Bible and publish successive volumes: *Living Prophecies* (1965), *Living Gospels* (1966), *Living Psalms* (1967), *Living Lessons of Life and Love* (1968), *Living Books of Moses* (1969), and *Living History of Moses* (1970). The *Living New Testament* was printed in 1966, and the entire *Living Bible* was published in 1971.

Using the American Standard Version as his working text, Taylor rephrased the Bible into modern speech—such that anyone, even a child, could understand the message of the original writers. Taylor explains his view of paraphrasing:

> To paraphrase is to say something in different words than the author used. It is a restatement of the author's thoughts, using different words than he did. This book is a paraphrase of the Old and New Testaments. Its purpose is to say as exactly as possible what the writers of the Scriptures meant, and to say it simply, expanding where necessary for a clear understanding by the modern reader.[1]

Even though many modern readers have greatly appreciated the fact that *The Living Bible* made God's word clear to them, Taylor's paraphrase has been criticized for being too interpretive. But that is the nature of paraphrases—and the danger as well. Taylor was aware of this when he made the paraphrase. Again, he clarifies:

> There are dangers in paraphrases, as well as values. For whenever the author's exact words are not translated from the original languages, there is a possibility that

[1] From the Preface to *The Living Bible.*

> the translator, however honest, may be giving the English reader something that the original writer did not mean to say.[1]

*The Living Bible* has been very popular among English readers worldwide. More than 40 million copies have been sold by the publishing house Taylor specifically created to publish *The Living Bible,* Tyndale House Publishers (named after William Tyndale, the father of modern English translations of the Bible).

## THE JERUSALEM BIBLE (JB), 1966

*The Jerusalem Bible* was published in England in 1966. *The Jerusalem Bible* is the English counterpart to a French translation entitled *La Bible de Jerusalem.* The French translation was "the culmination of decades of research and biblical scholarship,"[2] published by the scholars of the Dominican Biblical School of Jerusalem. This Bible, which includes the **Apocrypha** and deuterocanonical books, contains many study helps—such as introductions to each book of the Bible, extensive notes on various passages, and maps. The study helps are an intricate part of the whole translation because it is the belief of Roman Catholic leadership that laypeople should be given interpretive helps in their reading of the sacred text. The study helps in *The Jerusalem Bible* were translated from the French, whereas the Bible text itself was translated from the original languages with the help of the French translation. The translation of the text produced under the editorship of Alexander Jones is considerably freer than other translations, such as the Revised Standard Version, because the translators sought to capture the meaning of the original writings in a vigorous, contemporary literary

---

[1] Ibid.

[2] From the Preface to *The Jerusalem Bible.*

style. Consequently, *The Jerusalem Bible* offers many fresh and interesting renderings.

### GOOD NEWS BIBLE: TODAY'S ENGLISH VERSION (GNB or TEV), 1966, 1976

*The New Testament in Today's English Version*, also known as *Good News for Modern Man,* was published by the American Bible Society in 1966. The translation was originally done by Robert Bratcher, a research associate of the Translations Department of the American Bible Society, and then further refined by the American Bible Society. The translation, heavily promoted by several Bible societies and very affordable, sold more than 35 million copies within six years of being printed. The New Testament translation, based on the first edition of the United Bible Societies' *Greek New Testament* (1966 edition), is an idiomatic version in modern and simple English. The translation was greatly influenced by the linguistic theory of dynamic equivalence and was quite successful in providing English readers with a translation that, for the most part, accurately reflects the meaning of the original texts. This is explained by the translators of the New Testament:

> This translation of the New Testament has been prepared by the American Bible Society for people who speak English as their mother tongue or as an acquired language. As a distinctly new translation, it does not conform to traditional vocabulary or style, but seeks to express the meaning of the Greek text in words and forms accepted as standard by people everywhere who employ English as a means of communication. Today's English Version of the New Testament attempts to follow, in this century, the example set by the authors

> of the New Testament books, who, for the most part, wrote in the standard, or common, form of the Greek language used throughout the Roman Empire.[1]

Because of the success of the New Testament, the American Bible Society was asked by other Bible societies to make an Old Testament translation following the same principles used in the New Testament. The entire Bible was published in 1976, and is known as the *Good News Bible:* Today's English Version.

### THE NEW AMERICAN BIBLE (NAB), 1970

The first American Catholic Bible to be translated from the original languages is *The New American Bible* (not to be confused with the *New American Standard Bible*). Although this translation was published in 1970, work had begun on this version several decades before. Prior to Pope Pius's encyclical, an American translation of the New Testament based on the Latin Vulgate was published—known as the Confraternity Version. After the encyclical, the Old Testament was translated from the Hebrew Masoretic Text—with some divergence because the NAB translators accepted "the three-recension theory of Frank M. Cross. At times, they showed a definite preference for the Egyptian recension as witnessed by the agreement of LXX and some Qumran manuscripts. This is especially evident in its translation of the books of Samuel."[2]

When the New Testament was redone, it was based on the twenty-fifth edition of the Greek Nestle-Aland text. The New American Bible has short introductions to each book of the Bible and very few marginal notes. Kubo and Specht provide a just description of the translation itself:

---

[1] From the Preface to the *Good News Bible*.

[2] Scanlin, *Dead Sea Scrolls*, 16.

> The translation itself is simple, clear, and straightforward and reads very smoothly. It is good American English, not as pungent and colorful as the N.E.B. [*New English Bible*]. Its translations are not striking but neither are they clumsy. They seem to be more conservative in the sense that they tend not to stray from the original. That is not to say that this is a literal translation, but it is more faithful.[1]

The NAB has been well received by American Catholics. It is read in the churches and read in the homes. The NAB is unquestionably the most popular American edition of a Catholic Bible.

### THE NEW INTERNATIONAL VERSION (NIV), 1973, 1978

The New International Version is a completely new rendering of the original languages done by an international group of more than a hundred scholars. These scholars worked many years and in several committees to produce an excellent thought-for-thought translation in contemporary English for private and public use. The New International Version is called "international" because it was prepared by distinguished scholars from English-speaking countries such as the United States, Canada, Great Britain, Australia, and New Zealand, and because the translators sought to use vocabulary common to the major English-speaking nations of the world.

The translators of the New International Version sought to make a version that was midway between a literal rendering (such as the NASB) and a free, modern-speech edition (such as TEV). Their goal was to convey in English the thought of

---

[1] Kubo and Specht, *So Many Versions?*, 165.

the original writers. This is succinctly explained by the translators:

> Certain convictions and aims guided the translators. They are all committed to the full authority and complete trustworthiness of the Scriptures. Therefore, their first concern was the accuracy of the translation and its fidelity to the thought of the New Testament writers. While they weighed the significance of the lexical and grammatical details of the Greek text, they have striven for more than a word-for-word translation. Because thought patterns and syntax differ from language to language, faithful communication of the meaning of the writers of the New Testament demanded frequent modifications in sentence structure and constant regard for the contextual meanings of words.
>
> Concern for clarity of style—that it should be idiomatic without being idiosyncratic, contemporary without being dated—also motivated the translators and their consultants. They have consistently aimed at simplicity of expression, with sensitive attention to the connotation and sound of the chosen word. At the same time, they endeavored to avoid a sameness of style in order to reflect the varied styles and moods of the New Testament writers.[1]

The New Testament of the New International Version was published in 1973, and the en tire Bible in 1978. This version has been phenomenally successful. Millions and millions of readers have adopted the New International Version as their "Bible." Since 1987 it has outsold the King James Version,

---

[1] From the Preface to the *Holy Bible,* New International Version.

the best-seller for centuries—a remarkable indication of its popularity and acceptance in the Christian community. The New International Version, sponsored by the New York Bible Society (now the International Bible Society) and published by Zondervan Publishing House, has become a standard version used for private reading and pulpit reading in many English-speaking countries.

The success of the NIV is due, in part, to the fact that it struck a happy medium between the stiff and literal authorized versions and the modern, idiomatic versions. The NIV retained enough of the traditional language of the English Bible to make it familiar—especially in passages that are well known to Bible readers—while being modern enough to appeal to contemporary readers.

The textual basis for the Old Testament was the Masoretic Text, from which the translators were usually reluctant to depart. This is explained as follows:

> For the Old Testament the standard Hebrew text, The Masoretic Text as published in the latest editions of *Biblia Hebraica,* was used throughout. The Dead Sea Scrolls contain material bearing on an earlier stage of the Hebrew text. They were consulted, as were the Samaritan Pentateuch and the ancient scribal traditions relating to textual changes. Sometimes a variant Hebrew reading in the margin of the Masoretic Text was followed instead of the text itself. . . . The translators also consulted the more important early versions—the Septuagint; Aquila, Symmachus, and Theodotian; the Vulgate; the Syriac Peshitta; the Targums; and for the Psalms the *Juxta Hebraica* of Jerome. Readings from these versions were occasionally followed where the

> Masoretic Text seemed doubtful and where accepted principles of textual criticism showed that one or more of these textual witnesses appeared to provide the correct reading. Such instances are footnoted.[1]

In short, the NIV translators highly regarded the MT. But the Old Testament translators were willing to depart from it not only in cases where the translators concluded that the MT was corrupt, but also in cases where a less-well-attested witness yields a translation more in harmony with a New Testament quotation or allusion (e.g., Ps. 2:9/Rev. 2:27; Ps. 116:10/2 Cor. 4:13).

The New Testament translation, while based on an eclectic text, basically follows the United Bible Societies' first edition of the *Greek New Testament* (1966). The NIV diverges from this text in about three hundred fifty significant places—many in agreement with the TR. The translators took advantage of some very important manuscript discoveries (such as $\mathfrak{P}^{66}$ and $\mathfrak{P}^{75}$), but not full advantage. The translators were cautious in adopting readings from these manuscripts.[2]

### *THE NEW JERUSALEM BIBLE* (NJB), 1986

*The Jerusalem Bible* had become widely used for liturgical purposes, for study, and for private reading. This success spurred a new revision, both of the *Bible de Jerusalem* in French and *The Jerusalem Bible* in English. This new edition "incorporated progress in scholarship over the two decades since the preparation of the first edition. The introductions and notes were often widely changed to take account of linguistic, archaeological, and theological advances, and the text

[1] Ibid.

[2] A complete analysis of this is presented in Comfort, *Early Manuscripts*, 196–199.

itself in some instances reflected new understanding of the originals."[1] *The New Jerusalem Bible* (published in 1986) generally has been received as an excellent study text.

The translators of the Old Testament followed the Masoretic Text, except when this text presented problems—as stated in the preface: "Only when this text presents insuperable difficulties have emendations or the versions or other Hebrew manuscripts or the ancient versions (notably the LXX and Syriac) been used."[2] The New Testament offers some interesting variations from many other modern versions because it displays an eclectic text—especially in the book of Acts, where many "Western" readings were adopted.

### *THE REVISED ENGLISH BIBLE* (REB), 1989

*The Revised English Bible* (REB, 1989) is a revision of *The New English Bible* (NEB), which was published in 1971. Because the NEB had gained such popularity in British churches and was being regularly used for public reading, several British churches decided there should be a revision of the NEB to keep the language current and the text up-to-date with modern biblical scholarship.

For the Old Testament, the revisers used the Masoretic Text as it appears in *Biblia Hebraica Stuttgartensia* (1967, 1977). They also made use of the Dead Sea Scrolls and a few other important versions, including the Septuagint. Nonetheless, the REB translators were very conservative in their departures from the MT, as is made evident by their position stated in the preface—the statement of *The Revised English Bible* translators demonstrates a significant shift in their attitude towards the text, when compared with their predecessors:

---

1 From the Foreword to *The New Jerusalem Bible*.

2 Ibid.

> It is probable that the Massoretic Text remained substantially unaltered from the second century A.D. to the present time, and this text is reproduced in all Hebrew Bibles. The New English Bible translators used the third edition of Kittel's *Biblia Hebraica*. . . . Despite the care used in the copying of the Massoretic Text, it contains errors, in the correction of which there are witnesses to be heard. None of them is throughout superior to the Massoretic Text, but in particular places their evidence may preserve the correct reading.[1]

The revisers of the New Testament used Nestle-Aland's *Novum Testamentum Graece* (twenty-sixth edition, 1981) as their base text. This choice resulted in several textual changes from *The New English Bible* text, which followed a very eclectic text. The translators of the NEB adopted readings never before put into print by English translators. The scholars working on the REB adjusted many of these readings in the interest of providing a more balanced text. At the same time, they also made some significant textual changes. The most outstanding is what they did with the story of the woman caught in adultery (John 7:53–8:11). Reflecting the overwhelming evidence of the Greek manuscripts, this story is *not* included in the main body of John. Rather, it is printed as an appendix after the Gospel of John.

## CONTEMPORARY ENGLISH VERSION (CEV), 1991, 1994

Barclay Newman of the American Bible Society is the pioneer of a new translation for early youth. Working according to Eugene Nida's model of functional equivalence, Newman, in cooperation with other members of the American Bible Soci-

[1] From the Preface to the *New English Bible*.

ety, produced fresh translations of New Testament books based on the United Bible Societies' *Greek New Testament* (third, corrected edition, 1983). These first appeared as individual books: *A Book about Jesus* (containing passages from the four Gospels), *Luke Tells the Good News about Jesus,* and *Good News Travels Fast: The Acts of the Apostles.* Then the complete New Testament was published in 1991. With the aid of other scholars, Barclay Newman completed the entire Bible in 1994.

The CEV aims to be both reliable to the original languages and readable for modern English-speakers. In producing this kind of translation, the translators were constantly asking two questions: (1) "What do the words mean?" and (2) "What is the most accurate and natural way to express this meaning in contemporary English?" Since many technical terms such as "salvation," "grace," and "righteousness" do not readily communicate to modern readers, the CEV translators have sought natural English equivalents such as "God saves you," "God is kind to you," and "God accepts you." Sometimes translators cannot avoid using difficult terms in the text (such as "Pharisee," "Day of Atonement," and "circumcise"), because these words hold religious significance that cannot easily be conveyed in simpler terms. In order to help the reader with these words, the CEV defines such terms in a separate word list.

### NEW CENTURY VERSION (NCV), 1991

The New Century Version is a new translation of the original languages, published in two editions: one for children, called the *International Children's Bible,* and one for adults, first appearing in a New Testament edition called *The Word* and now available with the entire Bible text in an edition called *The Everyday Bible.*

The World Bible Translation Center developed the New Century Version by using an existing translation for the deaf, which used a limited vocabulary (published as *New Testament for the Deaf,* Baker Book House). The translators based the new version on the latest edition of *Biblia Hebraica Stuttgartensia* for the Old Testament and the third edition of the United Bible Societies' *Greek New Testament* for the New Testament.

Both the adults' and the children's editions of the NCV emphasize simplicity and clarity of expression. The children's edition, however, is stylistically simpler than the adults' edition. The translators of the NCV wanted to make "the language simple enough for children to read and understand for themselves."[1] Therefore, the translators used short, uncomplicated sentences, as well as vocabulary appropriate for children on a third-grade instructional level.

## NEW LIFE VERSION, 1993

The New Life Version, produced by Gleason H. Ledyard, was first published as the *Children's New Testament* (1966). While serving as missionaries in northern Canada, Ledyard and his wife, Kathryn, worked with Eskimos who were just starting to learn English. This experience encouraged them to make an English translation for people learning English as a second language. After translating a few books and distributing them to various people, they were told that their translation was excellent for children. Thus, the Ledyards continued their work, finishing first the New Testament and then the Old Testament. This work became the New Life Version, published by Christian Literature International.

The genius of this version's readability is that it uses a limited vocabulary and simplifies difficult biblical terms. With

[1] From the Preface to the New Century Version.

more than 6 million copies sold, the New Life Version has been published in many editions and has been distributed worldwide—especially to those who are learning English as a second language. This version is the text of the *Precious Moments Children's Bible,* published by Baker Book House (1993).

### THE MESSAGE, 1994

One of the most recent New Testament translations to come onto the publishing scene is *The Message* by Eugene H. Peterson (published by NavPress). Peterson was inspired to produce his idiomatic English translation because, as he says, he had been doing this throughout his vocational life:

> For thirty-five years as a pastor I stood at the border between two languages, biblical Greek and everyday English, acting as a translator, providing the right phrases, getting the right words so that the men and women to whom I was pastor could find their way around and get along in this world where God has spoken so decisively and clearly in Jesus.[1]

Peterson's goal in creating a translation of the New Testament was to convert the tone, the rhythm, the events, and the ideas of the Greek text into the way we actually think and speak in English. This is quite ambitious. In some places Peterson seems to have accomplished his goal, as in his rendering of Romans 1:25: "They traded the true God for a fake god, and worshiped the god they made instead of the God who made them." But in other places, Peterson seems simply to present the Greek text in very awkward English. This is most

---

[1] From the Preface to *The Message.*

apparent in the prologue to John's Gospel, where many expressions are often confusing to those unfamiliar with Greek. No doubt many readers will be hard-pressed to follow what Peterson is trying to do in John 1:1: "The Word was first, the Word present to God, God present to the Word." Likewise, in John 1:18 Peterson uses a fairly awkward phrase: "This one-of-a-kind God-Expression, who exists at the very heart of the Father, has made him plain as day."

While Peterson's translation reflects his good understanding of the Greek language, it is less certain whether it communicates in the way "we actually think and speak" (as posited in his preface). This goal is often better accomplished by other contemporary English translations.

## GOD'S WORD, 1995

The biblical translation most recently called *God's Word* has been referred to by several names in the past few years. It has been named *God's Word to the Nations: New Evangelical Translation,* and it has been called *New Evangelical Translation* (1988). It is now simply entitled *God's Word* (1995). Modeled after William Beck's version, *An American Translation* (New Testament, 1963; entire Bible, 1976), this translation is the publishing effort of a Lutheran group called God's Word to the Nations Bible Society.

The motivation behind this version was to provide English-reading people throughout the world with an accurate, clear, and easy-to-read translation of the Bible. With this in mind, the revisers avoided heavy theological jargon, which may not be meaningful to non-theologically-trained readers. Thus, they did not use words like *covenant, grace, justify, repent,* and *righteousness.* Rather, they employed common words to convey the meaning of the original text. They have called this theory of translation, "natural equivalence." It is supposed to avoid the extremes of formal equivalence (awkwardness due to strict literalness) and function equivalence (inaccuracy due to oversimplification).[1]

## NEW LIVING TRANSLATION (NLT), 1996

With over 40 million copies in print, *The Living Bible* has been a very popular version of the Bible for more than thirty years. But various criticisms spurred the translator of *The Living Bible,* Kenneth Taylor, to produce a revision of his paraphrase. Under the sponsorship of Tyndale House Publishers, *The Living Bible* underwent a thorough revision. More than ninety evangelical scholars from various theological backgrounds and denominations worked for seven years to produce the New Living Translation (NLT). As a result, the NLT is a version that is exegetically accurate and idiomatically powerful.

The scholars carefully revised the text of *The Living Bible* according to the most reliable editions of the Hebrew and Greek texts. For the Old Testament, the revisers used the Masoretic Text as it appears in *Biblia Hebraica Stuttgartensia* (1967, 1977). They also made use of the Dead Sea Scrolls and a few other important versions, including the Septuagint. The revisers of the New Testament used the text of NA$^{27}$/UBS$^{4}$ as their base text.

The translation method behind the NLT has been described as "dynamic equivalence" or "functional equivalence." The goal of this kind of translation is to produce in English the closest natural equivalent of the message of the Hebrew and Greek texts—both in meaning and in style. Such a translation should attempt to have the same impact upon

---

[1] From the Preface to *God's Word.*

modern readers as the original had upon its audience. To translate the Bible in this manner requires that the text be interpreted accurately and then rendered in understandable, current English. In doing this, the translators attempted to enter into the same thought pattern as the author and present the same idea, connotation, and effect in the receptor language. To guard against personal subjectivism and insure accuracy of message, the NLT was produced by a large group of scholars who were each well-studied in their particular area. To ensure that the translation would be extremely readable and understandable, a group of stylists adjusted the wording to make it clear and fluent.

A thought-for-thought translation created by a group of capable scholars has the potential to represent the intended meaning of the original text even more accurately than a word-for-word translation. This is illustrated by the various renderings of the Hebrew word *hesed.* This term cannot be adequately translated by any single English word because it can connote love, mercy, grace, kindness, faithfulness, and loyalty. The context—not the lexicon—must determine which English term is selected for translation.

The value of a thought-for-thought translation can be illustrated by comparing 1 Kings 2:10 in the KJV, the NIV, and the NLT.

> "So David slept with his fathers, and was buried in the city of David" (KJV).
>
> "Then David rested with his fathers and was buried in the City of David" (NIV).
>
> "Then David died and was buried in the City of David" (NLT).

Only the New Living Translation clearly translates the intended meaning of the Hebrew idiom "slept with his fathers" into contemporary English.[1]

In a recent work, entitled *The Journey from Texts to Translations,* Wegner provides an excellent comparative study between the original *Living Bible* and the New Living Translation. He applauds the scholarship that went into the New Living Translation—both in terms of the caliber of scholars who worked on the revision and in terms of the translation methodology (dynamic equivalence) that was applied. Wegner's estimation is that "the language of the New Living Translation is clear and intelligible; . . . its vastly improved accuracy over *The Living Bible* can be credited to the fine team of translators."[2]

---

[1] From the Introduction to the *Holy Bible,* New Living Translation.

[2] Wegner, *Texts to Translations,* 390.

CHAPTER SEVEN

# A Comparative Study of Major Translations of the Prologue to the Gospel of John

A comparative study of an intriguing passage like the prologue to John's Gospel set forth in several modern translations will help focus and substantiate all the foregoing discussions about how the translations differ. By doing this study we can see which translations tend to be literal, which tend to be more idiomatic, and which are dynamically equivalent; at the same time, we can see why each translation has its own strengths and weaknesses. It takes several translations to bring out the fullness and richness of the original language—and even then, at times, all of the translations together fail to convey the full meaning of the original words.

The following analysis of John's prologue (John 1:1-18) is detailed and, at times, complex because the analysis assesses translations of the Greek text and therefore makes constant reference to Greek words. The serious reader will be rewarded if he or she works through this chapter carefully.

## ENGLISH TRANSLATIONS: ANCIENT AND MODERN

### *John 1:1-5*

#### William Tyndale's Version

In the beginnynge was the worde, and the worde was with God: and the word was God. The same was in the beginnynge with God. All things were made by it, and with out it, was made nothinge, that was made. In it was lyfe, and the lyfe was the lyghte of men, and the lyght shyneth in the darckness, but the darckness comprehended it not.

#### King James Version

1 In the beginning was the Word, and the Word was with God, and the Word was God.

2 The same was in the beginning with God.

3 All things were made by him; and without him was not any thing made that was made.

4 In him was life; and the life was the light of men.

5 And the light shineth in darkness; and the darkness comprehended it not.

#### American Standard Version

1 In the beginning was the Word, and the Word was with
God, and the Word was God. 2 The same was in the beginning
with God. 3 All things were made through him; and without him
was not anything made that hath been made. 4 In him was life;
and the life was the light of men. 5 And the light shineth in the
darkness; and the darkness apprehended it not.

### Revised Standard Version

1In the beginning was the Word, and the Word was with
God, and the Word was God. 2He was in the beginning with
God; 3all things were made through him; and without him was
not anything made that was made. 4In him was life, and the life
was the light of men. 5The light shines in the darkness, and the
darkness has not overcome it.

### New American Standard Bible

1In the beginning was the Word, and the Word was with God,
and the Word was God.

2He was in the beginning with God.

3All things came into being by Him, and apart from Him
nothing came into being that has come into being.

4In Him was life, and the life was the light of men.

5And the light shines in the darkness, and the darkness did
not comprehend it.

### New International Version

1In the beginning was the Word, and the Word was with
God, and the Word was God. 2He was with God in the beginning.

3Through him all things were made; without him nothing
was made that has been made. 4In him was life, and that life
was the light of men. 5The light shines in the darkness, but the
darkness has not understood it.

### Today's English Version

1Before the world was created, the Word already existed; he
was with God, and he was the same as God. 2From the very beginning the Word was with God. 3Through him God made all
things; not one thing in all creation was made without him.
4The Word was the source of life, and this life brought light to
mankind. 5The light shines in the darkness, and the darkness has
never put it out.

### New Living Translation

1In the beginning the Word already existed. He was with
God, and he was God. 2He was in the beginning with God. 3He
created everything there is. Nothing exists that he didn't make.
4Life itself was in him, and this life gives light to everyone. 5The
light shines through the darkness, and the darkness can never
extinguish it.

### New English Bible

When all things began, the Word already was. The Word dwelt with God, and what God was, the Word was. The Word, then, was with God at the beginning, and through him all things came to be; no single thing was created without him. All that came to be was alive with his life, and that life was the light of men. The light shines on in the dark, and the darkness has never mastered it.

## The New Jerusalem Bible

1 In the beginning was the Word:
the Word was with God
and the Word was God.
2 He was with God in the beginning.
3 Through him all things came into being,
not one thing came into being
except through him.
4 What has come into being in him was life,
life that was the light of men;
5 and light shines in darkness,
and darkness could not overpower it.

## The New American Bible

1 In the beginning was the Word,
and the Word was with God,
and the Word was God.
2 He was in the beginning with God.
3 All things came to be through him,
and without him nothing came to be.
What came to be 4 through him was life,
and this life was the light of the human race;
5 the light shines in the darkness,
and the darkness has not overcome it.

## New Revised Standard Version

1 In the beginning was the Word, and the Word was with
God, and the Word was God. 2 He was in the beginning with
God. 3 All things came into being through him, and without him
not one thing came into being. What has come into being 4 in
him was life, and the life was the light of all people. 5 The light
shines in the darkness, and the darkness did not overcome it.

## A COMPARATIVE STUDY OF JOHN 1:1–18

### 1:1a

> In the beginning was the Word. (KJV, RSV, NASB, NIV)
>
> When all things began, the Word already was. (NEB)
>
> Before the world was created, the Word already existed. (TEV)
>
> In the beginning the Word already existed. (NLT)

From the outset the reader of John's Gospel is confronted with an enigmatic phrase, which in a word-for-word rendering becomes, "In beginning was the Word." The phrase "in beginning" most likely indicates the beginning before all beginnings, prior to the beginning of Genesis 1:1; it speaks of that eternal beginning in which the eternal Word existed. The NEB and TEV, understanding the phrase to have temporal significance, however, make this beginning equal to the beginning in Genesis 1:1. The paraphrases in the NEB and TEV might alarm the careful reader because, although their renderings indicate that the Word existed prior to Creation, they do not convey the idea that the Word existed from the beginning or from all eternity—which is the meaning probably intended by John. The NLT highlights this sense by using the verb "existed" to represent the Greek imperfect tense (a tense used to denote continuous action in past time).

All the versions render the Greek word *logos* as "the Word." There is probably no better term than "The Word" because it has become a traditional title of the Son of God before his incarnation, and it will probably remain a constant expression in English translations.

**1:1b**

> and the Word was with God (KJV, RSV, NASB, NIV)
> the Word dwelt with God (NEB)
> he was with God (TEV, NLT)

The rendering of this phrase depends upon how the Greek preposition *pros* is understood in this context. In classical usage, *pros* used in relationship between two people means "having regard to," and indicates "devotion."[1] Perhaps John intended to convey this meaning; but it is more likely that *pros* is to be understood according to koiné Greek usage. In koiné Greek, *pros* (short for *prosopon pros prosopon,* "face-to-face") was used to show personal relationships.[2] Accordingly, two other translations, that of Williams and that of Montgomery, rendered this passage, "and the Word was face-to-face with God." The NEB comes the closest to transferring this sense by adding "dwelt," and the REB is even better: "the Word was in God's presence." The translation "with" in the other translations is accurate but colorless.

**1:1c**

> and the Word was God. (KJV, RSV, NASB, NIV, NLT)
> and what God was, the Word was. (NEB)
> and he was the same as God. (TEV)

The Greek clause underlying these translations stipulates, according to a rule of grammar, that *logos* (the Word) is the subject and *theos* (God) is the predicate. Another particularity of Greek is that the definite article ("the" in English) is often used in Greek for defining individual identity and is

---

1 Abbott, *Johannine Grammar*, 274-275.

2 See Matt. 13:56; 26:18; Mark 6:3; 14:49; 1 Cor. 16:10; 2 Cor. 5:8; and Gal. 1:18.

thus absent when the purpose is to ascribe quality or character. In the previous clause ("the Word was with God"), there is an article before God (*ton theon*)—pointing to God the Father. In the present clause, there is no article before "God." The distinction may indicate that John did not want the reader to think the Son was the Father—but the same as the Father: that is, both are "God." The NEB reads, "and what God was, the Word was,"[1] and the TEV reads, "and he was the same as God." It can be argued, however, that the grammar simply indicates that "God" is the object of the verb rather than the subject, and the clause should be translated as in most of the versions: "the Word was God."

**1:2**

> He was in the beginning with God. (RSV, NASB, NLT)
> The same was in the beginning with God. (KJV)
> He was with God in the beginning. (NIV)
> The Word, then, was with God at the beginning. (NEB)
> From the very beginning the Word was with God. (TEV)

The first verse establishes three separate facts: (1) the Word existed in the beginning, (2) the Word was with God, and (3) the Word was God. The second verse, picking up from the third statement, joins facts two and one: the Word (who was God) existed in the beginning with God. All the versions, given their minor variations, convey this. Nevertheless, it

---

[1] Bruce says this: "The last clause of John 1:1 [in the NEB] reads: 'what God was, the Word was.' Is this what the clause really means? Or have the translators perhaps been moved by an unconscious desire to give a rather different rendering from the Authorized Version? On reflection, this is probably excellent exegesis of the words literally rendered in the older versions as 'the Word was God' " (*English Bible*, 245).

seems odd that the NEB and TEV would here use "at the beginning" or "from the very beginning" when in the first verse they paraphrased this phrase. Consistency would help the reader observe John's intended redundancy.

**1:3a**

> All things were made by him (KJV)
> All things were made through him (RSV)
> All things came into being through him (NRSV)
> All things came into being by Him (NASB)
> and through him all things came to be (NEB)
> Through him all things were made (NIV)
> Through him God made all things (TEV)
> He created everything there is (NLT)

The KJV and NASB's renderings, "all things were made/came into being *by him*," are unfortunate because the English preposition *by* in this context connotes authorship. The Word, according to this passage, was not so much the author of creation (i.e., the Creator) as the agent of creation. This agency or instrumentality is expressed in Greek by the preposition *dia,* best translated into English as "through."

Three of the translations (NRSV, NASB, NEB) have a literal rendering of the Greek verb *egeneto* (came into being or came to be); such expressions are perhaps more suggestive of creation than "made."

**1:3b–4a**

> and without him was not anything made that was made. [4]In him was life (KJV, RSV)

> and apart from Him nothing came into being that has come into being. [4]In Him was life (NASB)

> without him nothing was made that has been made.
> [4]In him was life (NIV)
>
> not one thing in all creation was made without him.
> [4]The Word was the source of life (TEV)
>
> no single thing was created without him. [4]All that came to be was alive with his life (NEB)
>
> Nothing exists that he didn't make. [4]Life itself was in him (NLT)

The variation in phrasing among the translations in verses 3 and 4 is due to a textual problem. The last phrase of verse 3 in the KJV and RSV has been placed with either verse 3 or verse 4 in the different versions by means of punctuation. Rendered literally, the two possible interpretations are as follows:

> (1) and without him was not anything created. [4]That which was created in him was life
> (2) and without him was not anything created that was created. [4]In him was life

The earliest manuscripts (the Bodmer Papyri—$\mathfrak{P}^{66}$ and $\mathfrak{P}^{75}$, Codex Sinaiticus, Codex Alexandrinus, Codex Vaticanus) do not have any punctuation in these verses. $\mathfrak{P}^{75}$ was later corrected, as was Codex Sinaiticus. In $\mathfrak{P}^{75}$ a punctuation mark was placed before the phrase, as in (1); in Codex Sinaiticus after it, as in (2).

The majority of the early church fathers interpreted John 1:3-4 according to the phrasing in (1). The passage was understood to mean that all created things were "life" by virtue of being "in him" (i.e., in Christ). The statement was somehow supposed to affirm that the Word (Christ) not only created the universe, he now sustains it with his life. This is the thought behind the rendering in the NLT: "Life itself was in him." Historically, interpretation generally changed after some gnostic heretics used the passage to say that the Holy Spirit was "a created thing." All the church fathers then shifted to the phrasing in (2). Most exegesis has followed this up to the present.

Of the translations listed above, only the NEB and the NLT follow the approach of (1).

We cannot be sure which of the two interpretations John intended. Since this is poetry, it is very likely that he wrote the phrase to have both meanings.

### 1:4

> In him was life, and the life was the light of men. (KJV, RSV, NASB)
>
> In him was life, and that life was the light of men. (NIV)
>
> The Word was the source of life, and this life brought light to mankind. (TEV)
>
> All that came to be was alive with his life, and that life was the light of men. (NEB)
>
> Life itself was in him, and this life gives light to everyone. (NLT)

Having discussed the problem of phrasing, let us examine other aspects of this verse. "In him was life" is a good, literal translation; but the TEV differs. Its first edition reads, "The Word had life in himself," but the third edition has, "The Word was the source of life." The first rendering is a paraphrase of John 5:26 and conveys the thought that life was located in the Word. The revision, an improvement, suggests that the Word is the source from which people can obtain life. Although this is in accord with the total thought of John's Gospel, it perhaps goes beyond what John intended here.

The second part of this verse, rendered literally, is clear enough. Most readers will recognize that the life was the light *to* people; but the TEV and NLT remove any uncertainty.

**1:5**

> The light shines in the darkness, and the darkness has not overcome it. (RSV)
>
> And the light shineth in darkness; and the darkness comprehended it not. (KJV)
>
> And the light shines in the darkness, and the darkness did not comprehend it. (NASB)
>
> The light shines in the darkness, but the darkness has not understood it. (NIV)
>
> The light shines in the darkness, and the darkness has never put it out. (TEV)
>
> The light shines on in the dark, and the darkness has never quenched it [mastered it, 2nd ed.]. (NEB)
>
> The light shines through the darkness, and the darkness can never extinguish it. (NLT)

All the versions essentially read the same in the first clause except the NEB and the NLT. The translation "shines on" seems correctly to capture the time element of verse 5 in conjunction with the sequence of verses 1-5. Since verses 1-2 deal with the eternal preexistence of the Word, they are prior to the time of Creation. Verse 3 involves the Creation; and verse 4 indicates the time period in which the Word was incarnate among men as "the light of life." Verse 5 then suggests that the light kept on shining, even after his departure.

In this second clause, the versions vary as to the translation of the predicate because the Greek word *lambano* can mean either "lay hold of, grasp, apprehend, comprehend" or "overcome, overpower." This Greek verb is used quite often in the New Testament to indicate obtainment or apprehension/understanding (see Acts 4:13; 10:34; Rom. 9:30; 1 Cor. 9:24; Eph. 3:18; Phil. 3:12-13). However, when the New Testament elsewhere has this word in relationship to darkness, the sense required is "overtake" or "overcome" (see John 12:35; 1 Thess. 5:4). It might be that John had both meanings in mind. He could have been asserting that the light keeps on shining because the darkness did not overtake it (as in the RSV, TEV, NEB, NLT); and he could have also been decrying the fact that the darkness (i.e., unenlightened humanity) did not apprehend or comprehend this light (as in the KJV, NASB, NIV, and NLT margin, which reads, "Or *and the darkness has not understood it*"). The remainder of the prologue and even the entire Gospel underscores this sense of misunderstanding and rejection.

### 1:6–8

> There was a man sent from God, whose name was John. The same came for a witness, to bear witness of the Light, that all men through him might believe. He was not that Light, but was sent to bear witness of that Light. (KJV)

> There was a man sent from God, whose name was John. He came for testimony, to bear witness to the light, that all might believe through him. He was not the light, but came to bear witness to the light. (RSV; similarly, NASB, NIV, NRSV)

> There appeared a man named John, sent from God; he came as a witness to testify to the light, that all might

> become believers through him. He was not himself the light; he came to bear witness to the light. (NEB)
>
> God sent his messenger, a man named John, who came to tell people about the light, so that all should hear the message and believe. He himself was not the light; he came to tell about the light. (TEV)
>
> God sent John the Baptist to tell everyone about the light so that everyone might believe because of his testimony. John himself was not the light; he was only a witness to the light. (NLT)

Given their minor semantic and syntactic variations, all the versions of this passage convey essentially the same message. The most notable differences are seen in the diverse renderings of the Greek verb *marturo.* The KJV, RSV, NASB, and NIV translate it "bear witness"—a somewhat outdated and/or religious expression that might bewilder the reader unfamiliar with its biblical usage. In the NRSV the expression is "came as a witness to testify." "Testify" (NEB) is more modern and more comprehensive; "tell" (TEV, NLT), while easy to understand, fails to convey the notion of verification and substantiation.

**1:9**

> That was the true Light, which lighteth every man that cometh into the world. (KJV)
>
> The true light that enlightens every man was coming into the world. (RSV)
>
> The true light that gives light to every man was coming into the world. (NIV)
>
> There was the true light which, coming into the world, enlightens every man. (NASB)

> The real light which enlightens every man was even then coming into the world. (NEB)
>
> This was the real light—the light that comes into the world and shines on all mankind. (TEV)
>
> The one who is the true light, who gives light to everyone, was going to come into the world. (NLT)

It should be noted that many of the translations provide an alternative rendering in the margin because, according to the grammar of this sentence, the verse can be constructed in two ways: (1) "the true light that gives light to every man was coming into the world," or (2) "He was the true light that gives light to every man coming into the world." According to the Greek, the participle for "coming" can agree with either "man" or "light"; and though "man" is closer to "coming" in the sentence, the next verses suggest that John was speaking of how the light came into the world. Thus, all modern translations have selected the first rendering.

The KJV translators, however, stayed closely to the syntax of the Greek and thereby provided a translation that asserts that Christ has given light to every person who has come into this world. One way to interpret this is to understand that Christ has brought the light of the gospel for all to see—not that all have seen or have been enlightened.

### 1:10

> He was in the world, and the world was made by him, and the world knew him not (KJV)
>
> He was in the world, and the world was made through him, yet the world knew him not (RSV, and similarly NASB and NIV; the NIV uses "recognize" in place of "knew")

> He was in the world; but the world, though it owed its being to him, did not recognize him (NEB)
>
> The Word was in the world and though God made the world through him, yet the world did not recognize him (TEV)
>
> But although the world was made through him, the world didn't recognize him when he came. (NLT)

Since the understood subject of this verse is "the Word," the TEV supplies it. Most of the translations correctly indicate that the world was made through him—a repetition of verse 3 (but observe the inconsistency in the NEB and NASB between "came into being" in verse 3 and "made" in this verse). The NEB's rendering ("the world . . . owed its being to him") means that the world was indebted to the Word for its existence; but this does not, in and of itself, necessarily indicate that Creation has occurred through his agency. Thus, Creation is obscured, as well as the Word's instrumentality in it. The KJV's rendering, "the world was made by him," connotes direct authorship, with no instrumentality.

In English, "recognize" (in NEB, TEV, NIV, NLT) is more poignant than "know" (RSV, NASB), which is a general term, especially in this context. After the Word's incarnation, mankind should have recognized the one through whom they were created, but they failed to do so—as is so poignantly reflected in the NLT: "But although the world was made through him, the world didn't recognize him when he came."

**1:11**

> He came unto his own, and his own received him not. (KJV)

> He came to his own home, and his own people received him not. (RSV)
>
> He came to His own, and those who were His own did not receive Him. (NASB)
>
> He came to that which was his own, but his own did not receive him. (NIV)
>
> He entered into his own realm, and his own would not receive him. (NEB)
>
> He came to his own country, but his own people did not receive him. (TEV)
>
> Even in his own land and among his own people, he was not accepted. (NLT)

The Greek idiom *ta idia* (literally, "one's own things") can designate one's own possession or domain (see NASB's footnote), but when John uses it he seems to mean domain (see John 16:32 and 19:27). Four versions (RSV, NEB, NLT, TEV) attempt to convey this in English by the phrases "own home," "own realm," "own land," or "own country" (respectively), while the other two leave it ambiguous (although NASB has a note). In the next phrase, the idiom *hoi idioi* denotes "one's own people." Again, the KJV, RSV, NEB, and TEV make this explicit, while the NASB and NIV leave it implicit. The NLT assumes that the Greek idioms *ta idia* and *hoi idioi* both refer to "the people."

**1:12**

> But as many as received him, to them he gave power to become the sons of God, even to them that believe on his name. (KJV)
>
> But to all who received him, who believed in his name, he gave power to become children of God (RSV)

> But as many as received Him, to them He gave the right to become children of God, even to those who believe in His name. (NASB)
>
> Yet to all who received him, to those who believed in his name, he gave the right to become children of God (NIV)
>
> But to all who did receive him, to those who have yielded him their allegiance, he gave the right to become children of God (NEB)
>
> Some, however, did receive him and believed in him; so he gave them the right to become God's children. (TEV)
>
> But to all who believed him and accepted him, he gave the right to become children of God. (NLT)

The Greek word rendered "receive" in this verse conveys the dual idea of acceptance and understanding. In English, one possible meaning of receive is "to permit to enter," and another is "to accept as true," which is related to the idea of believing.[1] All of the translations except the KJV and NASB rearrange the original syntax by joining the third clause to the first in order to show the association between receiving and believing. Reception is dependent upon and concurrent with belief: to believe is to receive. And to believe in Christ, according to John, means more than to "have yielded him allegiance" (NEB)—which sounds like a pledge of loyalty. (This has been corrected in the REB: "those who put their trust in him.")

To those who believed in Christ, "he" (God or Christ?) gave them "the right" or "the privilege" to become the children of God. The Greek word underlying "right" or "privilege"

---

[1] *Merriam Webster's New International Dictionary*, s.v. "receive."

(*exousia*) usually is translated "authority" in the New Testament; but in this context "right" is more natural. To translate it "power," as in the RSV, would require the Greek word to have been *dunamis,* a word that John never uses.

Modern versions were not trying to be gender inclusive when they used "children" instead of the KJV's "sons." Rather, the Greek word here is *tekna,* which means "children"—specifically, "born ones." There is an entirely different Greek word for "sons"—*huioi.*

**1:13**

> Which were born, not of blood, nor of the will of the flesh, nor of the will of man, but of God. (KJV; similarly RSV and NASB, which replace "which" with "who" and use different punctuation)
>
> children born not of natural descent, nor of human decision or a husband's will, but born of God. (NIV)
>
> not born of any human stock, or by the fleshly ["physical" in REB] desire of a human father, but the offspring of God himself. (NEB)
>
> They did not become God's children by natural means, that is, by being born as the children of a human father; God himself was their Father. (TEV)
>
> They are reborn! This is not a physical birth resulting from human passion or plan—this rebirth comes from God. (NLT)

In this verse John wanted to make it emphatically clear that becoming a child of God necessitates a divinely-initiated birth. Using four prepositional phrases, each beginning with the Greek preposition *ek* (which denotes source), John three times states what the origin of this birth is not and once states what the origin is. There is substantial variation among the versions as to how to translate these four prepositional phrases. The first prepositional phrase (literally, "not from bloods") comes from a Hebrew idiom that indicates physical bloodlines. Most commentators take this to mean natural descent, perhaps with reference to Abraham's lineage; thus, one is not a child of God because his genealogy traces to Abraham (this theme reappears later, John 8:31-47). The KJV, RSV, and NASB render this phrase almost literally, while others translate it idiomatically. The literal rendering, to modern readers, would be incomprehensible. The idiomatic renderings aid understanding.

The second phrase (literally, "not from the will [or desire] of the flesh") has been interpreted by some as implying sexual desire. Others, understanding the Greek word for "flesh" to designate that which is human, think this phrase signifies human volition. Again, the KJV, RSV, and NASB avoid making an exegetical commitment by translating literally. The NEB adopts the meaning of sexual desire; the NIV, on the other hand, takes the phrase to suggest human volition. Because the TEV translators understood this phrase as equivalent to the following phrase, "the one qualifying the other,"[1] the TEV condenses the two phrases into one.

The third phrase (literally, "nor from the will of a husband") is understood by most commentators to indicate the generative power of an adult male, a husband. The NIV, NEB, and TEV use the phrase "husband's will" or "human father" to convey this. The NLT has no reference to a husband.

The fourth prepositional phrase (literally, "from God") declares the divine origin of this birth. This is clear enough in the RSV, NASB, and NIV. The paraphrases in the NEB and

---

[1] Newman and Nida, *Translator's Handbook*, 20.

TEV are not necessary. The NEB's translation was changed in the REB to "of God." And Newman and Nida, who normally defend the TEV, suggest that a better thought-for-thought translation would be "God himself caused them to be his children."[1] Influenced by John 3, the NLT uses "rebirth" (and "reborn") in this verse, when the text speaks only of birth.

**1:14**

> And the Word was made flesh, and dwelt among us, (and we beheld his glory, the glory as of the only begotten of the Father,) full of grace and truth. (KJV)
>
> And the Word became flesh and dwelt ["lived" in the NRSV] among us, full of grace and truth; we have beheld his glory, glory as of the only Son from the Father. (RSV)
>
> And the Word became flesh, and dwelt among us, and we beheld His glory, glory as of the only begotten from the Father, full of grace and truth. (NASB)
>
> The Word became flesh and lived for a while [1st ed.; "made his dwelling," 2nd ed.] among us. We have seen his glory, the glory of the One and Only, who came from the Father, full of grace and truth. (NIV)
>
> So the Word became flesh; he came to dwell among us, and we saw his glory, such glory as befits the Father's only Son, full of grace and truth. (NEB)
>
> The Word became a human being and, full of grace and truth, lived among us. We saw his glory, the glory which he received as the Father's only Son. (TEV)
>
> So the Word became human and lived here on earth among us. He was full of unfailing love and faithfulness.

---

[1] Ibid.

> And we have seen his glory, the glory of the only Son of the Father. (NLT)

All the versions, with the exception of the TEB and NLT, read, "The Word became flesh." As this is a unique assertion of the Son of God's incarnation, it must be translated accurately. Fortunately, all the versions advance beyond the KJV's rendering, "was made," for this expression does not correctly translate the meaning of the Greek verb *egeneto,* which denotes the beginning of a new existence. The Word, who was God, became that which he had never been before—a man. When John says, "The Word became flesh," he must mean "The Word became a human being" (as in the TEV).[1] But this could imply that the Word, a divine person, assumed the personality of another, whereas the orthodox understanding of the incarnation is that the Word took on human nature (signified by the word "flesh"). Thus, it is better to say it as in the NLT: "the Word became human."

It should be noted that John probably avoided the Greek word *anthropos* (man) and instead used *sarx* (flesh) because he was battling against the *Docetic heresy*. The Docetists, a gnostic sect, believed that flesh was evil; therefore, they taught that the Son of God did not possess real flesh but only the guise of it. John wanted to make it unquestionably clear that the Word took on actual flesh. This historical background is critical for the proper interpretation and translation of this passage. Therefore, though it is linguistically appropriate to equate "flesh" with "man" or "human being," it is theologically inaccurate.

In the second clause of verse 14 (literally, "and tabernacled [or "pitched his tent"] in our midst"), all the translators chose

---

[1] Westcott defined flesh as follows: "Flesh expresses here human nature as a whole regarded under its aspect of its present corporal embodiment, including of necessity the 'soul' (12:27) and the spirit (11:33; 13:21) as belonging to the totality of man" (*Gospel According to St. John*, 11).

not to translate the Greek verb *eskenosen* literally because "tabernacled" sounds foreign to the English ear. Among the five translations, three chose "dwelt" (RSV, NASB, NEB) and two selected "lived" (TEV, so also NRSV) or "lived for a while" (NIV, 1st ed.). The NLT went with "lived here on earth." Although these adaptations may accommodate the English reader, they eclipse a word that was pregnant with meaning to the original readers. As a case in point, here is precisely where dynamic equivalence fails. While the average modern reader would probably be perplexed if he read "tabernacled," the ancient reader of this Gospel, when hearing *eskenosen,* would associate it with the Old Testament tabernacle. In the Old Testament account, God dwelt among his people, Israel, by pitching his tabernacle (his tent) among them. His presence and Shekinah glory filled that tabernacle; and wherever that tabernacle went in the journeys of Israel, God would also go (see Exod. 40). With this image in view, the writer, John, must have intended his readers to see the connection with the Old Testament tabernacle. If "tabernacled" (or "pitched his tent") is too peculiar to appear in the text of a translation, it should at least appear as a marginal reading accompanied by some explanation. And, finally, it should be pointed out that "made his dwelling" in the second edition of the NIV is much better than "lived for a while" (1st ed.), which captures only the transitory aspect of tabernacling while neglecting the act of dwelling.[1]

Before examining the next phrase ("we beheld his glory") and

[1] F. F. Bruce criticized the NIV for failing to capture the meaning of *eskenosen:* "In verse 14 the verb *eskenosen,* instead of being treated as an ingressive aorist, is rendered as though it were an imperfect: 'The Word lived for a while among us.'" The phrase 'for a while' is probably intended to bring out the idea of a temporary encampment in the verb *skenoo.* But why not retain the ingressive force by some such rendering as: "took up his temporary abode among us"? If a rendering of this verb in the present context, without becoming clumsy, could convey something of the shekinah idea also, that would be a further improvement" (*CHRISTIANITY TODAY,* Sept. 28, 1973, 26). The second edition of the NIV has a correction: "The Word became flesh and made his dwelling among us."

that which follows, we must note that among the versions there has been some rearrangement of the word order in the last part of verse 14. This is due to different interpretations of the grammatical identification of the Greek word *pleres* ("full"). As this word is often grammatically unmarked, it could agree with the Greek words for "only Son" or "his glory" or "Word." Since its connection with "the Word" is more natural and suitable to the context (see 1:16), the RSV repositions the clause "full of grace and truth" to follow immediately its logical antecedent, "the Word." This rearrangement or word order, however, separates the compounded idea of tabernacling and beholding his glory—which is clearly evident in the Greek text. The NEB handles it better, by keeping the last clause in its proper position and then clarifying its antecedent: "the Father's only Son, full of grace and truth." The TEV aligns "full of grace and truth" with "his glory." Two versions (NASB and NIV) retain the same syntax as in the Greek and, unfortunately, give the impression that "full of grace and truth" modifies "Father."

Most of the versions render the Greek word *charis* as "grace." The NLT, however, employs the expression "unfailing love" because the translators thought that John was attempting to convey the Hebrew notion of *hesed* with the Greek word *charis*. Here and in 1:17 *aletheia* uniformly becomes "truth." Yet, as Barclay Newman intimates, readers should not be surprised to see new versions changing "truth" to "reality."[1] In John's special terminology, *aletheia* does not, in all instances, simply mean "truth" (as versus falsehood) or "veracity." It more often signifies "divine reality revealed."[2]

---

[1] Newman and Nida, *Translator's Handbook*, 653-655.

[2] Bultmann wrote, "In John *aletheia* denotes 'divine reality' with reference to the fact (1) that this is different from the reality in which man first finds himself, and by which he is controlled, and (2) that it discloses itself and is thus revelation" (*Theological Dictionary of the New Testament*, vol. 1 [ed. Gerhard Kittel; trans. G. Bromiley], 245).

The last segment of this verse to be examined is, "We have beheld his glory, glory as of the only Son from the Father" (RSV). Beginning with verse 14, John introduces a testimony on behalf of the eyewitnesses of Jesus (see also 1 John 1:1-3). He declares, "We have beheld his glory." The Greek verb he uses (*etheasametha*) means more than "to see"; it means "to view, to gaze upon" (an English derivative is "theater"). Then John characterizes the glory that was seen as being special in that it belonged to one who possessed a unique relationship with the Father; that is, it was the glory of an only Son.

The Greek word underlying "only Son" is *monogenous*, which is derived from *monos* (only) and *genos* (kind, offspring). This word does convey the idea of birth but probably not as much as it emphasizes the notion of uniqueness. Therefore, the rendering "only begotten" (as in the KJV) can be misleading, for inherent in this term is the implication of generation—and much debate was incited in the early days of the church over how the Son was generated from the Father. It is better that the idea of generation be avoided in translation, as is done in the second edition of the NIV ("the One and Only") and in the NLT ("the only Son of the Father").

The rendering "only begotten" probably originated from Jerome's Latin translation when Jerome changed *unicus* (unique) to *unigenitus* (only begotten). Prior to Jerome's translation, the old Latin Codex Vercellensis (A.D. 365) had translated *monogenous* as *unicus*. The rendering "only begotten" was carried over to the KJV, then to the ERV and ASV, and on to several twentieth century versions, including the NASB. Fortunately, the phrase has been adjusted in Weymouth, Moffatt, Goodspeed, Williams, and other more recent versions (RSV, NIV, NEB, TEV, NLT).

This "one and only Son," according to the original, came from the Father. The NIV makes this explicit, while NEB and TEV say the glory came from the Father. But the Greek text does not indicate that the glory came from the Father to the Son (as in the NEB, TEV). Having just declared the incarnation of the Word, John is here viewing the Son as having come from the Father.

**1:15**

> John bare witness of him, and cried, saying, This was he of whom I spake, He that cometh after me is preferred before me: for he was before me. (KJV)
>
> (John bore witness to him, and cried, "This was he of whom I said, 'He who comes after me ranks before me, for he was before me.'") (RSV)
>
> John bore witness of Him, and cried out, saying, "This was He of whom I said, 'He who comes after me has a higher rank than I, for He existed before me.'" (NASB)
>
> John testifies concerning him. He cries out, saying, "This was he of whom I said, 'He who comes after me has surpassed me because he was before me.'" (NIV)
>
> Here is John's testimony to him: he cried aloud, "This is the man I meant when I said, 'He comes after me, but takes rank before me'; for before I was born, he already was." (NEB)
>
> John spoke about him. He cried out, "This is the one I was talking about when I said, 'He comes after me, but he is greater than I am, because he existed before I was born.'" (TEV)
>
> John pointed him out to the people. He shouted to the crowds, "This is the one I was talking about when I said, 'Someone is coming who is far greater than I am, for he existed long before I did.'" (NLT)

Following his own personal testimony, John (the evangelist) quotes the witness that John (the Baptist) made on the day he baptized Jesus (see 1:30). On one hand, this verse appears to interrupt the continuity between verses 14 and 16; as such, it is parenthetical in the RSV and a separate paragraph in the TEV and NIV. But, on the other hand, verse 15 seems to substantiate sequentially the testimony of 1:1-14, inasmuch as the Baptist's declaration refers to both the Word's eternal preexistence and incarnation, except in reverse order. At any rate, the message, as transmitted in all the versions, is essentially uniform in accuracy. They all relate that, while the incarnate Word came after John chronologically, he surpassed John (in rank) because he existed before him.

### 1:16

> And of his fulness have all we received, and grace for grace. (KJV)
>
> And from his fulness have we all received, grace upon grace. (RSV)
>
> For of His fulness we have all received, and grace upon grace. (NASB)
>
> From the fullness of his grace we have all received one blessing after another. (NIV)
>
> Out of his full store we have all received grace upon grace; (NEB)
>
> Out of the fullness of his grace he has blessed us all, giving us one blessing after another. (TEV)
>
> We have all benefited from the rich blessings he brought to us—one gracious blessing after another. (NLT)

The connection between 1:14 and 1:16 is obvious: 1:14 concludes with "full of grace and truth," and 1:16 begins with "because out of his fullness we all received." The Greek word translated "fullness" is *pleroma.* To Greek-speaking Christian readers, *pleroma* was a special term with particular significance. New Testament writers used it to describe the all-inclusive, all-sufficient Christ (see Col. 2:9). The NEB's rendering, "his full store," captures this idea. The NIV and TEV, based on a different interpretation, specify that the fullness is "the fullness of his grace." They made the addition "of his grace" in order to compensate for replacing the words "grace upon grace" with "one blessing after another" in the last part of this verse. The NLT makes this "one gracious blessing after another." From my perspective, these are unfortunate renderings because they obscure the meaning of "grace upon grace." This phrase does not mean that Christ gives us one blessing after another (in the sense that we keep getting good things); the expression means that there is no end to the supply of grace that comes from Christ's fullness. The phrase suggests constant replacement and replenishment: "continual accessions of grace, new grace coming upon and superseding the former."[1]

### 1:17

> For the law was given by Moses, but grace and truth came by Jesus Christ. (KJV)
>
> For the law was given through Moses; grace and truth came through Jesus Christ. (RSV, NIV)
>
> For the Law was given through Moses; grace and truth were realized through Jesus Christ. (NASB)

---

[1] Alford, *Greek Testament.*

> for while the Law was given through Moses, grace and truth came through Jesus Christ. (NEB)
>
> God gave the Law through Moses, but grace and truth came through Jesus Christ. (TEV)
>
> For the law was given through Moses; God's unfailing love and faithfulness came through Jesus Christ. (NLT)

In this verse, John seems to be distinguishing the New Testament dispensation from that of the Old Testament. The NEB adds "while," and the TEV adds "but," to make sure the reader notices the contrast. A few ancient scribes ($\mathfrak{P}^{66}$, $W^s$) and ancient translators (Old Latin and Coptic Bohairic) also added a contrastive *de.* While the Old Testament law was something "given" by God through the agent, Moses, grace and truth "came" or "were realized" through Jesus Christ. Since the Greek word *egeneto* can mean "came" (see 1:6), "came into being" (see 1:3, 10), or "became" (see 1:14), translators must decide which meaning is called for in each given context. In this verse, "came" was selected for most of the translations and "were realized" for one—namely, the NASB.

### 1:18

> No man hath seen God at any time; the only begotten Son, which is in the bosom of the Father, he hath declared him. (KJV)
>
> No one has ever seen God; the only Son, who is in the bosom of the Father, he has made him known. (RSV)
>
> No one has ever seen God; but God's only Son, he who is nearest to the Father's heart, he has made him known. (NEB)

> No man has seen God at any time; the only begotten God, who is in the bosom of the Father, He has explained Him. (NASB)
>
> No one has ever seen God, but God the One and Only, who is at the Father's side, has made him known. (NIV)
>
> No one has ever seen God. The only Son, who is the same as God and is at the Father's side, he has made him known. (TEV)
>
> No one has ever seen God. But his only Son, who is himself God, is near to the Father's heart; he has told us about him. (NLT)

The difference between the versions that read "only begotten Son" or "only Son" as opposed to the reading "the only begotten God" comes from a significant variance among the Greek New Testament manuscripts. The translation in the KJV, RSV, and NEB is based upon the reading *monogenes huios,* which has been translated as "only begotten Son" or "one and only Son"; the other translations are based upon *monogenes theos,* which has been translated as "only begotten God" (NASB) or "God the One and Only" (NIV). The latter reading has the support of the earliest manuscripts (the Bodmer Papyri—$\mathfrak{P}^{66}$ and $\mathfrak{P}^{75}$, Codex Sinaiticus, Codex Vaticanus, Codex Ephraemi Rescriptus). It is later manuscripts (Codex Alexandrinus, the Freer Gospel, and many later witnesses) that read, "the only begotten Son." The first reading is clearly the preferred reading because it is the most difficult of the two and best explains the origin of the variation. Scribes would not be inclined to change a common wording ("only begotten Son") to an uncommon wording ("only begotten God"—which is a literal translation). The reading in all the earliest manuscripts indicates that Jesus is here called "God," as well as "the one and only." Unfortunately, many translators feel compelled to add the word "Son" after "one and only," thereby creating, in effect, a conflated reading, as in the TEV: "the only Son, who is the same as God" (so also NLT).

The best rendering should convey that the Word is the one and only God. This perfectly corresponds to the first verse of the prologue, where the Word is called "God" and is shown as the Son living in intimate fellowship with the Father—literally, "in the bosom of the Father."

Among the translations, three translate this next phrase nearly word for word (KJV, RSV, NASB), and four paraphrase it. For others, the rendering "at the Father's side" (NIV, TEV) is far less picturesque than the translation "nearest to the Father's heart" (NEB) and "close the Father's heart" (NRSV; similarly NLT).

In the last clause of this verse is a Greek word, *exegesato,* that derives from the verb that means "to lead one through an explanation, to narrate." The English word *exegesis* is derived from this word. An exegesis in biblical studies means a detailed explanation of a Bible passage—literally "a leading through" a portion of Scripture. The Word is the one who leads people through a detailed explanation of God. To render the Greek verb "made him known" is too general and not very impressive. And the reader may not see the intended connection with "the Word" in 1:1. Indeed, 1:18 is a mirror of 1:1, for both speak of the Son's intimate relationship with the Father, of his being God, and of his being the expression—the explanation—of God. The best translation of them all, then, is the one in the NASB because it explicitly says, "He has explained Him."

The Son of God, called "the Word," came among people to explain the invisible God. Had he not come, God would have remained unknown by us. But the Word, who is himself God and knows God the Father, came to earth as a man among human beings to provide us with a full, living explanation of divinity.

## CONCLUSION

Having worked our way through this fascinating portion of the Bible, we could go on to do comparative studies of other portions. I would recommend that the serious reader use an interlinear Hebrew text and Greek text. The most up-to-date Hebrew-English interlinear is the *NIV Interlinear Hebrew-English Old Testament* (translator, John Kohlenberger), and the most up-to-date Greek-English interlinear is *The New Greek-English Interlinear New Testament* (translators, Robert Brown and Philip Comfort; ed. J. D. Douglas). Using an interlinear with lexicons and other modern translations, a serious Bible reader can do a very thorough and enlightening study of any portion of the Bible.

Such a study will also show you, firsthand, the differences in translation philosophy and methodology. Each of the translations that was discussed in the previous chapters was based on a particular philosophy of translation. For example, the Revised Standard Version and the *New American Standard Bible,* which share a common purpose (i.e., to revise and revive the American Standard Version), are more literal than most versions. The translators often adhered to a word-for-word methodology instead of a thought-for-thought. The New Revised Standard Version is a little more "free"—in fact, the guiding concept for this revision was "as literal as possible, as free as necessary." The New International Version is even more free than the New Revised Standard Version because the translators employed a thought-for-thought approach to translation. And yet the New International Version is not as free as Today's English Version and the New Living Translation because these versions were created to be as contemporary as possible. Of course, these are generalized observations; such exact distinctions between the translations cannot always be so clearly delineated. At times, the translations will cross over these boundaries. Nonetheless, it is possible to broadly classify several of the translations as follows:

**Classification of English Translations**

**Strictly literal**
*New American Standard Bible*

**Literal**
King James Version
American Standard Version
New King James Version
Revised Standard Version
*New American Bible*

**Literal with freedom to be idiomatic**
New Revised Standard Version

**Thought-for-thought**
New International Version
*New Jerusalem Bible*
*Revised English Bible*

**Functionally equivalent (modern speech)**
Today's English Version
New Living Translation
Contemporary English Version

**Paraphrastic**
*The Living Bible*
*The Message*

## WHICH VERSIONS SHOULD YOU USE?

A modern English reader (or student) of the Bible would do well to use five or six translations—one in each category listed above. For example, I use the American Standard Version, *New American Standard Bible,* and the New Revised Standard Version for detailed word studies; and the New International Version, the *New Jerusalem Bible,* and the New Living Translation for general study and reading pleasure. Other readers would make different selections from the various categories, depending on their needs and preferences. Those who use one translation exclusively would be enriched if they used a few others. This is especially true for those who are King James Version enthusiasts. They would discover that their Bible reading would be infused with fresh life and new light if they read a modern version as well.

In selecting a translation of the Bible, the reader should always make sure that the translation was based on the latest, most authoritative texts. Preferably, the Old Testament should have basically followed *Biblia Hebraica Stuttgartensia;* and the New Testament, the United Bible Societies' third or fourth edition of the *Greek New Testament* (the same text is published as the Nestle-Aland text; the twenty-sixth ($NA^{26}$) and twenty-seventh ($NA^{27}$) editions correspond to the third and fourth editions of the United Bible Societies' text). Many of the modern versions reflect these standard texts; whereas translations such as the King James Version and even the New King James are based on an inferior Greek text.

Finally, it must always be remembered that translations are nothing more than translations—they are not the same as the Bible in the original languages. Not one translation has been "inspired" by God in the same way the original text was. For those who want to read the Bible as it is in the original, inspired languages, they should learn Hebrew, Aramaic, and Greek. Those who do not learn these languages have to depend on translations.

Notice that I used the plural, "translations," not the singular, because I believe it is imperative for modern English readers to use several of the available English versions. By using different translations the reader can acquire a fuller understanding of the meaning of the original text.

CHAPTER EIGHT

# Extra Verses in the New Testament

The primary difference between the Textus Receptus (TR) and modern critical editions is that the TR (followed by the KJV/NKJV tradition) includes several passages that are considered spurious by most contemporary scholars. These differences are reflected in what is usually printed in modern translations. Thus, the purpose of this chapter is to examine all the added verses in the New Testament in an effort to determine how they got there and how we, as modern Christians, should respond to them. I think we are obligated to evaluate whether or not these additional verses are God-inspired and therefore profitable for teaching and instruction in the Christian church (see 2 Tim. 3:15-16).

In the following sections, I list the manuscripts that support a longer or shorter text, followed by a list of English versions that use each reading, and a discussion. A key to the manuscript symbols is given in Appendix B, "New Testament Manuscripts" (page 279). The symbol "mg" (margin) indicates that the English version has noted the other reading in a marginal note. In modern versions, this is usually done out of deference to the KJV tradition.

## MATTHEW 5:44

***What Were Jesus' Words in the Sermon on the Mount?***
Some manuscripts have a short version:

> pray for those who persecute you
> ℵ *B* $f^1$ *it*$^k$ *syr*$^{c,s}$ *cop*
> *NKJVmg RSV NRSV NASB NIV NEB NLT*

Other manuscripts have a longer version (additional words in italics):

> *bless those who curse you, do good to those who hate you,* pray for those who *despitefully use you and* persecute you
> *D L W* $f^{13}$ 𝔐—*TR*
> *KJV NKJV NIVmg NEBmg*

The extra words are not found in the two oldest manuscripts (ℵ B) and many other early translations. The additions in the variant reading came from Luke's account of Jesus' sermon (Luke 6:27-28). The TR incorporates most of these harmonizations, which were then translated into the KJV and NKJV.

## MATTHEW 6:13

***How Does the Lord's Prayer End?***
Some manuscripts end the Lord's Prayer in this fashion:

> but rescue us from evil.
> ℵ *B D Z 0170* $f^1$
> *RSV NRSV NIV NEB NLT*

Several manuscripts have additional endings. The fifth is the most common:

1. but rescue us from evil. *Amen.*
   *one minuscule (17) and one Vulgate manuscript*

2. but rescue us from evil, *because yours is the power and the glory forever. Amen.*
   *cop$^{sa, fay}$; Didache (which omits "Amen")*

3. but rescue us from evil, *because yours is the kingdom and the glory forever. Amen.*
   *syr$^{c}$*

4. but rescue us from evil, *because yours is the kingdom and the power and the glory forever.*
   *it$^{k}$, syr$^{p}$*

5. but rescue us from evil, *because yours is the kingdom and the power and the glory forever. Amen.*
   *L W 0233 f$^{13}$ 33 syr 𝔐—TR*
   *KJV NKJV NASB*

6. but rescue us from evil, *because yours is the kingdom of the Father and the Son and the Holy Spirit. Amen.*
   *one minuscule (1253), Chrysostom*

There are other minor variations than those listed above (see NA$^{27}$ and UBS$^{4}$), but these represent the six basic variations of the doxology that were added to the Lord's Prayer. The testimony of the earliest **extant witnesses** reveals that the prayer must have concluded with a petition for deliverance from evil. The variety among the variants speaks against the genuineness of any of the additions. What is presented above shows the continual expansion of the addition—from the simple "Amen" in variant 2 to the elaborate Trinitarian doxology in variant 6.

According to Westcott and Hort, this "doxology originated in liturgical use in Syria, and was thence adopted into the Greek and Syriac texts of the N.T."[1] The fifth variant became the most popular and was included in the TR and in the KJV. As a result, many Bible readers throughout the ages have become attached to it, and many churchgoers and prayerful Christians recite it as the conclusion to the Lord's Prayer. It is not easy to drop this doxology because such a profound prayer invites a glorious, uplifting conclusion—especially in oral reading and public recitation (although American Catholic Churches, following the NAB, have done so). Sensing this lack (or gap) in the text prompted many ancient scribes to add a doxology for the sake of reading it orally in the church. In the first stage of additions, it appears that scribes used "power and glory" (probably adapted from verses such as 1 Chron. 29:11; 1 Pet. 4:11; Jude 25). This is the reading in the Didache (the "Teaching of the Twelve"), which may account for its Syriac origin (inasmuch as most scholars think the Didache originated in Syria). In the next stage, "kingdom" was appropriated, and "Amen" was appended.

## MATTHEW 16:1-4

### *Did Jesus Speak of Weather Signs?*

In certain manuscripts, there is a full version of Matthew 16:1-4, as follows:

> One day the Pharisees and Sadducees came to test Jesus' claims by asking him to show them a miraculous sign from heaven. [2]He replied, *"You know the saying, 'Red sky at night means fair weather tomorrow, [3]red*

[1] Westcott and Hort, *Introduction*, 9.

> *sky in the morning means foul weather all day.' You are good at reading the weather signs in the sky, but you can't read the obvious signs of the times!* [4]Only an evil, faithless generation would ask for a miraculous sign, but the only sign I will give them is the sign of the prophet Jonah." Then Jesus left them and went away.
> *C D L W f[1] 𝔐 it syr[h,p] Eusebius (and several late MSS add "hypocrites")—TR*
> *KJV NKJV RSV NASB NIV NRSV NLT*

Other manuscripts testify to a shorter version, which does not include any mention of weather signs. This version reads as follows:

> One day the Pharisees and Sadducees came to test Jesus' claims by asking him to show them a miraculous sign from heaven. [2]He replied, "[4]Only an evil, faithless generation would ask for a miraculous sign, but the only sign I will give them is the sign of the prophet Jonah." Then Jesus left them and went away.
> *א B X f[13] syr[c,s] cop[sa, bo] Origen Jerome*
> *NEB*

This portion, bracketed in NA[27] and UBS[4], was probably not written by Matthew, but inserted later by a scribe who either borrowed from Luke 12:54-56 as a metaphor for "the signs of the times" or inserted these words from an oral or other written tradition to provide an actual example of what it meant for the ancients to interpret the appearance of the sky.[1]

Had the words been original, there is no reason why the scribes of א (Codex Sinaiticus), B (Codex Vaticanus), *et al.* would have deleted the words on purpose, and there is no way

---

[1] Ibid., 13.

to explain the omission as a transcriptional accident. According to Jerome, the words were absent in most manuscripts known to him, even though he included them in the Vulgate.

Some scholars, such as Scrivener, have argued that the copyists of א and B (both presumed to be of Egypt) omitted these verses because the Egyptian red sky in the morning does not signify the advent of rain.[1] For most of Egypt this may be true, but not for Alexandria, which sits on the Mediterranean Sea. In Alexandria, a red sky in the morning does signify the advent of rain. Since א and B were very likely produced in Alexandria, the scribes would not have objected to this language. Furthermore, the manuscripts that exclude the words are not all Egyptian—indeed Jerome must have had several "Western" manuscripts before him that did not have the words. Finally, it must be asked, even if the manuscripts that excluded the words were all Egyptian, wouldn't the Egyptian copyists have respected the cultural setting of the Gospel text? For example, the agricultural life of Egypt (being dependent on the Nile River) was quite different than that of Israel (being dependent on rain). Another New Testament passage, James 5:7, that speaks of an early rain and a later rain (a phenomenon in Palestine, not Egypt) was not changed in Egyptian manuscripts. Therefore, we cannot blame cultural expectations for a supposed deletion of the expression.

## MATTHEW 17:21

### *Did Jesus Command Prayer and Fasting?*

Several manuscripts do not include verse 21. Let us look at the textual evidence:

---

[1] Scrivener, *Plain Introduction*, 2.326-327.

exclude verse 21
*ℵ* B 33 it^e syr^{c,s} cop^{sa,bo}*
*RSV NRSV NIV NEB NLT*

Other manuscripts include the verse, which reads:

This kind does not come out except by prayer and fasting.
*ℵ^2 C D L W f^{1,13} 𝔐—TR*
*KJV NKJV NASB*

This verse was assimilated from Mark 9:29 in its long form, which has the additional words "and fasting." In fact, the same manuscripts that have the long form in Mark 9:29 (C D L W f^{1,13} 𝔐) have the additional verse here. Thus, some scribe(s) took the full verse of Mark 9:29 as presented in his manuscript and inserted it here; most other later manuscripts maintained this insertion in the transmission of the text.

## MATTHEW 18:11

***Did Matthew Write, "The Son of Man came to save the lost"?***

The textual evidence is as follows:

exclude verse 11
*ℵ B L* f^{1,13} 33 it^e syr^s cop^{sa} Origen*
*RSV NRSV NIV NEB NLT*

Other manuscripts add the verse, in one of two forms:

1. For the Son of Man came to save the lost.
*D L^c W 078^{vid} 𝔐 syr^{c,p}—TR*
*KJV NKJV NASB RSVmg NRSVmg NIVmg NEBmg NLTmg*

2. For the Son of Man came *to seek and* to save the lost.
*L$^{mg}$ 892$^{c}$ it$^{c}$ syr$^{h}$*
*no English translations*

The absence of this verse in several important and diverse witnesses attests that it was not part of the original text of Matthew. It was borrowed from Luke 19:10, a passage not at all parallel to this one. Most likely the addition first appeared in the shorter form (variant 1), and then the longer (variant 2), which concurs exactly with Luke 19:10. The manuscript L demonstrates all three phases: L* (without the verse), L$^{c}$ (with the shorter form of the addition), and L$^{mg}$ (with the longer form).

## MATTHEW 20:16

***Did Jesus Say, "For many are called, but few are chosen"?*** The textual evidence is as follows:

exclude this statement
*א B L Z 085 cop$^{sa}$*
*RSV NRSV NASB NIV NEB NLT*

For many are called, but few are chosen.
*C D W f$^{1,13}$ 𝔐 it syr—TR*
*KJV NKJV*

Some scholars have argued that this sentence was accidentally dropped from the text due to **homoioteleuton** ("similar endings")—the first sentence ends with *eskatoi* (last ones) and the second with *eklektoi* (chosen ones). However, it is far more likely that scribes added it from Matthew 22:14. But whereas the statement perfectly suits the conclusion to the parable of the wedding feast in Matthew 22:1-14 (where several are invited but only a few attend), it is an odd addendum to a parable in which all were called *and* chosen to work in the vineyard.

## MATTHEW 20:22-23

***Did Jesus Tell James and John That They Had To Be Baptized with His Baptism?***

Several manuscripts have the following reading:

> "Are you able to drink the cup which I am about to drink?" They say to him, "We are able." He says to them, "Indeed you will drink my cup."
> *ℵ B D L Z 085 $f^{1,13}$ it $syr^{c,s}$ $cop^{sa}$*
> *RSV NRSV NASB NIV NEB NLT*

Other manuscripts have a longer reading:

> "Are you able to drink the cup which I am about to drink *or be baptized with the baptism that I will be baptized with?*" They say to him, "We are able." He says to them, "Indeed you will drink my cup *and be baptized with the baptism that I will be baptized with.*"
> *C W 0197 𝔐 $syr^{h}$ $cop^{bo}$—TR*
> *KJV NKJV*

The variant reading is a scribal expansion borrowed verbatim from Mark 10:38-39. The manuscripts C and W are notorious for scribal harmonization of the Synoptic Gospels; the majority of manuscripts (𝔐) followed suit. So, to answer the question asked above—yes, Jesus told James and John that they had to experience his same baptism (which, in this context, refers to suffering)—but this is the wording in Mark, not Matthew.

## MATTHEW 23:14

***Did Jesus Condemn the Scribes and Pharisees for Making Long Prayers and Devouring Widows' Houses?***
Let's look at the textual evidence:

exclude verse 14
*א B D L Z Θ $f^1$ 33 $it^{a,e}$ $syr^s$ $cop^{sa}$*
*RSV NRSV NIV NEB NLT*

include verse 14
Woe to you, scribes and Pharisees, hypocrites, because you devour widows' houses and for a pretense make long prayers; therefore, you will receive the greater judgment.
*before verse 13:*
*W 0104 0107 0133 0138 𝔐 $it^f$ $syr^{h,p}$—TR*
*after verse 13:*
*$f^{13}$ it $syr^c$*
*KJV NKJV NASB*

This verse, not present in the earliest manuscripts, was taken from Mark 12:40 or Luke 20:47 and inserted in later manuscripts either before or after Matthew 23:13. This kind of gospel harmonization became prevalent after the fourth century. It is noteworthy that the KJV did not follow the TR in placing the verse before verse 13.

## MATTHEW 27:35

***Did Matthew Cite the Old Testament Scriptures as Being Fulfilled in the Casting of the Lots?***
Here is the textual evidence:

> And having crucified him, they divided his garments [by] casting lots.
> *א A B D L W 33*
> *RSV NRSV NASB NIV NEB NLT*

A longer reading is as follows:

> And having crucified him, they divided his garments [by] casting lots, *that it might be fulfilled what was spoken through the prophet, "they parted my garments among them, and for my vesture they cast lots."*
> Δ Θ *0250 f*[1,13] *1424 it—TR*
> *KJV NKJV*

Because of the excellent support for the shorter text, the long addition must have come from John 19:24 coupled with a typical Matthean introduction to a prophetic citation (see Matt. 4:14). It was natural for scribes to make this addition because Matthew had a penchant for showing how various events in Jesus' life and ministry fulfilled the Old Testament Scriptures (in this case, Psalm 22, the OT passage most quoted in the NT concerning the crucifixion). Some of the same scribes (Θ 0250 f[1,13]) also made this addition in Mark 15:27.

## MARK 7:16

### *Did Mark Write This Verse?*

Let us look at the evidence in the manuscripts:

> exclude verse 16
> *א B L 0274 28*
> *RSV NRSV NIV NEB NLT*

add verse 16
If anyone has ears to hear, let him hear.
*A D W $f^{1,13}$ 𝔐—TR*
*KJV NKJV NASB*

This verse was added by scribes, borrowing it directly from 4:23 (see also 4:9) to provide a conclusion to an otherwise very short pericope, 7:14-15. This addition was included in the TR and made popular by the KJV.

## MARK 9:43-48

***How Many Times Did Mark Write, "Where the Worm Does Not Die and the Fire Is Never Extinguished"?***

Several manuscripts have this statement appearing only once, in Mark 9:48:

include statement once in Mark 9:48
*א B C L W 0274 $f^1$ 28 565 $it^k$ $syr^s$ cop*
*RSV NRSV NIV NEB NLT*

Other manuscripts have it two more times, as extra verses, 44 and 46 (which are identical to 9:48):

add statement in Mark 9:44 & 46
*A D $f^{13}$ 𝔐—TR KJV NKJV NASB*

Although it could be argued that these verses were omitted by scribes who considered the repetition to be unnecessary, such an omission could hardly occur in manuscripts of such vast diversity as those that witness to the absense of these verses. Contrarily, verses 44 and 46 were probably added as a sort of prophetic refrain to enhance oral reading. Indeed, many textual variants entered the textual stream as the result of scribes "enhancing" the text for oral reading in the church.

## MARK 11:26

***Did Mark Write This Verse?***

Let us examine the textual evidence:

exclude verse 26
*א B L W 565 700 syr*$^{s}$
*RSV NRSV NIV NEB NLT*

include verse 26
But if you do not forgive, neither will your Father in heaven forgive your trespasses.
*A (C D) (f*$^{1,13}$*) 𝔐—TR*
*KJV NKJV NASB*

The addition of verse 26 is a natural scribal expansion of verse 25, borrowed from Matthew 6:15, a parallel verse.

## MARK 15:28

***Did Mark Cite the Old Testament Scriptures as Being Fulfilled in Jesus' Crucifixion with Thieves?***

Let's look at the textual evidence:

exclude verse 28
*א A B C D it*$^{k}$ *syr*$^{s}$ *cop*$^{sa}$
*RSV NRSV NIV NEB NLT*

include verse 28
And the Scripture was fulfilled that says, "He was counted among the lawless."
*L 0112 0250 f*$^{1,13}$ *𝔐 syr*$^{h,p}$*—TR*
*KJV NKJV NASB*

The documentary evidence decisively shows that this verse was not present in any Greek manuscript prior to the late sixth century (since 0112 is a late-sixth-century manuscript). Borrowing from Luke 22:37 (which is a quotation of Isa. 53:12), later scribes inserted this verse as a prophetic proof text for the phenomenon that Jesus died with the lawless.

## MARK 16:8-20

### *How Did Mark End His Gospel?*

The Gospel of Mark concludes in five different ways:

1) Conclude at 16:8, which reads as follows:

   So they went out and fled from the tomb, seized with terror and amazement; and they said nothing to anyone, for they were afraid.

   *א B sy]s it[avid] Clement Origen*
   *MSS[according to Eusebius, Jerome]*
   *This is noted in the margins of most modern versions.*

2) Shorter Ending, after 16:8:

   And all that had been commanded them they told briefly to those with Peter. And afterward Jesus himself sent out through them, from the east and as far as the west, the holy and imperishable proclamation of eternal salvation. Amen.

   *[see MSS supporting 5 below] it[k] syr[hmg] cop[sa] cop[bo] Irenaeus Diatessaron*
   *included in NASB NRSV NEB NLT; noted in RSVmg and NJBmg*

3) Traditional Longer Ending

   Mark 16:9-20

   *A C D K X $f^{13}$ 33 𝔐—TR*

*all English versions include this—usually along with other endings and/or notes; the KJV presents only this ending*

4) Traditional Longer Ending (Mark 16:9-20), with an addition after 16:14, which reads as follows: "Later he appeared to the eleven themselves as they were sitting at the table; and he upbraided them for their lack of faith and stubbornness, because they had not believed those who saw him after he had risen." To this is added: "And they excused themselves, saying, 'This age of lawlessness and unbelief is under Satan, who does not allow the truth and power of God to prevail over the unclean things of the spirits. Therefore reveal your righteousness now'—thus they spoke to Christ. And Christ replied to them, 'The term of years of Satan's power has been fulfilled, but other terrible things draw near. And for those who have sinned I was handed over to death, that they may return to the truth and sin no more, that they may inherit the spiritual and imperishable glory of righteousness that is in heaven'" (from NRSVmg).
   *W (Jerome)*
   *RSVmg NRSVmg NJBmg*

5) Both Shorter Ending and Traditional Longer Ending
   *L 099 0112 274$^{mg}$ 579 syr$^{hmg}$ cop$^{sa,bo}$*
   *RSVmg NRSV NLT*

Which of the five endings, as presented above, did Mark write? Or is it possible that the original ending to Mark's Gospel was lost (the last sheet of a codex could easily be torn away from the book), and that none of the above endings is the way the book originally ended?

The textual evidence for the first reading (stopping at verse 8) is the best, finding witness from the two earliest manuscripts, as well as other manuscripts. Of the church fathers, Clement, Origen, Cyprian, and Cyril of Jerusalem show no knowledge of any verses beyond 16:8. Eusebius said that the accurate copies of Mark ended with verse 8, adding that 16:9-20 were missing from almost all manuscripts (Quaestiones ad Marinum 1.22, 937). Jerome affirmed the same by saying that almost all the Greek codices did not have 16:9-20 (Epistle 120.3, *ad Hedibiam*). Several manuscripts (1, 20, 22, 137, 138, 1110, 1215, 1216, 1217, 1221, 1582) that include 16:9-20 have **scholia** (marginal notes) indicating that the more ancient manuscripts do not include this section. Other manuscripts mark off the longer reading with **obeli** (asterisks) to indicate its questionable status. The textual evidence, therefore, shows that Mark's Gospel circulated in many ancient copies with an ending at verse 8.

But this ending seemed to be too abrupt (and negative) for many readers, both ancient and modern. As a result, various endings were appended—both short and long, with a combination of the two. The most well-known ending is the longer, traditional ending of 16:9-20. The earliest witnesses to this ending come from Irenaeus and Tatian's Diatessaron. Thus, this ending was probably in circulation in the second century. According to Kurt Aland, the shorter and longer endings were composed independently in different geographical locations, and both readings were probably circulating in the second century.[1] The longer reading became the most popular of

---

[1] Aland and Aland, *Text of the New Testament*, 287–288.

the endings after the fourth century, and was copied again and again in many uncial manuscripts.

Scholarly consensus is that Mark did not write any of the endings that appear after 16:8 (variants 2-5 above); all are the work of other hands. Various readers, bothered that Mark ended so abruptly (or that the last portion was lost), completed the Gospel with an addendum. None of these endings is stylistically congruous with Mark's style, and none readily follows 16:8 (note the inconsistency between 16:8 and 16:9 in the traditional longer ending). Even though the composer of the traditional longer ending borrowed some material from the other Gospels and the book of Acts, some other elements (i.e., concerning divine protection for drinking poison and handling snakes) must not be considered as promises Jesus gave to the believers.

## LUKE 4:4

### *What Is Luke's Wording in Jesus' Temptation?*

The textual evidence is as follows:

> Man does not live by bread alone.
> *𝔓$^{75}$ ℵ B L W syr$^{s}$ cop$^{sa}$*
> *RSV NRSV NASB NIV NEB NLT*
>
> Man does not live by bread alone *but by every word of God.*
> *A (D) f$^{1,13}$ 𝔐—TR*
> *KJV NKJV*

The expanded reading in the variant is the result of scribal conformity to Matthew 4:4, the parallel passage. Such harmonizations fill the TR and KJV/NKJV.

## LUKE 9:54-56

*Shorter or Longer Text?*
Here is the textual evidence:

> shorter text
> James and John said, "Lord, do you want us to command fire to come down from heaven and destroy them?" And having turned around, he rebuked them.
> *𝔓45 𝔓75 א B L 700* syr[c,s]*
> *RSV NRSV NIV NEB NLT*
>
> longer text
> James and John said, "Lord, do you want us to command fire to come down from heaven and destroy them, as Elijah also did?" And he said, "You do not know of what spirit you are, for the Son of Man did not come to destroy men's lives but to save them."
> *(C D W) $f^{1,13}$ 700 it syr[c,h,p] 𝔐—TR*
> *KJV NKJV NASB*

The words of James and John would easily bring to mind Elijah's action of calling down fire from heaven (see 2 Kings 1:10, 12). Thus, this allusion may have first been written as an explanatory marginal note, which was later inserted by a scribe into the text. The verse was further expanded to explain why Jesus would not destroy people—for it was against his mission. If the words had originally been in the text, there is no good reason why they would have been deleted in the earliest manuscripts.

## LUKE 11:2

*Was Luke's Rendition of the Lord's Prayer Different Than Matthew's?*

Let's look at the evidence of the manuscripts. Some manuscripts include the phrase, "let your will be done on earth as it is in heaven":

include this phrase
*ℵ A C D W 33 $f^{13}$ 𝔐 it $syr^{h,p}$ $cop^{bo}$—TR*
*KJV NKJV*

exclude this phrase
*$\mathfrak{P}^{75}$ B L sy]c,s Origen*
*NKJVmg RSV NRSV NASB NIV NEB NLT*

Many scribes harmonized Luke's version of the Lord's Prayer to Matthew's. All the major early-fifth-century manuscripts (A C D W) display the harmonization, as does the late-fourth-century manuscript, ℵ (Codex Sinaiticus). For the Sermon on the Mount and the Lord's Prayer, scribes typically conformed Luke to Matthew.

## LUKE 17:36

***Did Luke write this verse?***
Let's look at the textual evidence:

exclude verse 36
*$\mathfrak{P}^{75}$ ℵ A B L W 33 $cop^{sa,bo}$*
*ASV RSV NRSV NIV NEB NLT*

include verse 36
Two men will be in the field; one will be taken and the other left.
*D $f^{13}$ 700 it syr—TR*
*KJV NKJV NASB*

The verse is a scribal interpolation borrowed from Matthew 24:40, with harmonization to the style of Luke 17:35. Though the verse is not present in the TR, it was included in the KJV (perhaps under the influence of the Latin Vulgate).

## LUKE 22:43-44

*Did Jesus Sweat Great Drops of Blood?*
Let's look at the textual evidence:

include verses 43-44
And an angel from heaven appeared to him, strengthening him. And being in agony, he prayed more earnestly, and his sweat became like great drops of blood falling down on the ground.
*א$^{*,2}$ D L 𝔐 (with obeli syr$^{c}$ 0171$^{vid}$ 892$^{c}$)—TR KJV NKJV ASV NRSV NASB NIV NEB NLT [note: $f^{13}$ 13* and some lectionaries include the verses after Matt. 26:39]*

exclude verses 43-44
*𝔓$^{69vid}$ 𝔓$^{75}$ א$^{1}$ B T W it$^{f}$ syr$^{s}$ cop$^{sa}$ Jerome RSV*

The earliest manuscripts exclude this passage. Other signs of its doubtfulness appear in manuscripts marking it with obeli or crossing out the passage (as was done by the first corrector of א). Writing in the fourth century, Epiphanius (Ancoratus 31.4-5) indicated that the verses were found in some "uncorrected copies" of Luke. But other early church fathers (Justin, Irenaeus, Hippolytus, Dionysius, Eusebius) acknowledged this portion as part of Luke's Gospel.

The debate about the genuineness of this passage has

focused on what view one takes concerning whether or not Jesus needed to have been strengthened by angels during his trial in the garden of Gethsemane. Some have said that the passage was excised because certain Christians thought that "the account of Jesus overwhelmed with human weakness was incompatible with his sharing the divine omnipotence of the Father." But it is more likely that the passage was an early (second-century) interpolation, added from an oral tradition concerning the life of Jesus.[1] Its transposition to Matthew 26 in some manuscripts and lectionaries indicates that it was a free-floating passage that could be interjected into any of the passion narratives.

## LUKE 23:17

### *Did Luke Write This Verse?*

Let us look at the textual evidence:

exclude verse 17
*𝔓$^{75}$ A B L T 892$^{txt}$ it$^{a}$ cop$^{sa}$*
*RSV NRSV NIV NEB NLT*

include verse 17
It was necessary for him to release one [prisoner] for them.
*א W 063 f$^{1,13}$ 892$^{mg}$ 𝔐 (D syr$^{c,s}$ after 23:19)—TR*
*KJV NKJV NASB*

Since this verse is absent from several manuscripts and is transposed in D syr$^{c,s}$, its presence in the other manuscripts is most likely the result of scribal interpolation—borrowing primarily from Mark 15:6, as well as from Matthew 27:15. The

[1] Westcott and Hort, *Introduction*, 64-67.

verse was added to provide a reason for the crowd's request that Pilate release Barabbas instead of Jesus (Luke 23:18).

## LUKE 23:34

***Did Jesus Say, "Father, forgive them for they know not what they are doing"?***

Let's examine the textual evidence. Some manuscripts include this verse:

> include verse 34
> And Jesus said, "Father, forgive them, for they do not know what they are doing."
> *א$^{*,2}$ (A) C $D^2$ (E with asterisks) L Ψ $f^{1,(13)}$ 𝔐 $syr^{c,h,p}$*
> *all English translations*

Other manuscripts exclude the verse:

> exclude verse 34
> *𝔓$^{75}$ א$^{1}$ B D* W Θ 0124 $it^{a}$ $syr^{s}$ $cop^{sa}$*
> *ASVmg NKJVmg RSVmg NRSVmg NASBmg NIVmg NEBmg NLTmg*

The omission of these words in early and diverse manuscripts (the earliest being 𝔓$^{75}$) cannot be explained as a scribal blunder. But were the words purposely excised? Westcott and Hort considered willful excision to be absolutely unthinkable.[1] But Marshall thinks of several reasons why scribes might have deleted the words—the most convincing of which is that scribes might have been influenced by an anti-Judaic polemic and therefore did not want the text saying that Jesus forgave the Jews who killed him.[2] If this was the case, however, we would

---

[1] Ibid., 68.

[2] Marshall, *Gospel of Luke*, 867-868.

think that Codex Beza (D) would have shown the omission because, of all the manuscripts, it is known for its anti-Judaic tendencies.[1]

It is more easy to explain that the words were not written by Luke, but were added later (as early as the second century—for it is attested to by Hegesippus, Marcion, the Diatessaron, and Justin). If the words came from an oral tradition, many scholars are of the opinion that they are authentic. Indeed, Westcott and Hort considered these words and Luke 22:43-44 to be "the most precious among the remains of the evangelic tradition which were rescued from oblivion by the scribes of the second century."[2]

## JOHN 5:3-4

### *Which Text Did John Write?*

John 5:3-4 are found in the manuscripts in both a shorter and a longer form. The textual evidence is as follows:

> In these [porches] lay a multitude of invalids, blind, lame, paralyzed.
> *𝔓66 𝔓75 א B C**
> *RSV NRSV NIV NEB NLT*

> In these [porches] lay a multitude of invalids, blind, lame, paralyzed, waiting for the movement of the water. 4For an angel of the Lord went down at certain seasons into the pool and stirred up the water; whoever then first stepped in, after the stirring up of the water, was made well from whatever disease he was afflicted with.
> *A C3 𝔐 it—TR (A* excludes 5:3b; Ac includes it)*
> *KJV NKJV NASB*

---

1 Epp, *Theological Tendency of Codex Bezae*, 51-62.

2 Westcott and Hort, *Introduction*, 67.

This portion (5:3b-4) was not written by John because it is not found in the earliest manuscripts, and where it does occur in later manuscripts it is often marked with obeli (asterisks) to signal probable spuriousness. The passage was a later addition—even added to manuscripts, such as A and C, that did not originally contain the portion. The expansion happened in two phases: first came the addition of 5:3b—inserted to explain what the sick people were waiting for, and then 5:4—inserted to provide an explanation about the troubling of the water mentioned in John 5:7.

## JOHN 7:53–8:11

***Did John Write the Story about the Woman Caught in Adultery?***

Let's examine the manuscript evidence:

omit the story of the adulteress

*$\mathfrak{P}^{66}$ $\mathfrak{P}^{75}$ ℵ $A^{vid}$ B $C^{vid}$ L N T W Δ Θ Ψ 0141 0211 33*
*$it^{a,f}$ $syr^{c,s,p}$ $cop^{sa,bo,ach}$ goth geo Tertullian Origen*
*RSV (first printing) NJB REB*

include the story of the adulteress

*D (F) G H K M U $it^{aur,c,d,e}$ $syr^{h,pal}$ $cop^{bo}$ $\mathfrak{M}$—TR*
*E [8:2-11 with asterisks]*
*$f^{1}$ arm [after John 21:25]*
*$f^{13}$ [after Luke 21:38]*
*$1333^{c}$ 8:3-11 after Luke 24:53*
*225 after John 7:36*
*KJV NKJV NASB RSV (second printing) NRSV NIV NLT*

The passage about the adulteress (John 7:53–8:11) is not included in any of the earliest manuscripts (second–fourth century), including the two earliest, 𝔓$^{66}$ and 𝔓$^{75}$. Its first appearance in a Greek manuscript is in D, but it is not contained in other Greek manuscripts until the ninth century. When this story is inserted in later manuscripts, it appears in different places (after Luke 21:38, Luke 24:53, John 7:36, John 7:52, and at the end of John); and when it does appear it is often marked off by obeli to signal its probable spuriousness. In most of the manuscripts that include this story, it appears at the beginning of John 8, probably because it provides an illustration of Jesus' resistance to pass judgment, which is spoken of in the following discourse (see 8:15ff.).

All the textual evidence unmistakably points to the conclusion that John did not write it. The inclusion of this story in the New Testament text is a prime example of how the oral tradition, originally not included in the text, eventually found its way into the written text. In its oral form the story may have been in circulation beginning in the early second century.

There is no doubt that John didn't write this passage and that it has no place whatsoever in the text of John's Gospel.[1] Of course, I am aware of how difficult it is to rid the Bible of spurious texts once they have gained a place in what people consider to be "Holy Scripture." When the RSV was first published, this pericope was taken out of the text and placed in a footnote, but the outcry against this was so vehement that it was placed back in the text in the next printing. No other English version, for fifty years, dared to remove it from the text. At long last, the translators of the REB took it out of John 7–8, placing it as addendum at the end of John.

---

[1] For a fuller discussion on this passage see my article, "The Pericope of the Adulteress (John 7:53–8:11)," in *The Bible Translator* 1989 (40).

## ACTS 8:37

***What Did Philip Tell the Ethiopian?***

Let's look at the textual evidence:

exclude verse 37
*𝔓45 𝔓74 ℵ A B C 33vid syrp copsa,bo Chrysostom Ambrose*
*RSV NRSV NIV NEB NLT*

include verse 37
And Philip said, "If you believe with all your heart, you may." And he replied, "I believe that Jesus Christ is the Son of God."
*E 1739 (it syrh**)—TR*
*KJV NKJV NASB*

If the verse was an original part of Luke's text, there is no good reason for explaining why it would have been omitted in so many early manuscripts. Rather, this verse is a classic example of scribal gap-filling, in that it supplied the apparent gap left by the unanswered question of the previous verse ("The eunuch said, 'Look, here is water! What is to prevent me from being baptized?'"). The interpolation puts an answer on Philip's lips that is derived from ancient Christian baptismal practices. Before being baptized, the new believer had to make a confession of his or her faith in Jesus as the Son of God.

There is nothing doctrinally wrong with this interpolation; it affirms belief with the heart (in accordance with verses like Rom. 10:9-10) and elicits the response of faith in Jesus Christ as the Son of God (in accordance with verses like John 20:31). But Luke didn't write it.

## ACTS 15:34

*Did Luke write this verse?*
Let's look at the evidence in the manuscripts:

exclude verse 34
*𝔓$^{74}$ ℵ A B E 𝔐 syr$^{p}$ cop$^{bo}$*
*ASV RSV NRSV NIV NEB NLT*

include verse 34, in one of two forms
1. But it seemed good to Silas to remain there.
*(C) 33 1739 it$^{c}$ syr$^{h**}$ cop$^{sa}$—TR*
*KJV NKJV NASB*

2. But it seemed good to Silas to remain with them, so Judas traveled alone.
*D it$^{d,w}$*

The extra verse, though it contradicts 15:33, was added to avoid the difficulty in 15:40, which indicates that Silas was still in Antioch. Thus, in trying to solve one problem the D-reviser (and other scribes) created another. Erasmus, probably aware of its inclusion in the Latin Vulgate, supposed that it had been omitted in the Greek manuscripts by an error of the scribes. From Erasmus's text it went into the TR, and was then translated in the KJV.

## Acts 24:6b-8a

*Which Version Did Luke Write?*
Let's look at the textual evidence:

6He even tried to profane the temple, and so we seized him. 8By examining him yourself you will be able to learn from him concerning everything of which we accuse him.

*$\mathfrak{P}^{74}$ א A B H L P 049 cop*
*ASV RSV NRSV NIV NEB NLT*

6He even tried to profane the temple, and so we seized
him. And we would have judged him according to our
law. 7But the chief captain Lysias came and with great
violence took him out of our hands, 8commanding his
accusers to come before you. By examining him yourself you will be able to learn from him concerning
everything of which we accuse him.
*$\mathfrak{M}$ 33 1739 $it^{gig}$ $syr^{(p/)}$ —TR*
*KJV NKJV NASB*

The longer reading is a late addition by some scribe who did not think it likely that Felix would have received the whole story from Paul. The text, without the interpolation, is bare but understandable: Paul was arrested so that he could be examined and tried by Felix.

## ACTS 28:29

### *Was This Verse Written by Luke?*

Let us examine the textual evidence:

exclude verse 29
*$\mathfrak{P}^{74}$ א A B E 049 33 1739 $syr^{p}$ cop*
*ASV RSV NRSV NIV NEB NLT*

include verse 29
And after he said these things, the Jews went away, arguing greatly among themselves.
*$\mathfrak{M}$ it $syr^{h**}$—TR*
*KJV NKJV NASB*

The additional verse passed from the Western text into the Byzantine text. It was added to fill in the narrative gap between 28:28 and 28:30. Most modern versions do not include it in the text.

## ROMANS 16:24

### *Did Paul Write This Verse?*

Let's examine the textual evidence:

exclude verse 24
*𝔓46 𝔓61 (א A) B C 1739 itb cop*
*RSV NRSV NIV NEB NLT*

include verse 24
The grace of our Lord Jesus Christ be with you all. Amen.
*D (F G) 𝔐 syrh—TR*
*KJV NKJV NASB*

The exclusion of this verse is strongly supported by all the earliest manuscripts. The verse was carried over from 16:20 by some scribe (or scribes) who thought it was better suited to follow the postscript. Since the TR and Majority Text include this verse, so do the KJV and NKJV, as well as the NASB. Other modern translations, following superior testimony, do not include the verse.

## 1 JOHN 5:6-8

### *Did John Write about Heavenly Witnesses?*

Let us examine the textual evidence:

shorter reading
because there are three testifying: the Spirit and the

water and the blood, and the three are for one [testimony].

*A B* $\mathfrak{M}$ *syr cop arm eth*
*RSV NRSV NASB NIV NEB NLT*

longer reading
because there are three testifying *in heaven: the Father, the Word, and the Holy Spirit, and these three are one. And there are three that testify on earth:* the Spirit and the water and the blood, and the three are for one [testimony].

*(61 629) 88*$^{v.r.}$ *221*$^{v.r.}$ *429*$^{v.r.}$ *636*$^{v.r}$ *918 2318 it*$^{l,q}$
*Vulgate*$^{mss}$ *Speculum (Priscillian Fulgentius)—*
*TR (third edition)*
*KJV NKJV*

This famous passage, called "the heavenly witnesses," probably came from a marginal note on 1 John 5:8 explaining that the three elements (water, blood, and Spirit) symbolize the Trinity (the Father, the Word [Son], and the Spirit). This gloss had a Latin origin and found its way into more and more copies of the Latin Vulgate. But "the heavenly witnesses" passage has not been found in the text of any Greek manuscript prior to the fourteenth century. Many of the Greek manuscripts listed above (in support of the variant reading) do not even include the extra verbage in the text but rather record these words as a "variant reading" in the margin.

Erasmus did not include "the heavenly witnesses" in the first two editions of his Greek New Testament. He was criticized for this by defenders of the Latin Vulgate. Erasmus, in reply, said that he would include it if he could see it in any one Greek manuscript. In turn, a manuscript (most likely the Monfort Manuscript, 61) was especially produced for the purpose of adding the passage. Erasmus kept his promise; he included it in the third edition. From there it became incorporated into the TR and hence was translated in the KJV. Both the KJV and NKJV have popularized this expanded passage.

## CONCLUSION

The key theological issue pertaining to these passages concerns their right to be considered "Scripture." If they are clearly scribal additions, then they cannot be considered part of the original text and therefore must not be treated on the same par as divinely-inspired Scripture.

It should be noted that some of the additional verses in the Gospels have been borrowed from other Gospels and therefore are God-inspired sayings (from the particular Gospels where they have excellent manuscript support). Thus, an expression like, "For the Son of Man has come to save the lost," genuine to Luke but not to Matthew, is a divinely-inspired saying. But other portions, not found elsewhere in the New Testament, must not be considered divinely-inspired and therefore must not be used for establishing Christian practice or doctrine. For instance, Christians should be careful *not* to use the longer ending of Mark (16:9-20) to support snake handling or poison drinking as religious practices warranted by Jesus.

APPENDIX A

# Glossary

**Apocrypha.**
A group of Old Testament books, hidden (*apocrypha* means "hidden") from public view. Many of these books were included in the Septuagint and Vulgate (and thus in Orthodox and Roman Catholic editions), but excluded from the Masoretic Text (and thus from Jewish and Protestant editions).

**apostolicity.**
Whether or not a particular early church document was considered to have been written by an apostle.

**assimilation.**
See *harmonization.*

**autograph.**
The original manuscript of an ancient document; the copy penned by the author or scribe who first wrote the document.

**canon.**
1. The collection of works understood to be authoritative ("the *canon* of Scripture").
2. A rule or guideline for a particular discipline ("the *canons* of textual criticism").

**canon, closed.**
An exclusive list of authoritative works; a *canon* that is not open for additions or deletions.

**catechetical teaching.**
Basic instruction in doctrine and the Christian faith, usually given to new church members.

**church fathers.**
Prominent leaders in the early church, from the second to the sixth centuries (from Ignatius to Augustine).

**codex (pl. *codices*).**
A manuscript arranged in the form of a *book*, with separate sheets bound in a stack at one edge.

**collation.**
The process of comparing and listing the *variant readings* in a particular manuscript or set of manuscripts.

**comparative philology.**
The study of a piece of literature by means of comparison with other languages.

**compositional-transmissional stage.**
The stage in the development and *transmission* of a manuscript in which the content is still being formed and edited.

**conflation.**
The scribal technique of resolving a discrepancy between two or more variant readings by including all of them.

**conjectural emendation.**
The text-critical technique of making an "educated guess" as to what the original text might have been, without direct manuscript evidence.

**consonantal text.**
The form of Hebrew text in which there are no vowels.

**Coptic.**
A language spoken in ancient Egypt.

**corpus.**
A collection of writings.

**critical edition.**
An edition of an ancient text that is based on a *collation* of *variant readings* and that includes editorial decisions about which readings are most likely original.

**cuneiform.**
An ancient Near Eastern script written by pressing a *stylus* into clay, forming a pattern of incised wedges in the clay.

**D-text.**
A family of texts (a *text type*) sharing similar readings to Codex Bezae (D). Also called the "Western" text type.

**Dead Sea Scrolls.**
A collection of very early (100 B.C.–A.D. 100) Old Testament and other Jewish manuscripts found in the late 1940s and early 1950s near the Dead Sea.

**deuterocanonical books.**
Ancient Jewish documents that are not considered part of the original *canon* of Scripture but were added later to the canon by the Roman Catholic church (*deuterocanonical* means "second canon").

**diaspora.**
1. The "scattering" of Jewish people from Palestine throughout the Near East and Europe.
2. Jews living outside of Palestine.

**diglot.**
A manuscript which presents a text in two languages at once.

**diorthotes.**
A "scribal corrector" who re-reads a copied manuscript to ensure accuracy.

**dittography.**
A scribal error involving the repetition of a word, letter, or phrase, caused by the eye skipping backward while copying.

**dynamic equivalence.**
A translation methodology in which the translator attempts to produce the same response in the "target" language readers as the original language text produced in the original readers.

**encyclical.**
A letter intended to be circulated among several recipients (or recipient communities) rather than being addressed to a particular individual or group.

**exegesis.**
Study of a text in order to understand its full meaning.

**exemplar.**
The manuscript from which a copy is made and against which the copy is corrected; a "parent" manuscript.

**extant manuscripts /extant witnesses.**
Manuscript copies that are currently available for study and collation.

**external evidence.**
Evidence for a given reading based on *extant witnesses.*

**folio.**
A leaf (sheet of paper, parchment, or papyrus) in a *codex.*

**formal equivalence.**
A translation methodology in which the translator attempts to produce in the "target" language a text that is as syntactically, lexically, and grammatically as close to the original language text as possible.

**functional equivalence.**
See *dynamic equivalence.*

**genizah.**
A storage room in an ancient synagogue in which worn or faulty copies of Scripture were hidden until they could be disposed of properly.

**haplography.**
A scribal error involving the omission of a word, letter, or phrase, due to the eye accidentally skipping that portion. See also *homoioteleuton.*

**harmonization.**
The process of editing a text while copying a certain passage or book of the Bible, in order to make it match the reading in another passage or book of the Bible.

**Hexapla.**
An edition of the Old Testament published by Origen, who arranged six versions of the Old Testament text in parallel columns in an effort to find the best text.

**homoioteleuton.**
A scribal error of omission (see *haplography*) in which the eye of

the copyist slips accidentally from one word to a similar word having a similar ending.

**indirect evidence.**
Textual evidence drawn from an indirect source, such as from an ancient *version* (translation) of the document.

**inspiration.**
The process by which God enabled the writers of Scripture to record his words and thoughts.

**intentional alterations.**
Scribal errors produced when the scribe edits the text in an (unsuccessful) attempt to make it more "accurate."

**intentional fallacy.**
The presumption that a reader can fully understand the original intentions of an author.

**internal criticism.**
Textual criticism conducted on the basis of *internal evidence.*

**internal evidence.**
Evidence for a given reading based on how that reading and other *variants* most likely occurred.

**interpolations.**
Scribal additions to a manuscript or translation that attempt to clarify the meaning.

**Koiné Greek.**
The "common," *vernacular* Greek that functioned as the lingua franca of the Greco-Roman world during the first Christian centuries.

**lacunae.**
Missing portions of a manuscript.

**lectionary.**
A collection or arrangement of Scripture readings used in Christian liturgies.

**lector.**
The man responsible for reading the Scriptures aloud in a synagogue or church.

**local text theories.**
Theories of the history of textual *transmission* that rely on the idea that diversity among manuscripts is based on geographical location.

**local-genealogical method.**
A method of textual criticism in which decisions are made on a case-by-case basis, taking into account all available *external* and *internal evidence* for the possible *variant readings.*

**Majority Text.**
The majority of extant manuscripts, representing the Byzantine text type.

**majuscules.**
Capital letters used in manuscript copying.

**manuscript.**
A copy of an ancient text in the language in which it was written.

**manuscript stemma.**
A genealogical tree of manuscripts with similar texts.

**Masoretes.**
A school of European Jewish scribes who helped preserve the Old Testament text between A.D. 500 and 1000 and who standardized *vowel pointings* for the *consonantal Hebrew text.*

**mechanical inspiration.**
A view of *inspiration* in which it is thought that God dictated each word verbally to those who wrote the Scriptural texts.

**minuscule manuscript.**
A manuscript written in lowercase cursive script.

**Nag Hammadi manuscripts.**
Manuscripts found at Nag Hammadi in Egypt.

**Neutral Text.**
The name Westcott and Hort gave to the early Alexandrian text type, as preserved particularly in Codex Vaticanus.

**nomina sacra.**
Special contractions (or abbreviations) used in early Christian manuscripts for the divine names—Lord, God, Jesus, Christ, and the Spirit.

**obeli.**
Astericks used by scribes to mark a passage in a manuscript as questionable.

**ostraca.**
Shards of pottery used in the ancient Near East to jot down notes, business receipts, and other short texts.

**paleo-Hebrew script.**
An archaic style of writing the Hebrew alphabet. See also *square script.*

**paleography.**
The study of ancient handwriting.

**palimpsest.**
An animal skin manuscript on which the original writing was later scraped off and replaced with a newer text; very often the older manuscript is much more valuable and can be recovered as an important textual witness.

**papyrology.**
The study of ancient *papyrus* manuscripts.

**papyrus.**
A manuscript writing surface prepared from strips of papyrus reed pounded to make a flat surface.

**parchment.**
A manuscript writing surface prepared from animal skins that have had the hair removed and have been rubbed smooth.

**Pentateuch.**
The first five books of the Old Testament (literally, "five in a case"—that is, five scrolls kept together in a box), consisting of the law of Moses; also called the *Torah.*

**Peshitta.**
The Syriac *version* of the Old and New Testaments, which became the common Scriptural text for the Syriac church.

**proto-Alexandrian manuscript.**
A New Testament manuscript that pre-dates the Alexandrian manuscripts but appears to have been used in composing those later manuscripts.

**proto-Masoretic manuscript.**
An Old Testament manuscript which pre-dates the Masoretic manuscripts but appears to have been used in composing those later manuscripts.

**quire.**
A group of four sheets in a *codex* that are folded together.

**rabbinic literature.**
The scholarly writings of Jewish rabbis.

**recensio.**
An accounting or tabulation of all of the manuscript data (see *collation*).

**recension.**
A purposely-created *critical edition* of a text, usually implying the exercise of editorial and textual judgment.

**reception tendencies.**
See *scribal reception tendencies.*

**redactor.**
A scribal editor who creates a *recension*, as opposed to simply copying a manuscript.

**reformed documentary hand.**
A handwriting style that displays the work of a scribe accustomed to preparing documents and attempting to present a "book" or professional hand.

**Samaritan Pentateuch.**
The Samaritan text for the five books of Moses, which shows a different text type from the Masoretic Text.

**scholia.**
Marginal notes written by the scribe in the margin of the manuscript.

**scribal reception tendencies.**
A description of the way a particular scribe or group of scribes tended to read and copy the exemplar he was using—for instance, whether he read and copied strictly or allowed himself liberty.

**scribes.**
Scholars whose vocation was to make new copies of earlier manuscripts.

**scriptoral practices.**
The methods and practices of a particular scribe or school (group) of scribes.

**scriptorium (pl. scriptoria).**
A room or building (usually attached to a library) set apart for scribes to do their work of copying.

**Semitic.**
A family of languages that includes Hebrew, Aramaic, and Arabic.

**Septuagint.**
A translation of the Old Testament into Greek, made in the third century B.C., and widely used in the early church (and in eastern Orthodox churches).

**singular reading.**
A textual *variant* that occurs in only a single manuscript witness.

**square script.**
Aramaic handwriting that was brought over to Hebrew, replacing the *paleo-Hebrew script.*

**stichoi / stichometrical notes.**
Notations at the end of a manuscript, recording how many lines were copied (as a means of measuring how much the scribe should be paid).

**stylus.**
A hard-pointed writing instrument.

**Talmud.**
Rabbinic commentaries on the Old Testament.

**Tanakh.**
The Jewish name for the Old Testament.

**Targums.**
Aramaic paraphrases of the Old Testament.

**tetragrammaton.**
The "four letters," *YHWH* (יהוה), which in Hebrew is the personal name of God, commonly translated "LORD."

**text type.**
A group of manuscripts that show similar characteristics.

**textual critic.**
A person who studies manuscripts and their transmission and helps make decisions about which reading among the *variants* is most likely the correct one.

**textual transmission.**
The process of manually transmitting a written text from copy to copy during the time period prior to the printing press.

**textual-transmission stage.**
The stage in the development and transmission of a manuscript in which the text is copied meticulously and handed down in more or less unchanged form.

**Textus Receptus.**
The "received text," an edition of the Greek New Testament which formed the basis of the King James Version.

**three-recension theory.**
A theory of Old Testament text types

which holds that there are three *recensions* of the Old Testament text. See *local text theories.*

**transposition.**
A scribal error in which two letters are accidentally reversed.

**uncials.**
Uppercase letters used in writing a manuscript copy.

**uncial manuscript.**
A manuscript written on vellum or parchment, as opposed to papyrus, usually displaying *uncials.*

**variant readings.**
All of the different readings for a given section of text present in different manuscripts.

**variation unit.**
The unit of a single text for which a set of variants is available.

**vernacular.**
The common language of the people.

**versions.**
Translations of ancient texts into other languages.

**vocalization.**
The correct pronunciation of a written text; indications of the correct pronunciation, written within the text.

**vowel pointing.**
Markings in a *consonantal text* showing which vowels should be used in *vocalizing* the text.

**Vulgate.**
The translation of the Hebrew and Greek Scriptures into common Latin by Jerome, ca. 400.

**"Western" text type.**
See *D-text.*

APPENDIX B

# New Testament Manuscripts

## MANUSCRIPT SYMBOLS

| Symbol | Manuscript | Description |
|---|---|---|
| $\mathfrak{P}^{1}\ldots\mathfrak{P}^{115}$ | papyrus manuscripts | all papyrus manuscripts, numbered in the order in which they were published |
| ℵ | Codex Sinaiticus | 4th c. |
| A | Codex Alexandrinus | 5th c. |
| B | Codex Vaticanus | 4th c. |
| C | Codex Ephraemi Rescriptus | 5th c. |
| $D^{ea}$ | Codex Bezae | 5th c., Gospels, Acts |
| $D^{p}$ | Codex Claromontanus | 6th c., Epistles |
| $E^{e}$ | Codex Basilensis | 8th c., Gospels |
| $E^{a}$ | Codex Laudianus | 6th c., Acts |
| $F^{e}$ | Codex Boreelianus | 9th c., Gospels |
| $G^{e}$ | Codex Seidelianus I | 9th c., Gospels |
| $G^{p}$ | Codex Boernerianus | 9th c., Epistles |
| $H^{e}$ | Codex Seidelianus II | 9th c., Gospels |
| $L^{ap}$ | Codex Angelicus | 9th c., Acts, Epistles |
| $L^{e}$ | Codex Regius | 8th c., Gospels |
| $P^{apr}$ | Codex Porphyrianus | 9th c., Acts, Epistles, Revelation |
| T | Codex Borgianus | 5th c., Luke–John |
| W | Codex Washingtonianus | 5th c. |
| X | Codex Monacensis | 10th c. |
| Z | Codex Dublinensis | 6th c. |
| Δ | Codex Sangallensis | 9th c. |
| Θ | Codex Coridethianus | 9th c. |
| Ψ | Codex Athous Lavrensis | 8th/9th c., Gospels, Acts, Epistles |
| $\mathfrak{M}$ | Majority of manuscripts | |
| *f1* | minuscules family 1 | 12th c., Gospels, Acts, Epistles |
| *f13* | minuscules family 13 | 13th c., Gospels |

| | | |
|---|---|---|
| arm | Armenian versions | 4th/5th c. |
| cop | Coptic versions | 3rd/4th c. |
| $cop^{bo}$ | Bohairic (Coptic) | 4th c. |
| $cop^{fay}$ | Fayyumic (Coptic) | 4th c. |
| $cop^{sa}$ | Sahidic (Coptic) | 3rd c. |
| eth | Ethiopic versions | 5th c. |
| geo | Georgian versions | 4th/5th c. |
| goth | Gothic versions | 5th c. |
| it | Old Latin (Itala) versions | 3rd/4th c. |
| $it^{a}$ | Latin Vercellensis | 4th c. |
| $it^{d}$ | Latin Cantabrigiensis | 5th c. |
| $it^{e}$ | Latin Palatinus | 5th c. |
| $it^{gig}$ | Latin Gigas | 13th c. |
| $it^{k}$ | Latin Bobiensis | ca. 400 |
| syr | Syriac versions | 4th–6th c. |
| $syr^{c}$ | Syriac Curetonian | 5th c. |
| $syr^{h}$ | Syriac Harklean | 6th c. |
| $syr^{p}$ | Syriac Peshitta | 5th/6th c. |
| $syr^{pal}$ | Syriac Palestinian | 6th–13th c. |
| $syr^{s}$ | Syriac Sinaiticus | 4th/5th c. |
| $MSS^{\text{according to N}}$ | The person named N reports having seen manuscripts with a given reading | |

## SYMBOL MODIFIERS

The following symbols "modify" the manuscript symbols, giving more specific information about their meaning. These modifiers appear in superscript following the manuscript symbol. The symbol _ in the chart below signifies any manuscript symbol.

| Symbol | Description |
|---|---|
| $\_^{*}$ | the first scribe |
| $\_^{1}$ | the first corrector |
| $\_^{2}$ | the second corrector |
| $\_^{3}$ | the third corrector, *etc.* |
| $\_^{c}$ | any corrector |
| $\_^{vid}$ | apparently (*ut videtur*) |
| $\_^{v.r.}$ | variant reading |
| $\_^{mss}$ | a number of manuscripts |

# BIBLIOGRAPHY

Abbott, Edwin. *Johannine Grammar.* London: Adam and Charles Black, 1906.

Ackroyd, P. R. and C. F. Evans. *The Cambridge History of the Bible,* Volume I, *From the Beginnings to Jerome;* Volume II, *The West from the Fathers to the Reformation,* Volume III, *The West from the Reformation to the Present Day.* Cambridge: Cambridge University Press, 1970, 1963, and 1969, respectively.

Aland, Barbara, Kurt Aland, Johannes Karavidopoulos, Carlo Martini, Bruce Metzger. *The Greek New Testament,* 4th edition. Stuttgart: Deutsche Bibelstiftung, 1993.

Aland, Kurt, and Barbara Aland. *The Text of the New Testament.* Grand Rapids: William B. Eerdmans Publishing Company, 1988.

Aland, Kurt, Matthew Black, Carlo M. Martini, Bruce M. Metzger, and Allen Wikgren. *Novum Testamentum Graece,* 26th edition. Stuttgart: Deutsche Bibelstiftung, 1979.

Aland, Kurt, Matthew Black, Carlo M. Martini, Bruce M. Metzger, and Allen Wikgren. *Novum Testamentum Graece,* 27th edition. Stuttgart: Deutsche Bibelstiftung, 1993.

Aland, Kurt. "The Significance of the Papyri for New Testament Research," in *The Bible in Modern Scholarship,* edited by J. P. Hyatt. Nashville: Abingdon Press, 1965.

________. "The Text of the Church?" in *Trinity Journal* 1987:8.

Alford, Henry. *The Greek Testament,* vol. 2 (1852). Grand Rapids: Guardian Press, 1976 (reprint).

Aune, David. *The New Testament in Its Literary Enviornment.* Philadelphia: Westminster Press, 1987.

Bauer, Walter. *A Greek-English Lexicon of the New Testament and Other Early Christian Literature,* trans. William F. Arndt and F. Wilbur Gingrich. 2nd revised edition by F. Wilbur Gingrich and Frederick W. Danker. Chicago: University of Chicago Press, 1979.

Beekman, John and John Callow. *Translating the Word of God.* Grand Rapids: Zondervan Publishing House, 1974.

Bengel, Johannes Albert. *Gnomon Novi Testamenti*, third edition, edited by J. Steudel. Tübingen, 1885.

Bruce, F. F. *The Books and the Parchments.* Old Tappan, N.J.: Fleming H. Revell Co., 1984.

________. *The Canon of Scripture.* Grand Rapids: William B. Eerdmans Publishing Co., 1988.

________. *The English Bible.* New York: Oxford University Press, 1970.

Bultmann, Rudolf. "Aletheia," in *Theological Dictionary of the New Testament,* vol. 1, edited by Gerhard Kittel, trans. Geoffrey Bromiley. Grand Rapids: William B. Eerdmans Publishing Co., 1964.

Burgon, John W. *The Revision Revised.* London: John Murray, 1883.

Burtchaell, James T. *From Synagogue to Church.* Cambridge: Cambridge University Press, 1992.

Carson, D. A. *The Inclusive Language Debate: A Plea for Realism.* Grand Rapids: Baker Book House, 1998.

________. *The King James Version Debate: A Plea for Realism.* Grand Rapids: Baker Book House, 1979.

Colwell, Ernest. "Scribal Habits in Early Papyri: A Study in the Corruption of the Text," in *The Bible in Modern Scholarship,* edited by J. P. Hyatt. Nashville: Abingdon, 1965. Reprinted as "Method in Evaluating Scribal Habits: A Study of $\mathfrak{P}^{45}$, $\mathfrak{P}^{66}$, $\mathfrak{P}^{75}$," in his *Studies in Methodology in Textual Criticism of the New Testament. New Testament Tools and Studies* 9. Leiden: E. J. Brill, 1969. (Reprint pages cited.)

________. "Hort Redivivus: A Plea and a Program" reprinted in *Studies in Methodology in Textual Criticism of the New Testament. New Testament Tools and Studies* 9. Leiden: E. J. Brill, 1969.

Comfort, Philip W. *The Complete Guide to Bible Versions,* revised edition. Wheaton: Tyndale House Publishers, 1996.

________. *Early Manuscripts and Modern Translations of the New Testament.* Wheaton: Tyndale House Publishers, 1990. Revised edition, Grand Rapids: Baker Book House, 1996.

________. "New Reconstructions of New Testament Manuscripts," in *Novum Testamentum* XLI, 3 (1999), 215-230.

________. "The Pericope of the Adulteress (John 7:53–8:11)," in *The Bible Translator* (1989), 40.

________. *The Quest for the Original Text of the New Testament.* Grand Rapids: Baker Book House, 1992.

________. "The Scribe as Interpreter: A New Look at New Testament Textual

Criticism according to Reader Response Theory," dissertation for D. Litt. et. Phil. Pretoria: University of South Africa, 1997.

Comfort, Philip W., ed. *The Origin of the Bible.* Wheaton: Tyndale House Publishers, 1992.

Comfort, Philip W. and David P. Barrett, eds. *The Complete Text of the Earliest New Testament Manuscripts.* Grand Rapids: Baker Book House, 1999.

Comfort, Philip W. and Wendell Hawley. *Opening the Gospel of John.* Wheaton: Tyndale House Publishers, 1994.

Cross, Frank. "New Directions in Dead Sea Scroll Research. I: The Text Behind the Text of the Hebrew Bible," in *Bible Review* 1 (1985), 2:12–25.

Deissman, Adolf. *Light from the Ancient East: The New Testament Illustrated by Recently Discovered Texts of the Greco-Roman World,* trans. L. Strachan. London: Hodder and Stoughton, 1909.

Edwards, Brian. *God's Outlaw.* Wheaton: Tyndale House Publishers, 1981.

Ehrman, Bart. *The Orthodox Corruption of Scripture.* Oxford: Oxford University Press, 1993.

Epp, Eldon. "The Eclectic Method in New Testament Textual Criticism: Solution or Symptom?" in *Harvard Theological Review* 69 (1976).

________. *The Theological Tendency of Codex Bezae Cantabringiensis in Acts.* Cambridge: Cambridge University Press, 1966.

________. "The Twentieth Century Interlude in New Testament Textual Criticism," in *Harvard Theological Review* (1974), 390-394.

Fee, Gordon. "$\mathfrak{P}^{75}$, $\mathfrak{P}^{66}$, and Origen: The Myth of the Early Textual Recension in Alexandria," in *New Dimensions in New Testament Study,* edited by R. N. Longenecker and Merrill C. Tenney. Grand Rapids: Zondervan Publishing House, 1974.

Frend, William H. C. *The Rise of Christianity.* Philadelphia: Fortress Press, 1984.

Gamble, Harry Y. *Books and Readers in the Early Church.* New Haven: Yale University Press, 1995.

Glassman, Eugene H. *The Translation Debate: What Makes a Translation Good?* Downers Grove: InterVarsity Press, 1981.

Goodspeed, Edgar J. *New Chapters in New Testament Study.* New York: Macmillan, 1937.

Grant, F. C. *An Introduction to the Revised Standard Version of the New Testament.* International Council of Religious Education, 1946.

Grudem, Wayne. "The Battle for the Bible," *World* (April 19, 1997), 14-18.

Grudem, Wayne and Grant Osborne. "Do Inclusive-Language Bibles Distort Scripture?" *CHRISTIANITY TODAY* (October 27, 1997).

Hanson, Richard S. "Paleo-Hebrew Scripts in the Hasmonean Age," *Bulletin of the American Schools of Oriental Research* 175 (1964): 26-42.

Hodges, Zane and Arthur Farstad, eds. *The Greek New Testament According to the Majority Text.* Nashville: Thomas Nelson Publishers, 1982.

Holmes, Michael. "New Testament Textual Criticism." Pp. 53-74 in *Introducing New Testament Interpretation.* Edited by Scot McKnight. Grand Rapids: Baker Book House, 1989.

Hunger, Herbert. "Zur Datierung des Papyrus Bodmer II ($\mathfrak{P}^{66}$)," in *Anzieger der oịsterreichischen Akademie der Wissenschaften.* Philologisch-Historischen Klasse (1960), Nr. 4, 12-23.

Hurtado, Larry. "The Origin of the *Nomina Sacra:* A Proposal." Pp. 655-673 in *Journal of Biblical Literature,* Winter 1998.

Kenyon, Frederic G. *The Chester Beatty Biblical Papyri: Descriptions and Texts of Twelve Manuscripts on Papyrus of the Greek Bible,* Fasciculus I. London: Emery Walker Ltd., 1933.

________. *The Chester Beatty Biblical Papyri: Descriptions and Texts of Twelve Manuscripts on Papyrus of the Greek Bible,* Fasciculus II: The Gospels and Acts. London: Emery Walker Ltd., 1933.

________. *The Chester Beatty Biblical Papyri:* Fasciculus III: Pauline Epistles. London: Emery Walker Ltd., 1934.

________. *The Chester Beatty Biblical Papyri:* Fasciculus III, Supplement. London: Emery Walker Ltd., 1937.

________. *The Story of the Bible.* New York: E. P. Dutton, 1937.

________. *Books and Readers in Ancient Greece and Rome.* Oxford: Clarendon Press, 1951.

________. *Our Bible and the Ancient Manuscripts.* New York: Harper and Row, 1958.

Knox, Ronald. *Trials of a Translator.* New York: Sheed and Ward, 1949.

Kubo, Sakae. "$\mathfrak{P}^{72}$ and the Codex Vaticanus" in *Studies and Documents* 27. Salt Lake City: University of Utah Press, 1965.

Kubo, Sakae and Walter Specht. *So Many Versions?* revised and enlarged edition. Grand Rapids: Zondervan Publishing House, 1983.

Lake, H. and K. Lake *Codex Sinaiticus Petropolitanus.* Oxford: Oxford University Press, 1911 (a photographic reproduction).

Lewis, Jack P. *The English Bible from KJV to NIV.* Grand Rapids: Baker Book House, 1982.

Liddell, Henry G. and Robert Scott. *Greek English Lexicon* (originally printed in 1843; revised, with supplement by Henry Jones and Roderick McKenzie in 1968). Oxford: Clarendon Press, 1968.

Lyon, Robert W. "A Re-examination of Codex Ephraemi Rescriptus." in *New Testament Studies* 5 (1958-1959), 260-272.

Marshall, I. Howard. *The Gospel of Luke.* Grand Rapids: William B. Eerdmans Publishing Co., 1978.

Martin, Victor and Rudolf Kasser. *Papyrus Bodmer II: Evangile de Jean, 1-14.* Cologny/Geneva: Bibliotheca Bodmeriana, 1956.

________. *Papyrus Bodmer II: Supplement, Evangile de Jean, 14-21.* Cologny/Geneva: Bibliotheca Bodmeriana, 1958.

________. *Papyrus Bodmer XIV-XV, I: XIV: Luc chap. 3-24; II: XV: Jean chap. 1-15.* Cologny/Geneva: Bibliotheca Bodmeriana, 1961.

Metzger, Bruce. *A Textual Commentary on the Greek New Testament.* New York: United Bible Societies, 1975.

________. *The Early Versions of the New Testament: Their Origin, Transmission, and Limitations.* Oxford: Clarendon Press, 1977.

________. *The Text of the New Testament,* 2nd edition. Oxford: Oxford University Press, 1992.

Milne, H. J. M. and T. C. Skeat. *The Scribes and Correctors of the Codex Sinaiticus.* Oxford: Oxford University Press, 1938.

________. *The Codex Sinaiticus and the Codex Alexandrinus.* London, the British Museum, 1951 and 1963.

Newman, Barclay and Eugene Nida, *Translator's Handbook on the Gospel of John.* New York: United Bible Societies, 1980.

Nida, Eugene and Charles Taber, *The Theory and Practice of Translation.* Leiden: E. J. Brill, 1969.

Paap, A. H. R. E. *Nomina Sacra in the Greek Papyri of the First Five Centuries A.D.* Leiden: E. J Brill, 1959.

Parker, D. C. *Codex Bezae: An Early Christian Manuscript and Its Text.* Cambridge: Cambridge University Press, 1992.

Porter, Calvin. "Papyrus Bodmer XV ($\mathfrak{P}^{75}$) and the Text of Codex Vaticanus" in *Journal of Biblical Literature* 81 (1962), 363-376.

Rhodes, Erroll. "The Corrections of Papyrus Bodmer II." in *New Testament Studies* 14 (1968), 271-281.

Roberts, Colin H. *An Unpublished Fragment of the Fourth Gospel in the John Rylands Library.* Manchester: Manchester University Press, 1935.

________. "Books in the Graeco-Roman World and in the New Testament."

in *The Cambridge History of the Bible*, Vol. 1, *From the Beginnings to Jerome*, edited by Pater R. Ackroyd and Christopher F. Evans. Cambridge: Cambridge University Press, 1970.

________. *Manuscript, Society, and Belief in Early Christian Egypt.* London: Oxford University Press, 1979.

Roberts, Colin H. and Theodore C. Skeat. *The Birth of the Codex.* London: Oxford University Press, 1987.

Robinson, James. *The Pachomian Monastic Library at the Chester Beatty Library and Bibliotheque Bodmer.* Occasional Papers 19. Claremont, California: Institute for Antiquity and Christianity, 1990.

Robinson, John A. T. *The Priority of John.* Oak Brook, Illinois: Meyer Stone Books, 1985.

Ropes, R. "The Acts of the Apostles," Part I in *The Beginnings of Christianity*, edited by F. J. Foakes Jackson and K. Lake. London: MacMillan and Co., 1926.

Sanders, Henry A. *The New Testament Manuscripts in the Freer Collection.* New York: MacMillan, 1912.

________. *The New Testament Manuscripts in the Freer Collection: Part I and Part II, The Washington Manuscript of the Fourth Gospel.* Ann Arbor: University of Michigan Studies, 1916 and 1918.

________. *A Third Century Papyrus Codex of the Epistles of Paul.* Ann Arbor: University of Michigan Press, 1935.

Scanlin, Harold. *The Dead Sea Scrolls and Modern Translations of the Old Testament.* Wheaton: Tyndale House Publishers, 1993.

Schaff, Philip and Henry Wace, eds. *The Nicene and Post-Nicene Fathers*, 2nd series, vol. 6: *St. Jerome: Letters and Select Works.*

Schwarz, W. *Principles and Problems of Biblical Translation.* Cambridge: Cambridge University Press, 1955.

Scrivener, F. H. A. *A Full Collation of Codex Sinaiticus*, 2nd ed. Cambridge, 1867.

________. *A Plain Introduction to the Criticism of the New Testament.* London, 1861.

Talmon, Shemaryahu. "The Old Testament Text" in *The Cambridge History of the Bible*, vol. 1, *From the Beginnings to Jerome*, edited by Pater R. Ackroyd and Christopher F. Evans. Cambridge: Cambridge University Press, 1970.

Tasker, R. V. G. "Notes on Variant Readings." in *The Greek New Testament.* London: Oxford University Press, 1964.

Testuz, Michael. *Papyrus Bodmer VII-IX: L'Epitre de Jude, Les deux Epitres de Pierre, Les Psaumes 33 et 34.* Cologny/Geneva: Bibliotheca Bodmeriana, 1959.

Thompson, E. M. *Facsimile of the Codex Alexandrinus.* London, 1879-1883.

Tischendorf, Constantin von. *Codex Sinaiticus Petropolitanus.* Leipzig, 1862.

________. *Codex Ephraemi Syri rescriptus sive Fragmenta Novi Testamenti.* Leipzig, 1843.

________. *Novum Testamentum Vaticanum.* Leipzig, 1867.

Tov, Emanuel. *Textual Criticism of the Hebrew Bible.* Minneapolis: Fortress Press, 1992.

________. *The Hebrew and Greek Texts of Samuel.* Jerusalem: Academon, 1980.

Traube, L. *Nomina Sacra.* Munich, 1906.

Ulrich, Eugene Charles. "Double Literary Editions of Biblical Narratives and Reflections on Determining the Form to Be Translated," in *Perspectives on the Hebrew Bible: Essays in Honor of Walter J. Harrelson,* edited by James L. Crenshaw. Macon, Georgia: Mercer University Press, 1988.

Vermes, G. "Bible and Midrash: Early Old Testament Exegesis" in *The Cambridge History of the Bible,* vol. 1, *From the Beginnings to Jerome,* edited by Pater R. Ackroyd and Christopher F. Evans. Cambridge: Cambridge University Press, 1970.

Wallace, Daniel B. "The Majority Text Theory: History, Methods, and Critique," in *The Text of the New Testament in Contemporary Research,* edited by B. Ehrman and M. Holmes. Grand Rapids: William B. Eerdmans Publishing Co., 1995.

Walter, Victor. "Versions of the Bible," in *The Origin of the Bible,* edited by Philip W. Comfort. Wheaton: Tyndale House Publishers, 1992.

Waltke, Bruce K. "The Textual Criticism of the Old Testament" in *Expositor's Bible Commentary,* vol. 1. Grand Rapids: Zondervan Publishing House, 1976.

________. "The New International Version and Its Textual Principles in the Book of Psalms" in *Journal of the Evangelical Theological Society* 32:17–26, 1989.

Wegner, Paul. *The Journey from Texts to Translations.* Grand Rapids: Baker Book House, 1999.

Westcott, B. F. *The Gospel According to St. John: With the Greek Text.* London: John Murray, 1908.

Westcott, B. F. and Fenton Hort. *The New Testament in the Original Greek.* New York: Harper and Brothers, 1881.

________. *Introduction to the New Testament in the Original Greek.* New York: Harper and Brothers, 1882.

Wilcken, Ulrich. *Archiv für Papyrusforschung* II (1935), 113.

Williams, C. S. C. *Alterations to the Text of the Synoptic Gospels and Acts.* Oxford: Basil Blackwell, 1951.

Wimsatt, W. K. and Monroe C. Beardsley. "The Intentional Fallacy," in *On Literary Intention,* edited by David Newton-deMolina. Edinburgh: University Press, 1976.

Würthwein, Ernest. *The Text of the Old Testament.* Grand Rapids: William B. Eerdmans Publishing Co., 1979.

Züntz, Gunther. *The Text of the Epistles.* London: Oxford University Press, 1953.

# INDEX